ITALIANISSIMO

ITALIANISSIMO

Over 600 Great Recipes from Every Region of Italy

McRae Books

ISBN 978-88-6098-055-7

This book was conceived, edited and designed by McRae Books Srl
Borgo Santa Croce, 8 – 50122 Florence, Italy
info@mcraebooks.com
www.mcraebooks.com

Publishers: Anne McRae, Marco Nardi
Project Director: Anne McRae
Art Director: Marco Nardi
Texts: Carla Bardi, Maria Paola Dèttore, Rosalba Gioffrè, Sara Vignozzi,
Gabriella Mari, Cristina Blasi
Translation: Osla Fraser
Photography: Marco Lanza, Walter Mericchi, Cristina Canepari, Keeho Casati,
Gil Gallo, Sandra Preussinger
Home Economist: Benedetto Rillo
Layouts: Laura Ottina
Pre-press: Filippo delle Monache

Printed by KNP(Thailand) supervised by Kyodo Printing Singapore

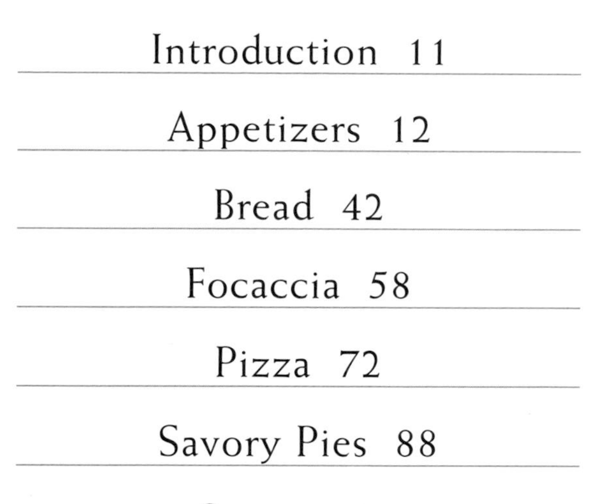

CONTENTS

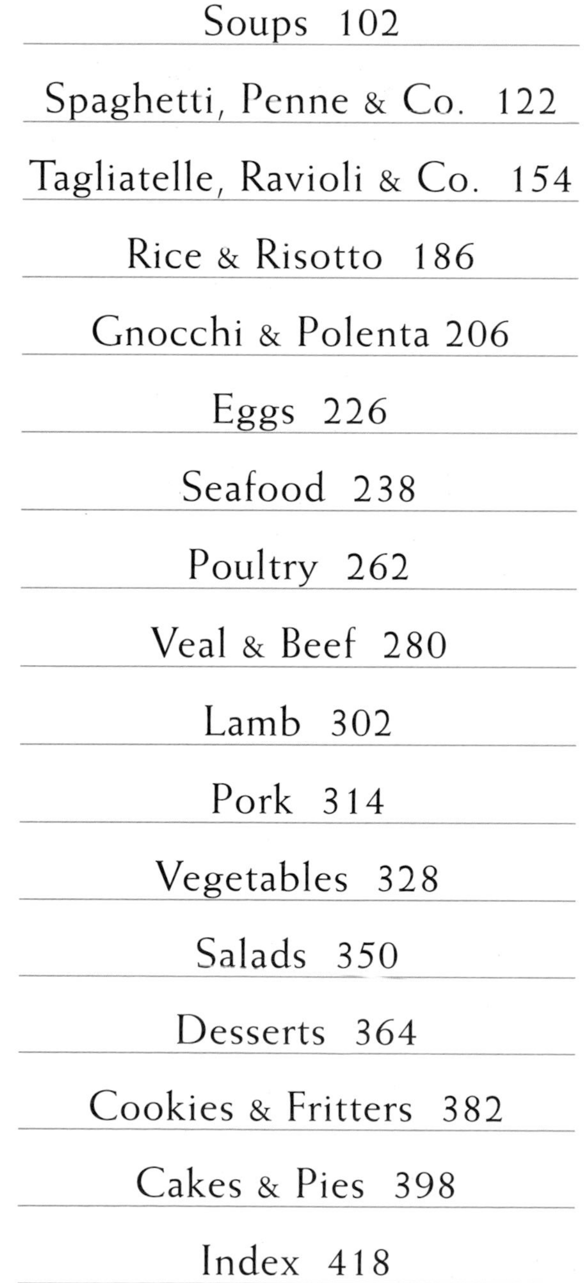

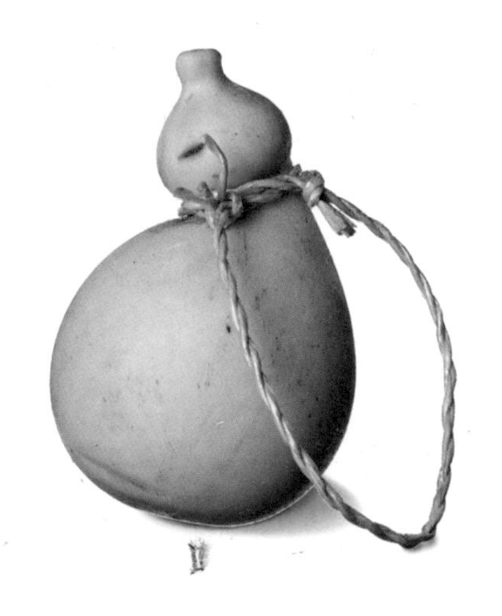

INTRODUCTION

Italian food is still the most popular of all the world cuisines that we enjoy today. This is hardly surprising, because not only is Italian cooking delicious, simple, and eye-catching, it is also nutritious and healthy. The Italian diet—the original Mediterranean diet—is based on grains, olive oil, seafood, fresh fruit and vegetables, legumes, and small amounts of red and white meats, all of which are enjoyed with a daily glass of red wine. With its strong regional traditions, Italian food is also extremely varied. For example, risotto and polenta are typical of the northern regions, while spaghetti, penne, and other dried pasta dishes are more typical of the south and the islands. But these are huge generalizations and the wonderful thing about Italian food is that every city, every province and town, and even every village and family home, has its own special dishes based on local traditions but adapted to personal tastes and the availability of fresh, high quality ingredients. In this book we bring you more than 600 of the best recipes from every region so that you can recreate all the flavors of Italy in your own kitchen.

APPETIZERS

Almost every Italian meal begins with one or more appetizers. These light and flavorsome little offerings are meant to stimulate the appetite without spoiling it. Traditionally divided into *antipasti freddi* (cold appetizers) and *antipasti caldi* (hot appetizers), there are literally hundreds of dishes to choose from. In this chapter we have selected just over 50 recipes from all over Italy. Prosciutto (Parma ham), salami, and other deli meats are the most common type of cold appetizer and every region has it specialties to offer. Crostini and crostoni are another classic choice; a slice of bread, usually toasted, can be rubbed with garlic, drizzled with extra-virgin olive oil, and sprinkled with salt to make a simple *bruschetta*, or covered with tomatoes, herbs, beans, sautéed vegetables, chicken liver pâté, cheese, or seafood to create an endless range of savory treats. Salads, grilled vegetables, shellfish, salmon, shrimps, olives, slices of focaccia or savory pie, fritters with fresh cheese and deli meats, Stuffed olives (see page 34), Stuffed rice cakes (see page 40), or Fried polenta crostini (see page 40)—the choice is yours!

Prosciutto with balsamic vinegar (see page 14)

Prosciutto with melon,
Salami with fresh figs

Prosciutto with melon

Prosciutto e melone

- 5 oz (150 g) prosciutto (Parma ham), thinly sliced
- 1 medium cantaloupe (rock melon)

Serve this simple and refreshing appetizer in the heat of summer when melons are at their fragrant best.

Wipe the cantaloupe with a damp cloth and cut it in half. Slice each half into 4 to 6 wedges and arrange them on a serving dish with the prosciutto. • If liked, cut the skin off the cantaloupe using a sharp knife and place the wedges of fruit back into the skins to serve.

Serves: 4–6 • Prep: 10 min • Level: 1

Salami with fresh figs

Salame e fichi

A late summer classic! The intense sweetness of ripe figs contrasts beautifully with the salt and spice of the salami.

Rinse the figs carefully under cold running water. Pat dry with paper towels. • Trim the stalks, then cut each fig into four. • Remove the rind from the salami. • If using, place the fig leaves on a large serving dish and arrange the salami and figs on top.

Serves: 4–6 • Prep: 10 min • Level: 1

- 8–12 large green or black figs
- 5 oz (150 g) salami, thinly sliced
- fresh fig leaves, to serve (optional)

Mixed prosciutto and deli meat platter

Affettati misti

- 4 oz (125 g) finocchiona (fennel-flavored Tuscan salami) sliced fairly thickly
- 5 oz (150 g) prosciutto (Parma ham)
- 4 oz (125 g) salami
- 6 small wild boar sausages
- 1 lb (500 g) firm-textured white bread, sliced
- green or black olives (optional)
- Mediterranean pickles (capers, pickled onions, gherkins, pickled chile peppers, etc) (optional)

Feel free to vary the types of ham and deli meats according to what is available. The important thing is to serve three or four types of cured meats that have different flavors, textures, and appearances.

Remove the rind from the salami and the finocchiona. If you can't find finocchiona replace it with another large, tasty salami with a flavor that contrasts with the smaller salami. • Arrange the prosciutto, salami, finocchiona, and sausages on a large serving platter. • Serve with the bread and, if liked, bowls of olives and pickles.

Serves: 6–8 • Prep: 10 min • Level: 1

Prosciutto with balsamic vinegar

Prosciutto all'aceto balsamico

Toast the pine nuts in a small frying pan over medium heat until golden brown, about 3 minutes. Remove from the heat. • Place the balsamic vinegar and sugar in a small frying pan over low heat. Simmer, stirring from time to time, until the mixture forms a light syrup. Add the cream and simmer for 5 minutes. • Add the grated Parmesan and mix well. Season with salt and pepper. Remove from the heat. • Arrange the prosciutto on a large serving dish. Drizzle with the balsamic vinegar dressing. Sprinkle with the toasted pine nuts and Parmesan flakes and top with the salad greens. Serve immediately.

Serves: 4–6 • Prep: 10 min • Cooking: 10 min • Level: 1

- 1/4 cup (45 g) pine nuts
- 1/3 cup (90 ml) balsamic vinegar
- 1 tablespoon sugar
- generous 3/4 cup (200 ml) heavy (double) cream
- 1/4 cup (30 g) freshly grated Parmesan cheese
- salt and freshly ground black pepper
- 4 oz (125 g) mixed salad greens
- 10 oz (300 g) sliced prosciutto (Parma ham)
- 1 oz (30 g) Parmesan cheese, cut into flakes

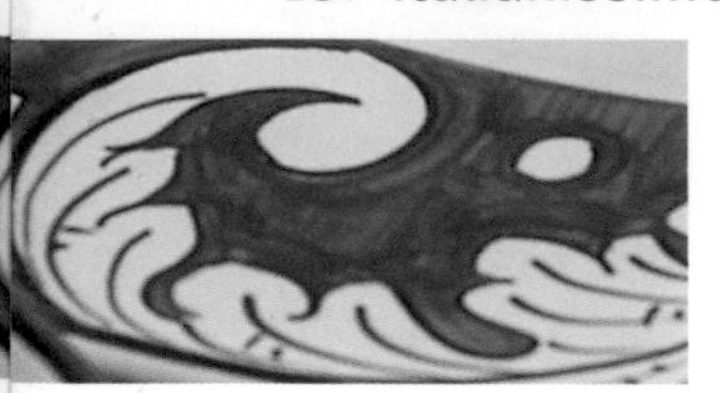

Bruschette with tomato and basil

Classic bruschette

Bruschette

- 4 large slices firm-textured bread
- 2 cloves garlic
- 1/4 cup (60 ml) extra-virgin olive oil
- freshly ground sea salt

You can toast the bread in the toaster, but using the oven dries it out more, adding an authentic touch. Be sure to use only the best cold-pressed oil as this dish depends on the quality of the oil.

Preheat the oven to 400°F (200°C/gas 6). • Toast the bread in the oven until crisp and golden brown, 5 minutes. • Rub each slice of toast with half a clove of garlic. • Drizzle with 1 tablespoon of oil and season with salt.

Serves: 4 • Prep: 5 min • Cooking: 5 min • Level: 1

Bruschette with cannellini beans

Bruschette coi fagioli

Preheat the oven to 400°F (200°C/gas 6). • Warm the beans, sage, and ½ (125 ml) water in a small saucepan over medium heat. • Toast the bread in the oven until crisp and golden brown, about 5 minutes. • Place slices of toast on individual serving plates and top with the beans, adding some of the cooking water to soften the bread. • Drizzle with the oil and season generously with pepper. • Serve warm.

Serves: 4 • Prep: 10 min • Cooking: 10 min • Level: 1

- 1 (14-oz/400-g) can cannellini (or white kidney) beans, drained
- 4 leaves sage
- salt and freshly ground black pepper
- 4 large slices firm-textured bread
- 1/4 cup (60 ml) extra-virgin olive oil

Bruschette with tomato and basil

Bruschette con pomodoro e basilico

- 4 medium salad tomatoes
- 4 large slices firm-textured bread
- 2 cloves garlic
- salt and freshly ground black pepper
- 1/3 cup (90 ml) extra-virgin olive oil
- 8–12 fresh basil leaves, torn

Cut the tomatoes in half, sprinkle with salt, and set them upside-down for 20 minutes to drain. • Toast the bread until golden brown over a barbecue or in the oven (so that it dries out and is very crisp). • Rub the slices with the garlic. Season with salt and pepper and drizzle with half the oil. • Chop the tomatoes in small cubes. Arrange them on the toast and garnish with the basil. Drizzle with the remaining oil and serve.

Serves: 4 • Prep: 10 min + 20 min to drain • Cooking: 5 min Level: 1

Sausage and cheese crostini

Crostini all'aretina

Preheat the oven to 400°F (200°C/gas 6). • Toast the bread in the oven, about 5 minutes. • Place the sausage meat in a medium bowl. Add the cheese and pepper and mix well with a fork. • Spread each slice of toast with the sausage and cheese mixture and transfer to a large oiled baking dish. • Bake until the cheese has melted and the topping is bubbling, 5–10 minutes. • Serve hot.

Serves: 4–6 • Prep: 5 min • Cooking: 10–15 min • Level: 1

- 1 long loaf firm-textured white bread (French loaf is ideal), sliced
- 8 oz (250 g) Italian sausage meat
- 8 oz (250 g) pecorino cheese, coarsely grated
- freshly ground black pepper

Sicilian crostini

Crostini siciliani

- 8 slices firm-textured bread, crusts removed
- 1/2 cup (125 ml) extra-virgin olive oil
- 2 tablespoons vinegar
- 1 tablespoon each sugar, capers, pine nuts, raisins, diced candied lemon peel
- 2 ripe tomatoes, diced

Heat the oil in a large frying pan and fry the bread until golden brown on both sides, 5–10 minutes. Drain on paper towels. • Bring the vinegar, sugar, and 2 tablespoons of water to a boil, then add the capers, pine nuts, raisins, lemon peel, and tomatoes. • Simmer for 5 minutes, stirring often. • Spread the fried bread with this mixture and serve.

Serves: 4–8 • Prep: 10 min • Cooking: 10–15 min • Level: 1

Crostini with black kale

Fettunta col cavolo nero

These crostini are made with cavolo nero, *or black Tuscan kale. Replace with Swiss chard (silver beet) if you can't find the black kale.*

Preheat the oven to 400°F (200°C/gas 6). • Boil the kale in salted water in a large deep saucepan until tender, 15–20 minutes. • Toast the bread in the oven and rub with garlic. • Place the kale on the toast. Season with salt, pepper, and oil.

Serves: 4 • Prep: 5 min • Cooking: 15–20 min • Level: 1

- 1 head black Tuscan kale, washed, stalked, and coarsely chopped
- 4 large slices firm-textured bread
- 1–2 cloves garlic
- salt and freshly ground black pepper
- 1/4 cup (60 ml) extra-virgin olive oil

Tuna appetizer with tomatoes and bell peppers

BROILED BELL PEPPERS WITH ANCHOVY DRESSING

Peperoni all'acciuga

- 2–3 large yellow and red bell peppers (capsicums)
- salt
- 2–3 cloves garlic, thinly sliced
- 1/3 cup (90 ml) extra-virgin olive oil
- 8–10 salt-cured anchovy fillets

Preheat the broiler (grill) to high. Cook the bell peppers whole under the broiler, giving them quarter turns as their skin scorches and blackens. This will take about 20 minutes. Wrap them in foil. Leave for 10 minutes then remove the skins. • Cut the bell peppers in half from top to bottom and discard the stalks, seeds, and pulpy inner core. Rinse gently and dry well. • Slice the bell peppers lengthwise into long strips (1–2 inches/3–6 cm wide). Place in a colander, sprinkling each layer with a little salt. Let drain for at least 1 hour. • Sauté the garlic in the oil in a small frying pan over low heat until pale gold, 3–5 minutes. • Add the anchovies, crushing them with a fork until they dissolve in the oil. • Transfer the bell peppers to a serving dish and drizzle with the anchovy dressing. • Serve at room temperature.

Serves: 4 • Prep: 30 min + 1 hr to drain • Cooking: 25 min Level: 2

TUNA APPETIZER WITH TOMATOES AND BELL PEPPERS

Tonno con pomodori e peperoni grigliati

Preheat the broiler (grill) to high. Cook the bell peppers whole under the broiler, giving them quarter turns as their skin scorches and blackens. This will take about 20 minutes. Wrap them in foil. Leave for 10 minutes then remove the skins. • Remove and discard the stalks, seeds, and pulpy inner core. Slice the peppers lengthwise into strips. • Arrange the tomatoes, bell peppers, tuna, and basil on a serving plate. Drizzle with the oil and season with salt. • Serve with freshly toasted bread.

Serves: 4–6 • Prep: 30 min • Cooking: 20 min • Level 2

- 3 large yellow bell peppers (capsicums)
- 4 large ripe tomatoes, thinly sliced
- 5 oz (150 g) canned tuna, drained
- fresh basil leaves, torn
- 1/4 cup (60 ml) extra-virgin olive oil
- salt
- freshly toasted bread, to serve

SWEET AND SOUR VEGETABLE APPETIZER

Caponata

- 2 lb (1 kg) eggplants (aubergine), cut into 1/2-inch (1-cm) cubes
- 1 tablespoon coarse sea salt
- 2/3 cup (150 ml) extra-virgin olive oil
- 4 stalks celery, cut into short lengths
- 1 large onion, sliced
- 1 (14-oz/400-g) can tomatoes, with juice
- 12 leaves fresh basil, torn
- 1 small, firm pear, peeled, cored, and diced (optional)

La Caponata is a classic Sicilian dish. Its subtle mix of sweet and sour flavors is typical of the island's cuisine and reflects it age old connections with the Orient.

Layer the eggplants in a colander, sprinkling with coarse salt, and leave for at least 1 hour. Rinse and dry on paper towels. • Heat about two-thirds of the oil in a frying pan and sauté the eggplant over a medium heat until tender, about 10 minutes. Set aside. • Blanch the celery in salted boiling water for 5 minutes. Drain and set aside. • Sauté the onion in the remaining oil until pale golden brown, about 5 minutes. • Add the tomatoes and half the basil. Simmer for 10 minutes. • Add the celery, pear (if using), capers, olives, pine nuts, sugar, and vinegar. Simmer for 20 minutes, stirring now and then. • Add the eggplant and the remaining basil. Simmer, stirring occasionally, for 10 minutes. • Remove from the heat and when the mixture is just warm, transfer to a serving dish, heaping it up into a mound. The eggplant should have absorbed most of the moisture. • Leave to stand for several hours or overnight. • Sprinkle with the almonds or bread crumbs and serve at room temperature.

Serves: 4–6 • Prep: 1 hr + several hr to stand • Cooking: 50 min • Level: 1

- 2 tablespoons capers
- 20 green or black olives, pitted and chopped
- 3 tablespoons pine nuts
- 2 tablespoons sugar
- scant 1/2 cup (100 ml) white wine vinegar
- 3 tablespoons coarsely chopped roasted almonds (or 3 tablespoons toasted bread crumbs)

Stuffed green peppers

STUFFED GREEN PEPPERS

Peperoni verdi ripieni

- 3 cups (180 g) fresh bread crumbs
- $1/4$ cup (60 ml) milk
- $1/2$ cup (60 g) freshly grated pecorino or Parmesan cheese
- generous $1/2$ cup (60 g) pitted black olives, finely chopped
- 2 tablespoons finely chopped parsley
- salt and freshly ground black pepper
- 8 long green peppers
- $1/4$ cup (60 ml) extra-virgin olive oil

Preheat the oven to 350°F (180°C/gas 4). • Oil a large baking dish. • Place the bread crumbs in a large bowl and drizzle with the milk. Add the pecorino, olives, and parsley. Mix well and season with salt and pepper. • Cut the tops off the peppers and scoop out the seeds and the fibrous white parts. Rinse the peppers and drain on paper towels. • Season each pepper with a little salt. Fill with some of the filling and then replace the top. • Arrange the filled peppers in the baking dish. Drizzle with the oil. • Bake until tender, about 30 minutes. • Serve hot or at room temperature.

Serves: 4 • Prep: 15 min • Cooking: 30 min • Level: 1

STUFFED BELL PEPPERS

Peperoni ripieni

Bell peppers can also be filled with ground beef, pork, or chicken and flavored with Parmesan or pecorino cheese, garlic, parsley, and other herbs. This simple vegetarian recipe makes a light and flavorful appetizer.

- 4 medium yellow bell peppers (capsicums), cut in half lengthwise, cleaned, seeds removed
- 2 tablespoons salt-cured capers, rinsed and chopped
- 2 cloves garlic, finely chopped
- 4 tablespoons fine dry bread crumbs
- 2 tablespoons finely chopped parsley
- 2 tablespoons raisins, soaked in warm water for 1 hour
- 2 tablespoons pine nuts
- $1/2$ cup (125 ml) extra-virgin olive oil
- salt and freshly ground black pepper

Preheat the oven to 400°F (200°C/gas 6). • Place the bell peppers in a roasting pan, skin-side down. Bake for 5 minutes. • Meanwhile, mix the capers, garlic, bread crumbs, parsley, raisins, pine nuts, oil, salt, and pepper in a medium bowl. • Spread the mixture on the partly-cooked bell peppers. • Bake until the filling begins to brown, about 15 minutes. • Serve hot or at room temperature.

Serves: 4 • Prep: 10 min • Cooking: 20 min • Level: 1

TOMATOES WITH CAPRINO CHEESE

Pomodorini cremosi

- 24 cherry tomatoes
- 1 tablespoon extra-virgin olive oil
- 10 green olives, pitted and chopped
- 1 clove garlic, finely chopped
- 6 fresh basil leaves, torn
- salt and freshly ground black pepper
- 8 oz (250 g) soft creamy caprino (Italian goat cheese)

Slice the tops off the tomatoes. Scoop out the pulp using a small teaspoon and set aside. • Sprinkle the shells lightly with salt and place upside-down in a colander to drain for 30 minutes. • In a bowl, mix the oil, tomato pulp, olives, garlic, basil, salt, pepper, and cheese until well mixed. • Stuff the tomatoes with the filling and chill in the refrigerator for at least 30 minutes before serving.

Serves: 4–6 • Prep: 15 min + 1 hr to drain and chill • Level: 1

BAKED TOMATOES WITH CHEESE

Pomodori gratinati al taleggio

- 8 medium tomatoes
- salt and freshly ground black pepper
- $1/4$ cup (60 ml) extra-virgin olive oil
- 1 tablespoon finely chopped parsley
- 1 tablespoon finely chopped basil
- 4 tablespoons all-purpose (plain) flour
- 2 cups (500 ml) milk
- dash of nutmeg
- 4 oz (125 g) taleggio, Fontina, or cheddar cheese, grated

Preheat the oven to 400°F (200°C/gas 6). • Cut the tomatoes in half, squeezing gently to remove the seeds. Place in an ovenproof baking dish and season lightly with salt and pepper. Drizzle with 1 tablespoon of oil and sprinkle with the parsley and basil. Bake for 20 minutes. • Heat the remaining oil in a small saucepan over low heat. Add the flour and stir constantly until thick. • Gradually add the milk, stirring constantly. Simmer until smooth and dense, 5–7 minutes. Season with salt, pepper, and nutmeg, and stir in the cheese. • Fill the tomatoes with this mixture and bake until the cheese is lightly browned, about 20 minutes.

Serves: 4–6 • Prep: 15 min • Cooking: 40 min • Level: 1

Piedmontese dip

Piedmontese Cheese Fondue

Fonduta piemontese

- 1 lb (500 g) (weight without crust) Fontina cheese
- 1¼ cups (300 ml) milk
- 3 tablespoons butter
- 5–6 egg yolks
- salt and freshly ground white pepper
- toasted bread or baked or fried polenta, cut in cubes

Cheese fondue is made throughout the European alps. This recipe comes from the Italian side, in Valle d'Aosta and Piedmont in the northwest. It should be made in the top half of a double boiler so that the ingredients never boil. To serve, transfer to a fondue pot over a low flame so that the cheese stays deliciously warm as your guests dip their pieces of bread or polenta. The gourmet version of this fondue is served with a sprinkling of wafer-thin slices of white truffles from the Alba region in Piedmont.

Slice the cheese thinly and place in a bowl with enough milk to cover. Leave to stand for 2–4 hours. • Half-fill a saucepan or the bottom pan of a double boiler with water and bring to a very gentle boil. Place a heatproof bowl or the top pan of the double boiler containing the butter over the top and leave to melt. • Drain the milk off the cheese, reserving the milk. Add the cheese to the melted butter, together with ¼ cup (60 ml) of the milk. • Stir continuously with a whisk or wooden spoon over the simmering water until the cheese has melted and threads start to form. At no point should the mixture be allowed to boil. • Adding them one at a time, stir 5 egg yolks into the cheese, incorporating each one very thoroughly. The mixture should now be glossy and smooth. If it still looks a little grainy, add the final, sixth egg yolk and stir well for 1 minute. • Season with salt and pepper to taste. • Transfer the mixture to a fondue pot and place at the center of the table. Give each guest a fondue fork for dipping the pieces of bread and polenta into the sauce.

Serves: 4–6 • Prep: 10 min + 2–4 hr to stand • Cooking: 30 min • Level: 2

Piedmontese Dip

Bagna cauda

In the days when walnut oil was widely available, it was used in place of the olive oil. Traditionally, Bagna Cauda is made in a small fireproof earthenware pot which is placed in the center of the table and kept hot over a spirit lamp (formerly a small brazier containing embers). This means that everyone seated round the table can easily reach over to dip the prepared raw vegetables into the sauce. The vegetables should be arranged on a large serving platter.

- ⅓ cup (90 g) sweet (unsalted) butter
- 6 cloves garlic, very finely chopped
- 1 cup (250 ml) extra-virgin olive oil
- 4 oz (125 g) salt-cured anchovy fillets
- selection of fresh, raw vegetables, including: cardoon stalks (peeled and kept in cold water acidulated with lemon juice until just before serving to prevent discoloration); celery stalks; tender Savoy cabbage leaves; cauliflower florets; sliced baby turnips; carrots (sometimes boiled until just tender); peeled, sliced artichokes; radishes; raw or roast sweet bell peppers (capsicums)

Melt the butter in a small earthenware pan or heavy saucepan. Add the garlic and cook over very low heat for 15 minutes. The garlic should not take on any color. • Add the oil and leave over very low heat for 10 minutes more. • Add the anchovy fillets and cook as gently as possible for 30–40 minutes. Stir frequently with a wooden spoon and use the back of it to mash the anchovies, which should gradually dissolve into the oil and butter. The sauce should never reach boiling point. • There are a number of delicious variations on the basic recipe. Try adding a scant ½ cup (100 ml) of heavy (double) cream 5 minutes before the end of cooking time for a very rich sauce. • Add wafer-thin slices of fresh truffle just before serving. • Crumble 3–4 walnut halves together with the oil to recreate the traditional flavor of walnut oil.

Serves: 4 • Prep: 10 min • Cooking: about 1 hr • Level: 2

Fresh salmon with lemon and capers

Tuna mousse

Mousse di tonno

- 12 oz (350 g) tuna, packed in oil
- 8 oz (250 g) mascarpone cheese
- 3 oz (90 g) pickled onions, well drained and finely chopped
- 1 tablespoon finely chopped parsley
- salt and freshly ground black pepper
- 1 tablespoon butter
- bunch fresh arugula (rocket)
- 12 black olives, pitted and chopped

Chop the tuna in a food processor for 1–2 minutes. • Transfer to a bowl and stir in the mascarpone. Add the pickled onions and parsley and mix well. Season with salt and pepper. • Lightly butter an 8-inch (20-cm) pudding mold and line with aluminum foil. Fill with the tuna mixture and chill in the refrigerator for 6 hours. • Wash and dry the arugula and arrange on a serving dish. Invert the mousse onto the bed of arugula. Garnish with the olives and serve.

Serves: 4–6 • Prep: 15 min + 6 hr to chill • Level: 1

Seafood salad

Insalata di mare

Soak the mussels in a large bowl of water for 1 hour. Pull off their beards, scrub, and rinse under cold running water. • Cook the mussels in a large pot over medium heat until they open up, 5–10 minutes. Discard any that do not open. Shell and set aside. • Cook the octopus in 3 cups (750 ml) of salted boiling water, 1 tablespoon of oil, and the vinegar over medium heat until tender, about 30 minutes. • Drain and chop coarsely. • Cook the shrimp with the garlic and 1 tablespoon of oil in a large saucepan over medium heat for 2 minutes. Shell and let cool. • Steam the cod until tender, about 5 minutes. Let cool. • Beat the lemon juice, remaining oil, and salt in a small bowl. • Arrange the mussels, shrimp, cod, octopus, onion, and celery in a large salad bowl. Drizzle with the oil and lemon. • Chill in the refrigerator until ready to serve.

Serves: 4–6 • Prep: 30 min • Cooking: 50 min • Level: 2

- 12 oz (350 g) mussels, in shell
- 12 oz (350 g) baby octopus, cleaned
- 12 oz (350 g) shrimp (prawns)
- 1 clove garlic, finely chopped
- 1/4 cup (60 ml) extra-virgin olive oil
- 12 oz (350 g) cod fillets
- 1 tablespoon white wine vinegar
- 1 tablespoon fresh lemon juice
- salt
- 1 large onion, finely sliced, soaked in cold water for 10 minutes, drained
- 1 head celery, finely chopped

Fried mozzarella

Mozzarella fritta

- 4 slices of mortadella (Bologna sausage), 1/4-inch (5-mm) thick
- 2 cups (500 ml) warm milk
- 2/3 cup (100 g) all-purpose (plain) flour
- 1 egg
- salt and freshly ground black pepper
- 1/8 teaspoon freshly grated nutmeg
- 3/4 cup (100 g) fine dry bread crumbs
- 1 cup (250 ml) sunflower oil, for frying

Cut the mortadella slices into quarters and place in a bowl. Add enough milk to cover and let stand for 2 hours. • Drain the mortadella. Dry with paper towels and coat with flour. • Lightly beat the egg and season with salt, pepper, and nutmeg. • Dip the mortadella in the egg, followed by the bread crumbs. • Heat the oil in a large frying pan to very hot. • Fry the mortadella in two batches until golden brown on both sides, about 5 minutes per batch. • Drain on paper towels and serve hot.

Serves: 4 • Prep: 15 min + 2 hr to soak • Cooking: 10 min Level: 1

Fresh salmon with lemon and capers

Carpaccio di salmone

Coarsely pound the salt and half the pepper corns in a mortar and pestle. Add the thyme and mix well. • In a small bowl, beat together 1/3 cup (90 ml) of the oil with the lemon juice and salt mixture. • Arrange the salmon in a shallow serving dish and pour the dressing over the top. • Cover with plastic wrap (cling film) and chill in the refrigerator for 4 hours. • Remove the plastic wrap and drizzle with the remaining oil. • Garnish with the remaining pepper corns and the lemon wedges and serve.

Serves: 6–8 • Prep: 15 min + 4 hr to chill • Level: 1

- 1 teaspoon coarse sea salt
- 2 tablespoons whole green pepper corns, preserved in brine
- 1 teaspoon fresh thyme leaves
- 1/2 cup (125 ml) extra-virgin olive oil
- juice of 1 lemon
- 1 1/2 lb (750 g) very fresh salmon fillet, thinly sliced
- 1 lemon, cut into wedges, to garnish

Marinated olives with orange

Olive nere all'arancia

- 3 cups (300 g) large ripe black olives
- 2 cloves garlic, finely sliced
- 2 teaspoons dried oregano
- shredded zest of 1 large orange
- 1/4 cup (60 ml) extra-virgin olive oil

Rinse the olives in very hot water. Dry and transfer to a shallow dish. • Sprinkle with the garlic, oregano, and orange zest. • Drizzle with the oil and mix well. • Marinate overnight before serving.

Serves: 6–8 • Prep: 5 min + 12 hr to marinate • Level: 1

Savory hearts

Sfoglie saporite

- 4 sprigs fresh parsley
- 4 sprigs fresh basil
- 1/2 cup (90 g) pine nuts
- 4 tablespoons freshly grated pecorino cheese
- salt
- 1/2 cup (125 ml) extra-virgin olive oil
- 1/4 cup (60 ml) black olive paste (or tapenade)
- 4 tablespoons freshly grated Parmesan cheese
- 1/2 teaspoon sweet paprika
- 8 oz (250 g) frozen puff pastry, thawed

In a food processor, chop the parsley, basil, half the pine nuts, the pecorino, and 1/8 teaspoon salt to a smooth paste. Add 5 tablespoons of the oil and mix well. • Separately, process the olive paste, remaining pine nuts, Parmesan, paprika, and remaining oil until smooth. • Cut the pastry in half. Roll out each half on a lightly floured surface to make a rectangle 1/8 inch (3 mm) thick. • Spread one of the rectangles with the herb paste. Roll up the pastry, rolling from both of the outside edges at the same time until the two rolls meet in the center. • Spread the other rectangle with the olive paste. Roll up the pastry, rolling from both of the outside edges at the same time until the two rolls meet in the center. • Preheat the oven to 400°F (200°C/gas 6). • Cover two baking sheets with waxed paper. • Slice the pastry rolls 1/4 inch (5 mm) thick. • Arrange the slices, well spaced, on the baking sheets. • Bake until golden brown, about 15 minutes. • Serve hot or at room temperature.

Serves: 6–8 • Prep: 20 min • Cooking: 15 min • Level: 2

Stuffed olives

Olive alla ascolana

This recipe comes from the little known but stunning Roman and medieval town of Ascoli Piceno, in the Marches.

- 4 oz (125 g) lard
- 2 tablespoons extra-virgin olive oil
- 5 oz (150 g) lean ground (minced) pork
- 4 oz (125 g) lean ground (minced) beef
- 1 medium tomato, peeled and finely chopped
- 2 oz (60 g) chicken livers, chopped
- 1/4 cup (15 g) fresh breadcrumbs
- 2–3 tablespoons stock (bouillon cube)
- 3 large eggs
- 1/3 cup (50 g) freshly grated Parmesan cheese
- pinch of freshly grated nutmeg
- pinch of ground cinnamon
- salt and freshly ground black pepper
- 60 large green olives
- 1/2 cup (75 g) all-purpose (plain) flour
- 1 cup (125 g) fine dry bread crumbs
- 1 lemon, sliced, to garnish (optional)
- 2 cups (500 ml) olive oil, for frying

Put the lard and 2 tablespoons of the oil in a large frying pan over medium heat. Add the pork and beef. Sauté until browned, 5–7 minutes. • Add the tomato and 2 tablespoons of water. Mix well and simmer until the meat is cooked, about 15 minutes. • Add the chicken livers and simmer until cooked, 5–7 minutes. • Transfer the mixture to a food processor and chop to make a smooth paste. • Drizzle the fresh bread crumbs with the stock and mix well. Transfer the paste to a bowl and add the moist bread crumbs. Add 1 egg, the Parmesan, nutmeg, and cinnamon. Season with salt and pepper and mix well. • Slit the olives down one side and remove the pit. Open each olive a little and stuff it with some of the filling. • Beat the remaining eggs in a small bowl. • Place the flour and fine dry bread crumbs on separate plates. • Roll each olive in the flour, dip it in the egg, then roll it in the bread crumbs, making that it is evenly coated. Repeat with all the olives. • Heat the frying oil in a deep fryer or frying pan until very hot. Fry the olives in small batches until golden brown all over, 5–7 minutes per batch. • Transfer to paper towels using a slotted spoon and let drain. • Serve hot, garnish with sliced lemon (if liked).

Serves: 8–10 • Prep: 45 min • Cooking: 45 min • Level: 3

Fried parmesan packets

FRIED PARMESAN PACKETS

Chizze

- 3 cups (450 g) all-purpose (plain) flour
- salt
- 1 teaspoon baking powder
- 5 oz (150 g) butter. chopped
- $1/2$ cup (125 ml) warm water
- 5 oz (150 g) Parmesan cheese, thinly sliced
- 2 cups (500 ml) olive oil, for frying

This hearty appetizer comes from Emilia-Romagna, the homeland of Parmesan cheese.

Place the flour, salt, and baking powder in a large bowl and mix well. • Add half the butter and use your fingertips to work it into the flour. • Pour in enough water to obtain a firm dough. • Place the dough on a lightly floured work surface and knead for 5 minutes. • Roll the dough out into an 8 x 15-inch (20 x 40-cm) rectangle. • Place pieces of Parmesan on one half of the dough about 2 inches (5 cm) apart. Top the cheese with a piece of the remaining butter. • Fold the piece of dough without cheese on it over the other half. • Use a fluted pastry cutter or sharp knife to cut out rectangles around each piece of cheese. • Heat the oil in a deep fryer or frying pan to very hot. • Fry the fritters in batches until golden brown, 5–7 minutes per batch. Drain on paper towels and serve hot.

Serves: 8–10 • Prep: 10 min • Cooking: 20 min • Level: 2

SAVORY PASTRY FRITTERS

Crescenti

Serve these fritters very hot with a platter of prosciutto (Parma ham), salami, and fresh creamy cheeses.

Dissolve the yeast in the warm water and set aside to rest for 15 minutes. • Sift the flour and salt into a large bowl. Pour in the lard and yeast mixture. Stir with a fork, gradually working in the flour, adding a little more water if needed. • Transfer to a floured work surface and knead until the dough is smooth and elastic, 10–15 minutes. • Shape into a ball and leave to rise in the bowl, covered with a clean cloth, for about 1 hour. • Roll out the dough into a sheet $1/8$ inch (3 mm) thick. Cut into diamonds or rectangles about 2 inches (5 cm) long. • Heat the oil in a deep fryer or frying pan to very hot. • Fry the fritters in batches until golden brown, 5–7 minutes per batch. • Drain on paper towels and serve hot.

Serves: 8–10 • Prep: 40 min + 1 hr to rest the dough
Cooking: 20 min • Level: 2

- $1\frac{1}{2}$ oz (45 g) fresh yeast or 3 ($1/4$-oz/7-g)) packages active dry yeast
- 1 cup (250 ml) warm water
- $3\frac{1}{3}$ cups (500 g) all-purpose (plain) flour
- salt
- $1/4$ cup (60 ml) melted lard
- 1–2 cups (250–500 ml) olive oil, for frying

GARBANZO BEAN FRITTERS

Panelle

- 2 quarts (2 liters) cold water
- $2\frac{2}{3}$ cups (400 g) garbanzo bean (chickpea) flour
- salt
- 5 tablespoons finely chopped parsley
- 1–2 cups (250–500 ml) olive oil, for frying

Pour about two-thirds of the water into a blender. Add the garbanzo bean flour and process, adding more water as needed to form a pouring batter. • Pour the mixture into a saucepan. Season with salt and bring slowly to a boil, stirring constantly. • Simmer, stirring often, until very thick, soft, and smooth, about 30 minutes. Stir in the parsley. • Lightly oil a baking sheet or large shallow pan. • Use a spatula to spread the mixture evenly to a thickness of about $1/4$ inch (5 mm). • Let cool completely, then cut into short strips or squares. • Heat the oil to very hot in a frying pan or deep fryer. • Fry the fritters in batches until golden brown, about 5-7 minutes per batch. • Drain well and serve hot.

Serves: 4 • Prep: 15 min • Cooking: 40 min • Level: 2

FRIED MOZZARELLA TRIANGLES

Mozzarella in carrozza

Beat the eggs in a bowl. Season with salt and pepper. • Cut the slices of bread and the mozzarella into triangles. Arrange an anchovy and a slice of mozzarella on each slice of bread. Fasten them to the bread with a toothpick. • Dip the bread slices in flour and then in the beaten egg. • Heat the oil in a large frying pan to very hot. Fry the bread, mozzarella-side down, for 1 minute. Turn and fry until golden brown all over. • Drain well on paper towels. Remove the toothpicks before serving. • Serve hot.

Serves: 4 • Prep: 10 min • Cooking: 10 min • Level: 2

- 3 eggs
- salt and freshly ground black pepper
- 8 slices sandwich bread
- 12 oz (350 g) fresh mozzarella cheese, sliced
- 2 oz (60 g) salt-cured anchovy fillets, rinsed
- $1/3$ cup (50 g) all-purpose (plain) flour
- 1 cup (250 ml) olive oil, for frying

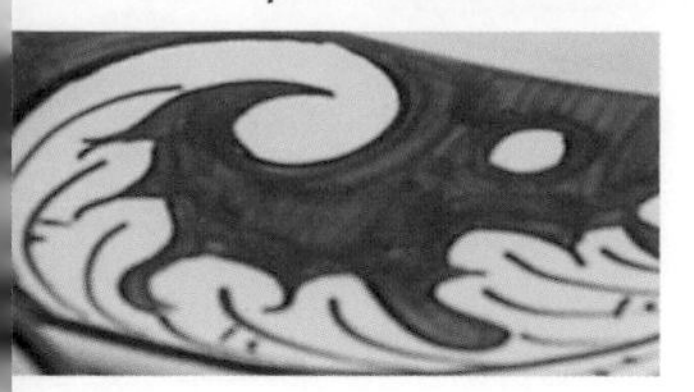

Stuffed rice cakes

Stuffed rice cakes

Arancine di riso

- 3 eggs
- 3 tablespoons extra-virgin olive oil
- $\frac{1}{3}$ cup (90 g) butter
- 1 small onion, finely chopped
- 3 oz (90 g) chicken giblets, finely chopped
- 4 oz (125 g) minced beef
- 1 cup (150 g) frozen peas
- $\frac{1}{4}$ cup (60 ml) canned tomato sauce
- $\frac{1}{4}$ cup (125 ml) beef stock, homemade (see page 104), or bouillon cube
- 2 tablespoons finely chopped basil
- 2 tablespoons finely chopped parsley
- 1 stalk celery, finely chopped
- salt and freshly ground black pepper
- $1\frac{1}{2}$ cups (300 g) short-grain rice
- pinch of saffron strands
- 3 tablespoons freshly grated Parmesan cheese
- $\frac{1}{3}$ cup (50 g) all-purpose (plain) flour
- 1 cup (125 g) fine dry bread crumbs
- 2–3 cups (500–750 ml) olive oil, for frying

*These stuffed fried rice cakes are a Sicilian specialty. In Messina and Catania they are pear shaped but most often they are made in the form of small balls the size of mandarins and this is what gives them their Italian name—*arancine*— which means "little oranges."*

Place one of the eggs in a small saucepan and cover with water. Bring to a boil over medium heat; simmer for 8 minutes from the moment the water reaches the boil. Drain and cool under cold running water. Shell the egg and chop coarsely. • Heat the extra-virgin oil and 1 tablespoon of butter in a large frying pan over medium heat. Add the onion and sauté until softened, 3–4 minutes. • Add the chicken and beef and sauté until lightly browned, 5 minutes. • Add the peas, tomato sauce, stock, basil, parsley, and celery. Mix well and season with salt and pepper. Cover and simmer over low heat until the sauce is very thick, 35–40 minutes. • Cook the rice in a large pot with 2 cups (500 ml) of salted water until very al dente and the water is absorbed, about 10 minutes. If the rice is still very uncooked add a little more boiling water and cook for 1–2 minutes more, until it has absorbed the added water. Remove from the heat and let cool slightly. • Add one of the remaining eggs, the remaining butter, the saffron, and the cheese. Mix well. • Shape the mixture into balls the size of large walnuts using your hands. Press your finger into the center of each ball to make a hole. Fill the hole with a piece of boiled egg and a little of the meat mixture. Close the rice mixture over the filling, making sure it is well sealed. • Beat the remaining egg in a small bowl. Place the flour and bread crumbs on separate plates. • Roll each rice cake in the flour, then dip it in the egg, and roll it in the bread crumbs, making sure it is evenly coated. • Heat the frying oil in a deep fryer to very hot. • Fry the arancine in two batches until golden brown all over, 7–10 minutes per batch. • Drain on paper towels and serve hot.

Serves: 4–6 • Prep: 25 min • Cooking: 1 hr 20 min • Level: 3

Mozzarella and tomato crostoni

Crostoni con mozzarella

- 2 cloves garlic, finely chopped
- $\frac{1}{4}$ cup (60 ml) extra-virgin olive oil
- 1 (14-oz/400-g) can tomatoes, with juice
- 6 leaves fresh basil, torn
- 1 teaspoon dried oregano
- salt
- 4 large slices firm-textured bread
- 6 oz (180 g) fresh mozzarella cheese, thinly sliced

Preheat the oven to 400°F (200°C/gas 6). • Heat 2 tablespoons of oil in a medium saucepan. Add the garlic and sauté until pale gold, 3 minutes. • Add the tomatoes, basil, half the oregano, and salt, and simmer for 30 minutes. • Cut the slices of bread in half, cover with mozzarella, and place in an oiled baking dish. Sprinkle with the remaining oregano, drizzle with the remaining oil, and bake until the mozzarella is lightly browned, 10–15 minutes. • Spread with the tomato sauce. • Serve hot.

Serves: 4 • Prep: 15 min • Cooking: 40 min • Level: 1

Fried polenta crostini

Crostini di polenta fritta

- 1 quantity polenta, cold (see recipe, page 220)
- 1 cup (250 ml) olive oil, for frying

Fried or baked polenta crostini are a good way to use up leftover polenta. They can be served as they are or with a variety of toppings. The polenta should be made at least 12 hours in advance; it needs time to firm up.

Prepare the polenta. • Turn the cooked polenta out onto a platter or board and leave to cool for at least 12 hours. • Cut the polenta in $\frac{1}{2}$-inch (1-cm) thick slices. • Heat the oil in a large frying pan to very hot and fry the polenta slices in batches until golden brown on both sides, 5–7 minutes per batch. • Serve hot.

Serves: 8 • Prep: 15 min • Cooking: 20 min • Level: 2

BREAD

Bread is a staple food in every region of Italy. In restaurants and trattorias a bread basket appears on the table without your asking, while in homes slices of bread or rolls are served with every meal. In many regions bread forms the basis of some classic dishes. In Tuscany, especially, bread is widely used to make soups, such as *Pappa al pomodoro* (see page 110) and *Ribollita* (see page 112), and salads, like *Panzanella* (see page 360). Tuscan bread is also famous because it contains no salt—which makes it the perfect foil for the highly flavored pecorino cheeses, hams, and liver crostini for which the region is also famous. But then every region has it specialties, from the crisp, flat *carta da musica* bread of Sardinia and the dense, tasty *ferrarese* rolls of Emilia-Romagna, to the crusty, firm-textured *pugliese* loaves of Puglia and the sesame seed-topped breads of Sicily. In this chapter we have included breads from every region that can be made with relative ease in home kitchens.

Parmesan loaves with seeds (see page 54)

Olive and rosemary bread

Basic olive oil bread

Pane all'olio

- 1 oz (30 g) fresh yeast or 2 ($\frac{1}{4}$-oz/7-g) packages active dry yeast
- 1 teaspoon sugar
- about $1\frac{1}{4}$ cups (300 ml) lukewarm water
- 4 cups (600 g) all-purpose (plain) flour
- 2–3 teaspoons salt
- 5 tablespoons extra-virgin olive oil

Proceed as for white bread (see next recipe), adding the oil to the yeast mixture at the beginning. Instead of kneading, mix the soft, sticky dough in the bowl with a wooden spoon. • When the rising time has elapsed (about 1 hour 30 minutes), mix the dough again for a few minutes. • Use a spatula to transfer it to an oiled baking pan about 12 inches (30 cm) in diameter. Cover with a cloth and leave to rise for 30 minutes. • Preheat the oven to 400°F (200°C/gas 6). • Bake until well risen and golden brown, about 35 minutes.

Makes: about 2 lb (1 kg) of bread • Prep: 30 min + about 2 hr to rise • Cooking: 35 min • Level: 2

Olive and rosemary loaves

Pane con olive e rosmarino

- 1 oz (30 g) fresh yeast or 2 ($\frac{1}{4}$-oz/7-g) packages active dry yeast
- 2 teaspoons salt
- about $1\frac{1}{2}$ cups (375 ml) lukewarm water
- 5 cups (750 g) all-purpose (plain) flour
- 1 cup (150 g) whole-wheat (wholemeal) flour
- $\frac{1}{2}$ cup (125 ml) extra-virgin olive oil
- 2 cups (200 g) black olives, pitted
- 3 tablespoons finely chopped rosemary

Dissolve the yeast and salt in $\frac{1}{2}$ cup (125 ml) of water and set aside until foamy, about 15 minutes. • Sift both flours into a large bowl. • Stir in the yeast mixture and enough of the remaining water to make a firm dough. • Knead the dough until smooth and elastic, 10–15 minutes. • Shape into a ball, place in an oiled bowl, and cover with a clean cloth. Let rise for 45 minutes in a warm place. • Oil a 12-inch (30-cm) ring baking pan. • Knead the dough again, just long enough to work in the olives and rosemary. • Place in the prepared baking pan. Cover with a cloth and let rise until doubled in bulk, about 30 minutes. • Preheat the oven to 350°F (180°C/gas 4). • Bake until well risen and lightly browned, about 35 minutes. • Cool for 10 minutes in the pan. Turn out onto a rack and let cool completely.

Makes just over 2 lb (1.2 kg) of bread • Prep: 30 min + 1 h 15 min to rise • Cooking: 35 min • Level: 2

Basic white bread

Pane bianco

- 1 oz (30 g) fresh yeast or 2 ($\frac{1}{4}$-oz/7-g) packages active dry yeast
- 1 teaspoon sugar
- about $1\frac{1}{2}$ cups (375 ml) lukewarm water
- $4\frac{2}{3}$ cups (700 g) all-purpose (plain) flour
- 2–3 teaspoons salt

This is a basic recipe for a versatile white bread. To freeze, wrap the loaves or rolls tightly in foil and place in the freezer. When serving frozen bread, don't let it thaw. Place it directly in a preheated oven at 350°F (180°C/gas 9) for 15–25 minutes (less time for rolls than for the larger loaves).

Place the yeast in a small bowl. Add the sugar and half the warm water and stir until dissolved. • Set aside for 15 minutes. It will look creamy when ready. Stir well. • Place the flour in a large bowl and add the yeast mixture, salt, and enough of the remaining water to obtain a firm dough. • Shape the dough into a ball and place on a lightly floured work surface. Knead the dough until smooth and elastic, 10–15 minutes. When ready the dough will show definite air bubbles beneath the surface and will spring back if you flatten it. • Place the kneaded dough in a clean bowl and cover with a clean cloth. Let rise in a warm place until doubled in bulk, about 1 hour 30 minutes. • Transfer the risen dough to a lightly floured work surface. Knead for 2–3 minutes. • Place the dough on an oiled baking sheet, and shape it into a long oval loaf. • Sprinkle the surface with flour and, using a serrated knife, cut several diagonal slashes about $\frac{1}{2}$-inch (1-cm) deep in the top. • For a large, ring-shaped loaf, about 12 inches (30 cm) in diameter, gently flatten the dough and make a hole in the middle with your fingers. Carefully enlarge the hole, shaping the dough into a ring. • For rolls, divide the dough into 8 equal portions and shape into rolls. Position the rolls at least $1\frac{1}{2}$ inches (5 cm) apart. • Cover with a cloth and leave to rise, 40–50 minutes. • Preheat the oven to 400°F (200°C/gas 6). • Bake in the oven. Large loaves will need about 40 minutes, the ring-shaped loaf about 30 minutes, and the rolls 20–25 minutes.

Makes about 2 lb (1 kg) of bread • Prep: 30 min + 2 hr 20 min to rise • Cooking: 25–40 min • Level: 2

Oregano bread

Oregano bread

Pane all'origano

- 1 oz (30 g) fresh yeast or 2 ($^1/_4$-oz/7-g) packages active dry yeast
- 1 teaspoon sugar
- about $1^1/_4$ cups (300 ml) lukewarm water
- 5 cups (750 g) all-purpose (plain) flour
- 1–2 tablespoons finely chopped fresh oregano or 1–2 teaspoons dried oregano
- 2 teaspoons salt
- $^1/_4$ cup (60 ml) extra-virgin olive oil

Place the yeast in a small bowl. Add the sugar and half the water and stir until dissolved. Set aside for 15 minutes. It will look creamy when ready. • Place the flour in a large bowl with the oregano, yeast mixture, salt, oil, and enough of the remaining water to obtain a fairly firm dough. • Shape the dough into a ball and place on a lightly floured work surface. Knead until smooth and elastic, 10–15 minutes. • Place in a clean bowl and cover with a cloth. Let rise in a warm place until doubled in bulk, about 1 hour 30 minutes. • Transfer the risen dough to a lightly floured work surface. Knead for 2–3 minutes. • Divide the dough into 4–6 equal portions and shape each one into a loaf about 14 inches (35 cm) long. • Place the loaves on two oiled baking sheets. Pull the ends of each loaf round and join them to make circular loaves, or leave them straight, as preferred. • Use a serrated knife to make a $^1/_2$-inch (1-cm) deep slash along the top of each loaf. • Cover with a cloth and let rise for 30 minutes. • Preheat the oven to 400°F (200°C/gas 6). • Bake until golden brown and hollow-sounding when tapped on the bottom, 25–30 minutes.

Makes: about 2 lb (1 kg) of bread • Prep: 30 min + about 2 hr to rise • Cooking: 25–30 min • Level: 2

Ciabatta

Ciabatta

Ciabatta is one of the most versatile and best loved of Italian breads. It is named for its shape, which is said to resemble a slipper, called a ciabatta *in Italian. Although this bread takes some time to make (about 20 hours in all), it can be made at home.*

- 1 oz (30 g) fresh yeast or 2 ($^1/_4$-oz/7-g) packages active dry yeast
- 1 cup (250 ml) lukewarm water
- $3^1/_2$ cups (500 g) + 2 tablespoons all-purpose (plain) flour
- 1 teaspoon natural or organic honey
- $^1/_2$ cup (125 ml) warm water
- 1 teaspoon salt
- $^1/_4$ cup (60 ml) extra-virgin olive oil
- durum wheat flour, to dust

Dissolve the yeast in half the water. Let stand until foamy, about 15 minutes. • Sift 3 cups (450 g) of flour onto a work surface and make a well in the center. Add the yeast mixture and enough of the remaining water to make a smooth dough. • Knead the dough until smooth and elastic, about 5 minutes. Place in a well floured bowl and cover with a clean cloth. Set aside in a warm place for 18 hours. • Turn the dough out onto a lightly floured work surface. Make an indentation in the center. • Dissolve the honey in the second measure of water. Mix in the remaining flour and salt. Knead the honey mixture into the dough until until well blended. Transfer the dough to an oiled bowl. Cover with a clean cloth and let rise for 30 minutes. • Turn out onto a lightly floured surface. Shape into a long oval, or ciabatta, shape. Sprinkle the top and sides of the dough with durum wheat flour. • Cover with a cloth and set aside for 1 hour. • Preheat the oven to 425°F (220°C/gas 7). • Place the dough on a baking sheet. • Bake for 10 minutes. Lower the oven temperature to 350°F (180°C/gas 4) and bake until golden brown, about 40 minutes more.

Makes: about 2 lb (1 kg) of bread • Prep: 40 min + 20 hr to rise • Cooking: 50 min • Level: 3

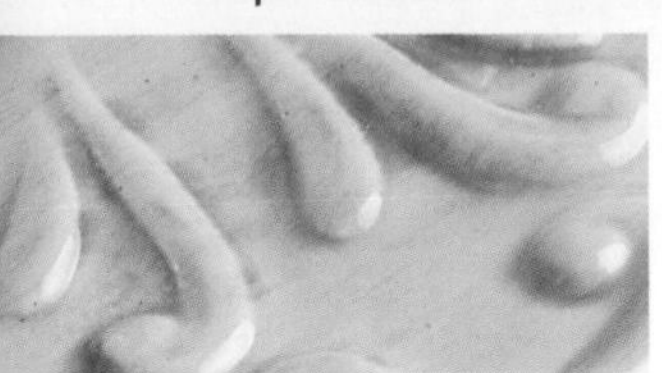

Potato bread

Pane con patate

- 5 oz (150 g) potatoes, peeled and cut in cubes
- 1 oz (30 g) fresh yeast or 2 (¼-oz/7-g) packages active dry yeast
- 1 teaspoon sugar
- about 1 cup (250 ml) lukewarm water
- 3⅓ cups (500 g) all-purpose (plain) flour
- 2 teaspoons salt
- 2 tablespoons extra-virgin olive oil

Cook the potatoes in a small pot of salted boiling water until tender, 15–20 minutes. • Drain and mash until smooth. • Place the yeast and sugar in a small bowl with ⅓ cup (90 ml) of the water. Stir well and let rest until foamy, about 15 minutes. • Sift the flour and salt into a large bowl. Use a wooden spoon to gradually stir in the yeast mixture, potatoes, and oil. Add enough of the remaining water to make a fairly soft dough. • Transfer to a lightly floured work surface and knead until smooth and elastic, 5–10 minutes. • Shape into a ball and place in an oiled bowl. Cover with a cloth and place in a warm place to rise until doubled in bulk, about 1 hour. • Turn the dough out onto a floured work surface and knead for 2–3 minutes. • Divide the dough into 6 balls and arrange, well spaced, on a large oiled baking sheet. Let rise for 30 minutes. • Preheat the oven to 400°F (200°C/gas 6). • Bake until risen and golden brown, 20–30 minutes..

Makes: just under 2 lb (1 kg) of bread • Prep: 45 min + 2 hr to rise • Cooking: 35–50 min • Level: 2

Sweet rosemary rolls

Pan di ramerino

This is an old Florentine recipe. These rolls were traditionally eaten at Easter, when the local bakers would set up stalls at church doors so that people could buy them on their way home from mass.

- 2 tablespoons fresh rosemary leaves
- 5 tablespoons extra-virgin olive oil
- ½ oz (15 g) fresh yeast or 1 (¼-oz/7-g) package active dry yeast
- 2 tablespoons sugar
- about ¾ cup (200 ml) lukewarm water
- 4 cups (600 g) all-purpose (plain) flour
- 1 teaspoon salt
- ½ cup (100 g) seedless raisins

Sweat the rosemary in ¼ cup (60 ml) of oil in a small pan over low heat for 10 minutes. Remove from the heat, discard the rosemary, and set the oil aside to cool. • Place the yeast in a small bowl. Add the sugar and half the water and stir until dissolved. Set aside for 15 minutes. It will look creamy when ready. • Put the flour in a large bowl with the salt, rosemary oil, yeast mixture, sugar, and enough of the remaining water to obtain a fairly firm dough. • Shape the dough into a ball and place on a lightly floured work surface. Knead until smooth and elastic, 10–15 minutes. • Place in a clean bowl and cover with a cloth. Let rise in a warm place until doubled in bulk, about 1 hour. • Rinse the raisins, drain, and pat dry on a clean cloth. • When the rising time has elapsed, transfer the dough to a lightly floured work surface and knead for 2–3 minutes. Incorporate the raisins into the dough as you knead. • Divide the dough into 6–8 equal portions, drizzle with the remaining oil, and shape into round rolls. • Place on an oiled baking sheet, keeping them well spaced (they will double in size as they rise). • Cover with a cloth and let rise for 30 minutes. • Preheat the oven to 400°F (200°C/gas 6). Bake until risen and golden brown, about 20 minutes.

Makes: just over 1 lb (500 g) of bread • Prep: 30 min + 2 hr to rise • Cooking: 20 min • Level: 2

Walnut bread

Italian corn bread

Pane di mais

- 1½ oz (45 g) fresh yeast or 3 (¼-oz/7-g) packages active dry yeast
- 1 teaspoon sugar
- about 1 cup (250 ml) lukewarm milk
- 2 cups (300 g) all-purpose (plain) flour
- 2 cups (300 g) finely ground cornmeal
- 2 teaspoons salt
- 1 egg, lightly beaten

Place the yeast in a small bowl. Add the sugar and half the milk and stir until dissolved. Set aside until creamy, about 15 minutes. • Combine both flours in a large bowl with the salt, egg, yeast mixture, and enough of the remaining milk to obtain a firm dough. • Place on a lightly floured work surface and knead until smooth and elastic, 10–15 minutes. Set aside to rise in an oiled bowl for 1 hour. • Knead again on a lightly floured work surface for 2–3 minutes. Divide the dough in half and shape into two round loaves. Sprinkle with flour and transfer to an oiled baking sheet. • Cover with a cloth and let rise for 30 minutes. • Preheat the oven to 400°F (200°C/gas 6). • Bake until golden brown, 25–35 minutes.

Makes: about 2 lb (1 kg) of bread • Prep: 30 min + 1 hr 30 min to rise • Cooking: 25–35 min • Level: 2

Walnut bread

Pane nociato

- 1 oz (30 g) fresh yeast or 2 packages (¼-oz/7-g)) active dry yeast
- about ¾ cup (200 ml) lukewarm water
- 3⅓ cups (500 g) all-purpose (plain) flour
- 1 teaspoon salt
- 3 tablespoons extra-virgin olive oil
- generous ¾ cup (100 g) freshly grated pecorino or parmesan cheese
- ½ cup (75 g) coarsely chopped walnuts
- ½ teaspoon freshly ground black pepper

Place the yeast in a small bowl. Add the sugar and half the water and stir until dissolved. Set aside for 15 minutes. It will look creamy when ready. • Sift the flour into a large bowl with the salt and stir in the yeast mixture, oil, cheese and enough of the remaining water to obtain a fairly firm dough. • Knead on a floured work surface until smooth and elastic, about 10 minutes. • Add the walnuts and pepper and knead for 5 minutes more. • Place the dough in a deep 10-inch (25-cm) oiled springform pan and let rise for 2 hours. • Preheat the oven to 425°F (220°C/ gas 7). • Bake until well risen and golden brown, 30–35 minutes. • Remove from the oven and let cool for 5 minutes before releasing the sides of the pan.

Makes: just over 1 lb (500 g) of bread • Prep: 35 min + 2 hr to rise • Cooking: 35 min • Level: 2

Walnut and rosemary bread

Pane alle noci e rosmarino

- 1 oz (30 g) fresh yeast or 2 (¼-oz/7-g) packages active dry yeast
- 1 teaspoon sugar
- about 1½ cups (375 ml) lukewarm water
- 2 cups (300 g) all-purpose (plain) flour
- 3 cups (450 g) whole-wheat (wholemeal) flour
- 1 tablespoon finely chopped rosemary or 1 teaspoon dried rosemary
- 1–2 teaspoons salt
- 2 tablespoons extra-virgin olive oil
- 1 clove garlic, finely chopped
- 3 oz (90 g) walnuts, coarsely chopped
- ½ teaspoon freshly ground black pepper

Place the yeast in a small bowl. Add the sugar and half the water and stir until dissolved. Set aside for 15 minutes. It will look creamy when ready. • Combine both flours with the rosemary and salt in a large bowl. • Stir half the oil into the yeast mixture then gradually stir it into the flour mixture together with enough of the remaining water to obtain a fairly firm dough. • Shape the dough into a ball and place on a lightly floured work surface. Knead until smooth and elastic, 10–15 minutes. • Place in a clean bowl and cover with a cloth. Let rise in a warm place until doubled in bulk, about 1 hour 30 minutes. • Meanwhile, sauté the garlic in the remaining oil in a small frying pan over medium heat for 2–3 minutes. Stir in the walnuts and pepper. Remove from heat and set aside to cool. • When the rising time has elapsed, place the dough on a lightly floured work surface and shape into a 12-inch (30-cm) disk. Spread the walnut mixture over the top then fold the dough over it. Knead to distribute the walnuts evenly, about 3 minutes. • Shape the dough into a ball and place on an oiled baking sheet. Cover with a floured cloth and let rise for about 30 minutes. It should almost double in bulk. • Preheat the oven to 375°F (190°C/gas 5). • Bake until the bread is golden brown and hollow-sounding when tapped on the bottom, about 45 minutes.

Makes: about 2 lb (1 kg) of bread • Prep: 30 min + 2 hr to rise • Cooking: 35min • Level: 2

QUICK SPICY BREAD ROLLS

Panini veloci piccanti

- 1/3 cup (90 ml) extra-virgin olive oil
- 1 cup (250 g) canned tomatoes, drained and crushed with a fork
- 1 cup (100 g) pitted black olives, chopped
- 1–2 dried chile peppers, crumbled
- 2 onions, finely chopped
- 3 1/3 cups (500 g) all-purpose (plain) flour
- 1 tablespoon baking powder
- 1 teaspoon salt

Substitute the chile pepper with 1–2 tablespoons finely chopped fresh herbs.

Mix the oil, tomatoes, olives, chile pepper, and onions in a large bowl. • Add the flour, baking powder, and salt and stir to make a fairly firm dough. • Knead the dough on a lightly floured work surface for 2–3 minutes. Shape into a ball and let rest for 10 minutes. • Preheat the oven to 450°F (250°C/gas 8). • Lightly oil a baking sheet. • Divide the dough into 10–12 balls and arrange on the baking sheet. • Bake until risen and golden brown, about 15 minutes. • Serve hot.

Makes: 10–12 rolls · Prep: 30 min · Cooking: 15 min
Level: 1

GARBANZO BEAN ROLLS

Panini ai ceci

- 1 oz (30 g) fresh yeast or 2 (1/4-oz/7-g) packages active dry yeast
- 1 teaspoon sugar
- about 1 cup (250 ml) lukewarm water
- 8 oz (250 g) canned garbanzo beans (chickpeas), drained
- 6 cups (600 g) all-purpose (plain) flour
- 2 teaspoons salt
- 1/3 cup (90 ml) extra-virgin olive oil

Place the yeast in a small bowl. Add the sugar and half the water and stir until dissolved. Set aside until creamy, about 15 minutes. • Chop the garbanzo beans in a food processor with the remaining water. • Combine the flour in a large bowl with the salt, yeast mixture, garbanzo beans, and 1/4 cup (60 ml) of oil. • Knead on a floured work surface until smooth and elastic, 10–15 minutes. Place in a bowl and let rise until doubled in bulk, about 1 hour 30 minutes • Knead for 2 minutes. Divide the dough into 16–20 equal portions and shape into round rolls. • Smear each roll with a little of the remaining oil. Use a serrated knife to cut a cross in the top of each roll. • Place on 2 oiled baking sheets, keeping the rolls well spaced. Cover with a cloth and let rise for 1 hour. • Preheat the oven to 425°F (225°C/gas 7). • Bake until risen and golden brown, 18–20 minutes.

Makes: about 16–20 rolls · Prep: 30 min + 2 hr 30 min to rise
Cooking: 18–20 min · Level: 2

Garbanzo bean rolls

Garbanzo bean flatbread

Italian flatbread

Piadine al formaggio

- 4 cups (600 g) all-purpose (plain) flour
- 1 teaspoon baking soda
- $1/2$ teaspoon salt
- $1/3$ cup (90 g) lard, at room temperature, thinly sliced
- $1/2$ cup (125 ml) lukewarm water

Piadine are made in Emilia-Romagna. Serve them hot with a platter of Parma ham and fresh, creamy cheeses.

Sift the flour, baking soda, and salt into a large bowl. Mix in the lard and enough water to make a firm dough. • Knead the dough on a lightly floured work surface until smooth and elastic. • Return to the bowl, cover with a cloth, and let rest for 30 minutes. • Divide the dough into pieces about the size of an egg. Sprinkle with flour and roll into $1/8$-inch (3-mm) thick disks about 6 inches (15 cm) in diameter. Prick well with a fork. • Cook, one at a time, in a very hot griddle or cast-iron pan, without adding any fat. After 2–3 minutes, turn the flatbread and cook for 2–3 minutes more. • Stack the flatbread on a plate and serve warm.

Makes: about 8 flatbreads • Prep: 15 min + 15 min to rest
Cooking: 25 min Level: 1

Garbanzo bean flatbread

Cecina

- 4 cups (600 g) garbanzo bean (chickpea) flour
- $1\frac{1}{2}$ cups (375 ml) lukewarm water
- $2/3$ cup (180 ml) extra-virgin olive oil
- salt and freshly ground black pepper

Put the garbanzo bean flour in a large mixing bowl and, using a wooden spoon or a balloon whisk, gradually stir in enough water to form a thick pouring batter with no lumps. • Beat in the oil and a generous pinch of salt. • When the batter is smooth, pour it into a pizza pan or similar ovenproof dish, filling to a depth of about $1/4$ inch (5 mm). • Preheat the oven to 400°F (200°C/gas 6). • Bake until golden brown and a thin crust forms on the surface, 10–15 minutes. • Transfer to a heated serving dish, sprinkle with freshly ground pepper, and serve hot.

Serves: 6–8 • Prep: 10 min • Cooking: 10–15 min • Level: 1

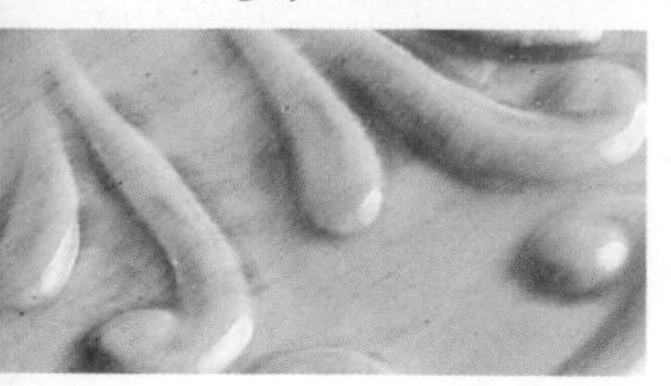

WHOLE-WHEAT HERB BREAD

Pane integrale alle erbe

- 1 oz (30 g) fresh yeast or 2 (1/4-oz/7-g) packages active dry yeast
- 1 teaspoon sugar
- about 1 cup (250 ml) lukewarm water
- 2 2/3 cups (400 g) whole-wheat (wholemeal) flour
- 1 cup (150 g) all-purpose (plain) flour
- 2 teaspoons salt
- 1 tablespoon finely chopped oregano
- 1 tablespoon finely chopped marjoram

Place the yeast in a small bowl. Add the sugar and half the water and stir until dissolved. Set aside for 15 minutes. It will look creamy when ready. • Sift both flours and the salt into a large bowl. Use a wooden spoon to gradually stir in the yeast mixture, oregano, and marjoram. Add enough of the remaining water to make a fairly soft dough. • Transfer to a lightly floured work surface and knead until smooth and elastic, 5–10 minutes. • Shape into a ball and place in an oiled bowl. Cover with a cloth and leave in a warm place to rise until doubled in bulk, about 1 hour and 30 minutes. • Turn out onto a floured work surface and knead for 2–3 minutes. • Divide the dough into 6 equal portions and shape into 12-inch (30-cm) long loaves. Let rise for 30 minutes. • Preheat the oven to 425°F (220°C/gas 7). • Bake until well risen and golden brown, 20–30 minutes.

Makes: just over 1 lb (500 g) of bread • Prep: 30 min + 2 hr to rise • Cooking: 20–30 min • Level: 2

PARMESAN LOAVES WITH SEEDS

Pane al formaggio

Parmesan cheese works beautifully in these loaves but you can replace it with the same quantity of any other aged grating cheese.

- 1 oz (30 g) fresh yeast or 2 (1/4-oz/7-g) packages active dry yeast
- about 1 1/4 cups (300 ml) lukewarm milk
- 1 teaspoon sugar
- 4 cups (600 g) all-purpose (plain) flour
- 8 oz (250 g) freshly grated Parmesan
- 1 teaspoon salt
- 1/2 teaspoon freshly ground white pepper
- 1 large egg, lightly beaten
- 2–3 tablespoons poppy seeds
- 2–3 tablespoons sesame seeds

Place the yeast in a small bowl. Add the sugar and half the milk and stir until dissolved. Set aside for 15 minutes. It will look creamy when ready. • Place the flour, cheese, salt, and pepper in a large bowl. Make a well in the center and stir in the yeast mixture and enough of the remaining milk to obtain a fairly soft dough. • Knead on a lightly floured work until smooth and elastic, 10–15 minutes. • Place in a clean bowl and cover with a cloth. Let rise in a warm place until doubled in bulk, about 2 hours. • When the rising time has elapsed, transfer the dough to a lightly floured work surface and knead for 2–3 minutes. • Divide the dough into 4 equal portions. Roll each one into a loaf about 16 inches (40 cm) long. Brush with the egg. Fold each one in half and braid (plait) the pieces of dough loosely. • Arrange the loaves on an oiled baking sheet. Sprinkle 2 of the loaves with poppy seeds and 2 with sesame seeds. Let rise for 1 hour. • Preheat the oven to 400°F (200°C/gas 6). • Bake until golden brown, 20–30 minutes.

Makes: about 2 lb (1 kg) of bread • Prep: 30 min + 3 hr to rise • Cooking: 20–30 min • Level: 2

BUCKWHEAT LOAVES

Pane saraceno

- 1 oz (30 g) fresh yeast or 2 (1/4-oz/7-g) packages active dry yeast
- 1 teaspoon sugar
- 1 1/2 cups (375 ml) lukewarm water
- 4 cups (600 g) buckwheat flour
- 1 1/3 cups (200 g) all-purpose (plain) flour
- 2 teaspoons salt
- 1/4 cup (60 ml) extra-virgin olive oil

Place the yeast in a small bowl. Add the sugar and half the water and stir until dissolved. Set aside until creamy, about 15 minutes. • Sift both flours and the salt into a large bowl. Stir in the yeast mixture, oil, and enough of the remaining water to obtain a firm dough. • Knead on a floured work surface until smooth and elastic, 10–15 minutes. • Place in an oiled bowl and let rise until doubled in bulk, about 1 hour. • Knead again for 2–3 minutes. • Divide the dough in 4 equal portions and shape into round loaves. Sprinkle with flour and use a serrated knife to cut a 1/2-inch (1-cm) deep cross in the top of each. • Transfer to two oiled baking sheets. Let rise for 1 hour. • Preheat the oven to 400°F (200°C/gas 6). • Bake until golden brown, 30–35 minutes.

Makes: about 2 lb (1 kg) of bread · Prep: 30 min + 2 hr to rise · Cooking: 30–35 min · Level: 2

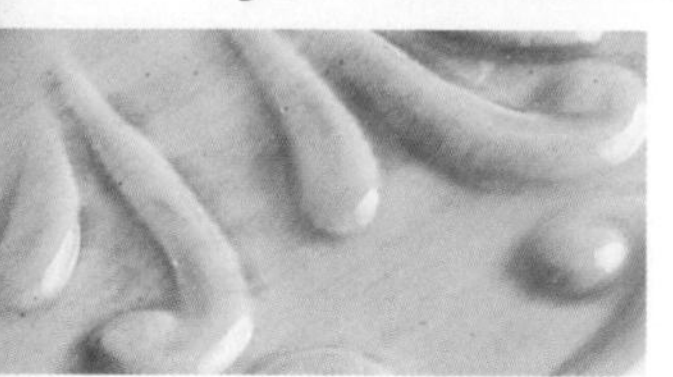

Bread rings

Tarallucci

- $6^2/_3$ cups (1 kg) all-purpose (plain) flour
- 2–3 teaspoons salt
- $1^1/_4$ cups (300 ml) dry white wine
- about 1 cup (250 ml) extra-virgin olive oil
- 1 teaspoon fennel seeds
- 1–2 dried chile peppers, crumbled

These very crisp little cracker-like snacks come from Puglia where they are known as taralli *or* tarallucci. *They are not especially easy to make at home, mainly because they need to be boiled for a minute or two before going into a hot oven to be baked. They can be plain or flavored with freshly ground pepper, chile pepper, cumin seeds, fennel seeds, or finely chopped sun-dried tomatoes, among other things. Here we have made plain, fennel-flavored, and spicy tarallucci. This recipe makes a large quantity but stored in an airtight container they will last for up to two weeks. Serve as a snack or with a glass of wine or pre-dinner drink.*

Sift the flour and salt into a large bowl. Stir in the wine and enough of the oil to make a firm dough. • Knead the dough on a lightly floured work surface until smooth and elastic, 15–20 minutes. Cover and let rest for 20 minutes. • Preheat the oven to 400°F (200°C/gas 6). • Oil 3 large baking sheets. • Bring a large pan half filled with water to a boil. • Divide the dough into three equal portions. Knead the fennel seeds into one portion and the chile pepper into the other. • Shape the dough into small batons, about ½-inch (1 cm) in diameter and 3 inches (8 cm) in length. Shape into rings, pinching the ends together with your fingertips. • Simmer the rings in small batches in the boiling water for 2–3 minutes. • Remove with a slotted spoon and place on a clean cloth to dry. • Arrange on the baking sheets. • Bake until crisp and golden brown, about 30 minutes.

Makes: about 60–70 tarallucci • Prep: 45 min + 20 min to rest • Cooking: about 1 h • Level: 3

Bread sticks

Grissini

- $^3/_4$ oz (20 g) fresh yeast or $1^1/_2$ ($^1/_4$-oz/7-g) packages active dry yeast
- 1 teaspoon sugar
- about $^3/_4$ cup (200 ml) lukewarm water
- $3^1/_2$ cups (500 g) all-purpose (plain) flour
- 1 teaspoon salt

Bread sticks, or grissini, *are from the northern region of Piedmont. According to legend, they were invented in 1679 by the Turinese baker Antonio Brunero when the doctor at the royal court asked for a long, crisp type of bread for his young patient and future king, Vittorio Amedeo di Savoia. Whatever their origin, they are strongly associated with Turin where they can be served at breakfast, lunch, and dinner. Thick or thin, plain or flavored with onion, cheese, or seeds, they make a delicious snack.*

Place the yeast in a small bowl. Add the sugar and half the water and stir until dissolved. Set aside for 15 minutes. It will look creamy when ready. • Sift the flour into a bowl with the salt and stir in the yeast mixture and enough of the remaining water to obtain a firm dough. • Shape the dough into a ball and place on a lightly floured work surface. Knead until smooth and elastic, 10–15 minutes. • Place in a clean bowl and cover with a cloth. Let rise in a warm place until doubled in bulk, about 1 hour. • When the rising time has elapsed, transfer the dough to a lightly floured work surface and knead for 2–3 minutes. • Divide the dough into portions about the size of an egg, then shape into sticks about the thickness of your little finger. • Sprinkle with flour and transfer to three oiled baking sheets, keeping them a finger's width apart. • Cover with a cloth and set aside to rise for 1 hour. • Preheat the oven to 450°F (250°C/gas 8). • Bake until well-browned but not too dark, about 5 minutes. • Leave to cool before removing from the sheets.

Makes: just over 1 lb (500 g) bread sticks • Prep: 30 min + 2 hr to rise • Cooking: 5 min • Level: 2

FOCACCIA

Focaccia is a delicious type of Italian bread made by spreading ordinary bread dough out flat and covering it with various toppings, from a simple layer of extra-virgin olive oil and coarse sea salt, to layers of herbs, vegetables, or cheese. It can be baked in round pizza or cake pans or rectangular jelly-roll pans or simply spread out on a well oiled baking sheet. The dough can also be broken into pieces and shaped into *focaccine* (small focaccias). However you bake it, it is important to always spread the dough using your fingertips to create dimples in the surface of the dough where the topping can accumulate. The earliest focaccias date back 2000 years to Roman times when they consisted of just a simple disk of bread baked in a hot oven. Since then, dozens of different regional "classics" have developed, including *Focaccia di Recco* (with fresh cheese, see page 67) and *Sfincione* (Palermo-style focaccia, see page 64). In this chapter we have included a selection of modern and classic focaccias from every region of Italy.

Herb focaccia (see page 67)

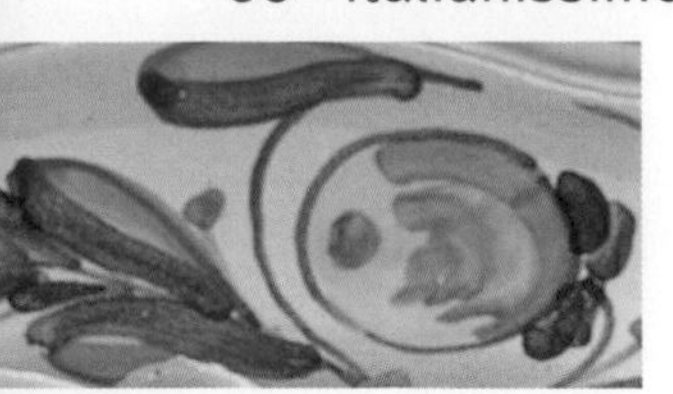

Basic dough

Impasto per pizza e focaccia

- 1 oz (30 g) fresh yeast or 2 ($^1/_4$-oz/7-g) packages active dry yeast
- 1 teaspoon sugar
- about $^3/_4$ cup (200 ml) lukewarm water
- $3^1/_3$ cups (500 g) all-purpose (plain) flour
- $^1/_2$ teaspoon salt

The dough used to make most focaccias and pizzas is basically the same. Unless otherwise stated in individual recipes, use this basic dough for all the focaccia and pizza recipes in this book. It makes about 1 lb (500 g) of dough, usually enough for two to four people, depending on whether you are serving the dish as a starter, main, or snack.

Place the yeast in a small bowl. Add the sugar and half the water and stir until dissolved. Set aside until creamy, about 15 minutes. • Place the flour and salt in a large bowl. Pour in the yeast mixture and enough of the remaining water to obtain a fairly firm dough. • Kneading: Sprinkle a work surface, preferably made of wood, with a little flour. Place the dough on the work surface. Curl your fingers around it and press together to form a compact ball. Press down on the dough with your knuckles to spread it a little. Take the far end of the dough, fold it a short distance toward you, then push it away again with the heel of your palm. Flexing your wrist, fold it toward you again, give it a quarter turn, then push it away. Repeat, gently and with the lightest possible touch, for about 10 minutes. When the dough is firm and no longer sticks to your hands or the work surface, lift it up and bang it down hard against the work surface a couple of times. This will develop the gluten. The dough should be smooth and elastic, show definite air bubbles beneath the surface, and spring back if you flatten it with your palm. • Place in a large oiled bowl and cover with a cloth. Set aside to rise. The dough should double in volume, about 1 hour 30 minutes. To test if ready, poke your finger gently into the dough; if the impression remains, then it is ready. Remember that yeast is a living ingredient, affected by temperature and humidity, among other things. Some days it will take longer to rise than others.

Makes: enough dough for a 12-inch (30-cm) pizza or focaccia
Prep: 30 min + 1 hr 30 min to rise • Level: 1

Onion focaccia with sage

Focaccia con salvia e cipolla

- 1 quantity basic dough (see recipe on this page)
- 3 large white onions, thinly sliced
- $^1/_2$ teaspoon salt
- 15 leaves fresh sage
- $^1/_3$ cup (90 ml) extra-virgin olive oil

Prepare the focaccia dough following the instructions on this page. • Spread the onions out on a baking sheet, sprinkle with salt, and let rest for 1 hour. • Rinse and drain well. • Oil a large rectangular baking pan (a 10 x 15-inch/25 x 38-cm jelly-roll pan is ideal). • Place the risen dough in the pan and use your fingertips to spread it evenly over the bottom. • Top with the onions and sage leaves. Drizzle with the oil and season with salt. • Let rise for 30 minutes. • Preheat the oven to 400°F (200°C/gas 6). • Bake until golden brown, about 25 minutes. Serve hot or at room temperature.

Serves: 2–4 • Prep: 30 min + 1 hr 30 min to rise • Cooking: 35 min • Level: 1

Basil focaccia

Focaccia al basilico

- 1 quantity basic dough (see recipe on this page)
- 6–8 tablespoons finely chopped basil
- 2 tablespoons extra-virgin olive oil
- 1 teaspoon coarse sea salt

Prepare the dough following the instructions on this page, working the basil into the dough as you knead. • Oil a large rectangular baking pan (a 10 x 15-inch/25 x 38-cm jelly-roll pan is ideal). • Place the risen dough in the pan and use your fingertips to spread it evenly over the bottom. • Set aside in a warm place and let rise for 30 minutes. • Preheat the oven to 400°F (200°C/gas 6). • Brush the focaccia with the oil and sprinkle with the coarse sea salt. • Bake until golden brown, about 25 minutes. • Serve hot or at room temperature.

Serves: 4–6 • Prep: 25 min + 2 hr to rise • Cooking: 25 min
Level: 1

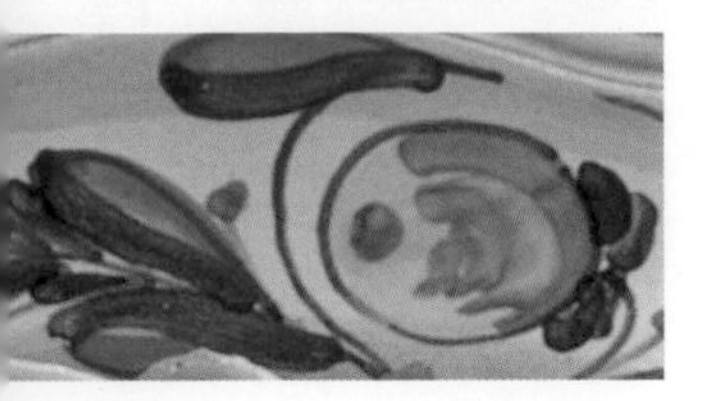

QUICK FOCACCIA WITH CHEESE AND ARUGULA

Focaccia veloce con stracchino e rucola

- 3 1/3 cups (500 g) all-purpose (plain) flour
- 1 teaspoon salt
- 1/3 cup (90 ml) extra-virgin olive oil
- 2/3 cup (150 ml) water
- 14 oz (400 g) stracchino or other fresh, creamy cheese
- 4 oz (125 g) arugula (rocket), coarsely chopped
- 1/2 teaspoon dried oregano
- 2 large ripe tomatoes, sliced

Sift the flour and salt into a large bowl. Stir in 1/4 cup (60 ml) of oil and enough water to make a soft dough. • Knead on a floured work surface until smooth and elastic, 5–10 minutes. • Cover and let rest for 30 minutes. • Preheat the oven to 425°F (220°C/ gas 7). • Oil a 12-inch (30-cm) baking pan. • Break the dough into two equal portions.Roll out on a floured work surface into 2 disks the same size as the baking pan. Place 1 disk in the pan. • Spread with the cheese, arugula, oregano, and tomatoes. Cover with the remaining piece of dough. Make cuts in the surface with a knife so that steam can escape during baking. Drizzle with the remaining oil. • Bake until golden brown, 15–20 minutes. • Serve hot or at room temperature.

Serves: 2–4 • Prep: 35 min + 30 min to rest • Cooking: 15–20 min • Level: 1

FOCACCIA WITH TOMATOES AND PECORINO

Focaccia con pomodori e pecorino

- 1 quantity basic dough (see page 60)
- 1/4 cup (60 ml) extra-virgin olive oil
- 10–12 cherry tomatoes
- salt and freshly ground black pepper
- 8 oz (250 g) fresh mozzarella cheese, thinly sliced
- 1/2 teaspoon dried oregano
- 8 leaves fresh basil, torn
- 1/2 cup (60 g) aged pecorino cheese, thinly sliced

Prepare the focaccia dough following the instructions on page 60. Gradually work 2 tablespoons of the oil into the dough as you knead. Let rise in a warm place until doubled in volume, about 2 hours. • Slice the tomatoes and place in a colander. Sprinkle with salt and let drain for 10 minutes. • Preheat the oven to 425°F (220°C/gas 7). • Oil a baking sheet. • Roll out the dough on a lightly floured work surface into a 12-inch (30-cm) disk. Place on the prepared baking sheet. Dimple the surface with your fingertips. • Bake until pale golden brown, about 20 minutes. • Remove from the oven and cover with the tomatoes and mozzarella. Season with salt and pepper. Sprinkle with oregano and basil and drizzle with the remaining oil. • Bake for 5 minutes more. • Top with the pecorino and serve hot or at room temperature.

Serves: 2–4 • Prep: 35 min + 2 hr to rise • Cooking: 25 min Level: 1

Quick focaccia with cheese and arugula

Potato focaccia with cherry tomatoes and oregano

Potato focaccia with cherry tomatoes and oregano

Focaccia di patate con pomodorini e origano

- 1 large floury (baking) potato, peeled and cut into small cubes
- 1 quantity basic dough (see page 60)
- 1/4 cup (60 ml) extra-virgin olive oil
- 20 cherry tomatoes, cut in half
- 1 teaspoon coarse salt
- 1 tablespoon finely chopped oregano

Cook the potato in a small pot of salted boiling water until tender, about 10 minutes. Drain and mash until smooth. • Prepare the focaccia dough following the instructions on page 60. Gradually work the mashed potato and 2 tablespoons of oil into the dough as you knead. Let rise in a warm place until doubled in volume, about 2 hours. • Oil a 10-inch (25-cm) baking pan and press the dough into it using your fingertips. Sprinkle with the tomatoes, coarse salt, and oregano. • Drizzle with the remaining oil and let rise for 30 minutes. • Preheat the oven to 425°F (220°C/gas 7). • Bake until golden brown, 25–30 minutes. • Serve hot or at room temperature.

Serves: 2–4 • Prep: 35 min + 2 hr 30 min to rise • Cooking: 25–30 min • Level: 1

Garlic focaccia with mortadella and cheese

Focaccia all'aglio con mortadella e pecorino

- 2 large floury (baking) potatoes, peeled and cut into small cubes
- 1 quantity basic dough (see page 60)
- 1/4 cup (60 ml) extra-virgin olive oil
- 4 cloves garlic, sliced
- 12 cherry tomatoes, sliced
- 1 teaspoon dried oregano
- 4 oz (125 g) mortadella or ham, sliced
- 4 oz (125 g) Provolone or other firm mature cheese, sliced

Cook the potatoes in a small pot of salted boiling water until tender, about 10 minutes. Drain and mash until smooth. • Prepare the focaccia dough following the instructions on page 60. Gradually work the mashed potato and 1 tablespoon of oil into the dough as you knead. Let rise in a warm place until doubled in volume, about 2 hours. • Preheat the oven to 400°F (200°C/gas 6). • Turn the dough out onto a lightly floured work surface and knead for 5 minutes. • Oil a 12-inch (30-cm) pizza or quiche pan and press the dough into it using your fingertips. • Sprinkle with the garlic, pressing it into the dough. Top with the tomatoes. Sprinkle with salt and oregano. Drizzle with the remaining oil. • Bake until golden brown, 20–25 minutes. • Top with the mortadella and cheese and serve hot or at room temperature.

Serves: 2–4 • Prep: 25 min + 2 hr to rise • Cooking: 20–25 min • Level: 1

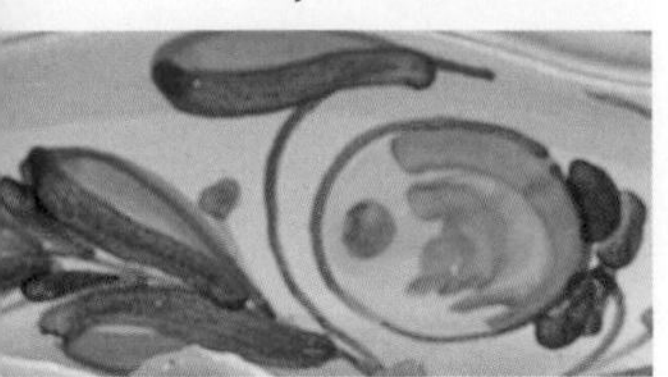

Palermo-style focaccia

Sfincione di San Vito

Dough
- 1 oz (25 g) fresh yeast or 2 (1/4-oz/7-g) packages active dry yeast
- 1 teaspoon sugar
- about 3/4 cup (200 ml) lukewarm water
- 3 1/3 cups (500 g) all-purpose (plain) flour
- 1/3 cup (50 g) freshly grated pecorino cheese
- 1/2 teaspoon salt
- 1/4 cup (60 ml) extra-virgin olive oil
- juice of 1/2 lemon

Topping
- 1/2 cup (125 ml) extra-virgin olive oil
- 1 onion, finely chopped
- 4 tablespoons finely chopped parsley
- 5 salt-cured anchovies, chopped
- 1 (14-oz/400-g) can tomatoes, with juice
- 4 oz (125 g) pecorino , chopped
- 1/4 cup (30 g) fresh bread crumbs

This hearty focaccia is a specialty from Palermo, the regional capital of Sicily. According to tradition it was invented by the nuns at the San Vito convent.

Dough: Place the yeast in a small bowl. Add the sugar and half the water and stir until dissolved. Set aside until creamy, about 15 minutes. • Place the flour, cheese, and salt in a large bowl. Pour in the yeast mixture, oil, lemon juice, and enough of the remaining water to obtain a fairly firm dough. • Knead on a lightly floured work surface until smooth and elastic, 10–15 minutes. Place in a large lightly oiled bowl, cover, and let rise until doubled in bulk, about 2 hours.
• Topping: Heat 1/4 cup (60 ml) oil in a saucepan over medium heat. Add the onion and sauté until softened, 3–4 minutes.
• Add the tomatoes and season with salt and pepper. Cover and simmer over low heat for 1 hour. • Add the parsley, half the anchovies, and the pecorino cheese. Simmer for 10 minutes, then remove from the heat.
• Preheat the oven to 350°F (180°C/gas 3).
• Oil a 10-inch (25 cm) baking pan. • Place the risen dough in the prepared pan and spread using your fingertips, making dimples all over the surface of the dough. • Bake for 10 minutes. Remove from the oven and spread with half the sauce. Bake until the base is almost cooked through, 15–20 minutes. • Heat 2 tablespoons of oil in a small frying pan over medium heat. Add the bread crumbs and sauté until crisp and golden brown, about 5 minutes. • Spread the remaining sauce over the base. Sprinkle with the remaining anchovies and the sautéed bread crumbs. Drizzle with the remaining oil and bake until the top is lightly browned, 5–10 minutes. Serve warm.

Serves: 4–6 • Prep: 50 min + 2 hr to rise • Cooking: 2 hr • Level: 2

Filled focaccia with onion and olives

Focaccia ripiena con cipolle e olive

- 1 1/2 quantities basic dough (see page 60)
- 1/3 cup (90 ml) extra-virgin olive oil
- 3 large sweet red onions, finely sliced
- salt
- 1 1/2 cups (150 g) pitted black olives, coarsely chopped
- 1 tablespoon finely chopped rosemary
- 1 tablespoon coarse sea salt

Prepare the focaccia dough following the instructions on page 60. Gradually work 2 tablespoons of the oil into the dough as you knead. Let rise in a warm place until doubled in bulk, about 2 hours. • Oil a baking sheet.
• Turn the dough out onto a lightly floured work surface and knead for 5 minutes. • Roll out into a large oval about 1/2-inch (1-cm) thick. • Mix together the onions, olives, and 1/2 tablespoon of rosemary in a medium bowl.
• Add 2 tablespoons of the remaining oil and a pinch of salt. Mix well. • Spoon the mixture over half the dough, leaving a 3/4-inch (2-cm) border free around the edges. • Brush the edges with water and then fold the remaining dough over the filling. Press the edges together to seal. Make a few slits in the dough with a sharp knife to allow steam to escape during baking. • Sprinkle with the sea salt and remaining rosemary. Brush with the remaining oil. Let rise for 30 minutes. • Preheat the oven to 350°F (180°C/gas 4). • Bake until risen and golden brown, 30–35 minutes. • Serve hot or at room temperature.

Serves: 4–6 • Prep: 45 min + 2 hr 30 min to rise • Cooking: 35 min • Level: 2

RUSTIC FOCACCIA

Focaccia rustica

- 1 quantity basic dough (see page 60)
- 3 eggs
- 1 cup (200 g) ricotta cheese, drained
- 8 oz (250 g) Italian sausage meat, crumbled
- 10 green olives, pitted and chopped
- 1 teaspoon dried oregano
- salt
- 1 dried chile pepper, crumbled
- 1/3 cup (90 ml) extra-virgin olive oil

Prepare the dough following the instructions on page 60. • Oil a 12-inch (30-cm) pizza pan. • Place the risen dough in the pan and use your fingertips to spread it evenly over the bottom. • Boil the eggs for 8–10 minutes. • Drain, shell, and slice them. • Spread the ricotta over the dough with the back of a spoon. Arrange the eggs, sausage meat, and olives over the ricotta. Sprinkle with oregano, salt, and chile pepper. Drizzle with the remaining oil and let rise for 30 minutes. • Preheat the oven to 425°F (220°C/gas 7). • Bake until golden brown, 20–30 minutes. • Serve hot.

Serves: 2–4 • Prep: 30 min + 1 hr 30 min to rise • Cooking: 20–30 min • Level: 1

BROWN FOCACCIA WITH ROSEMARY

Focaccia integrale con rosmarino

- 1/2 oz (15 g) fresh yeast or 1 (1/4-oz/7-g) package active dry yeast
- 2/3 cup (180 ml) lukewarm water
- 1 2/3 cups (250 g) whole-wheat (wholemeal) flour
- 1/2 cup (75 g) all-purpose (plain) flour
- salt
- 1 tablespoon finely chopped rosemary
- 1/4 cup (60 ml) extra-virgin olive oil

Dissolve the yeast in the water. • Sift both flours and the salt into a large bowl. Add the yeast mixture and mix to make a firm dough. • Knead on a lightly floured work surface until smooth and elastic, 5–10 minutes. • Transfer to an oiled bowl and let rise until doubled in volume, about 2 hours. • Turn the dough out onto a lightly floured work surface and knead, adding the rosemary as you work, for 5 minutes. • Oil a-12 inch (30-cm) pizza or quiche pan. • Press the dough into the pan using your fingertips. Prick with a fork and drizzle with the oil. • Let rise for 30 minutes. • Preheat the oven to 400°F (200°C/gas 6). • Bake until golden brown, 25–30 minutes. • Serve hot or at room temperature.

Serves: 2–4 • Prep: 25 min + 2 hr 30 min to rise • Cooking: 25–30 min • Level: 1

HERB FOCACCIA

Focaccia alle erbe

- 1 quantity basic dough (see page 60)
- 1/4 cup (60 ml) extra-virgin olive oil
- 1 medium onion, very finely chopped
- 2 cloves garlic, very finely chopped
- 3 tablespoons finely chopped parsley
- 2 tablespoons finely chopped basil
- 1 tablespoon finely chopped rosemary
- 1/2 teaspoon dried oregano
- salt and freshly ground black pepper
- 1 (14-oz/400-g) can tomatoes, with juice

Prepare the focaccia dough following the instructions on page 60. Gradually work 2 tablespoons of the oil into the dough as you knead. Let rise in a warm place until doubled in volume, about 2 hours. • Preheat the oven to 425°F (220°C/gas 7). • Turn the dough out onto a lightly floured work surface and knead for 5 minutes. • Press the dough into an oiled 8 x12-inch (20 x 30-cm) baking pan using your fingertips. • Mix together the onion, garlic, parsley, basil, rosemary, and oregano in a small bowl. Add 2 tablespoons of the remaining oil and season with pepper. Spread the tomatoes over the focaccia and top with the herb mixture. Season with salt. • Bake until golden brown, 20–25 minutes. • Serve hot or at room temperature.

Serves: 4 • Prep: 30 min + 2 hr to rise • Cooking: 20–25 min • Level: 1

CHEESE-FILLED FOCACCIA

Focaccia di Recco

This unleavened focaccia comes from Recco, near Genoa. Try other fillings, but always use ingredients that cook quickly, such as sliced champignons or ham.

- 3 1/2 cups (500 g) all-purpose (plain) flour
- 1 teaspoon salt
- 1/3 cup (90 ml) extra-virgin olive oil
- 1 cup (250 ml) water
- 1 1/4 cups (300 g) stracchino (or other fresh, creamy) cheese, melted with 1 tablespoon milk

Preheat the oven to 400°F (200°C/gas 6). • Oil an 8 x 12-inch (20 x 30-cm) baking pan. • Sift the flour and salt into a large bowl and make a well in the center. Stir in 1/4 cup (60 ml) of oil and enough water to form a fairly soft dough. Divide in half and shape into two balls, cover with a clean cloth, and set aside for 15 minutes. • Roll both pieces of dough out to fit the pan. Place one in the pan. Cover with the cheese, leaving a 1/2-inch (1-cm) border. Cover with the other piece of dough, pressing down to seal the edges. • Brush with the remaining oil and sprinkle with salt. • Bake until lightly browned, about 20 minutes. If the dough puffs up while baking, prick with a fork.

Serves: 4 • Prep: 30 min • Cooking: 15–20 min • Level: 1

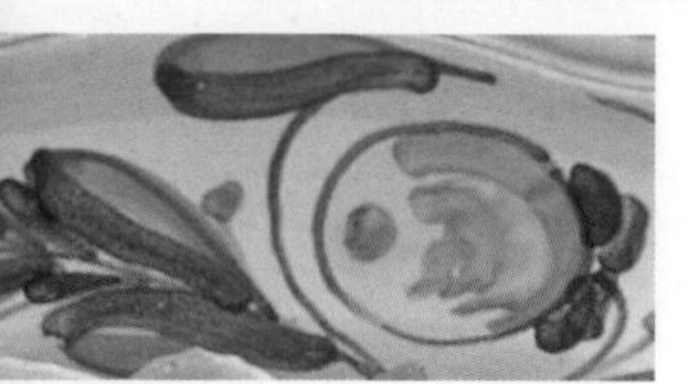

Filled focaccia with zucchini

FILLED FOCACCIA WITH ZUCCHINI

Focaccia ripiena con zucchini

- 1 quantity basic dough (see page 60)
- 2 tablespoons extra-virgin olive oil
- 2 tablespoons lard, melted
- 2 tablespoons fresh rosemary leaves
- 3 medium zucchini (courgettes), sliced thinly lengthwise
- 8 oz (250 g) fresh mozzarella cheese, drained and cut into small cubes
- salt and freshly ground black pepper
- 1–2 tomatoes, thinly sliced

Prepare the focaccia dough following the instructions on page 60. Gradually work the oil, lard, and 1 tablespoon of rosemary into the dough as you knead. Let rise in a warm place until doubled in volume, about 2 hours. • Preheat a grill pan or griddle over medium heat. Grill the zucchini on both sides until tender and lightly browned. • Oil an 8-inch (20-cm) square baking pan. • Divide the dough into 2 equal portions. Press half the dough into the base and sides of the prepared pan. • Cover with the mozzarella and zucchini. Season with salt and pepper. • Roll out the remaining dough on a lightly floured work surface until it is large enough to cover the pan. Place in the pan over the filling. Press the edges together to seal. Prick the dough with a fork. Let rise for 45 minutes. • Preheat the oven to 425°F (220°C/gas 7). • Brush the focaccia with the remaining oil. Place the tomatoes on top of the focaccia. Sprinkle with the remaining rosemary and season with salt. • Bake until the focaccia is golden brown, 25–30 minutes. • Serve hot.

Serves: 4 • Prep: 45 min + 2 hr 45 min to rise • Cooking: 30–35 min • Level: 1

FILLED FOCACCIA WITH BELL PEPPERS

Focaccia ripiena con peperone

- 1 quantity basic dough (see page 60)
- 1/4 cup (60 ml) extra virgin olive oil
- 1 large red bell pepper (capsicum)
- 1 large yellow bell pepper (capsicum)
- 1 clove garlic, finely sliced
- 8 oz (250 g) Gorgonzola cheese, sliced
- salt and freshly ground black pepper
- 16 cherry tomatoes, cut in half
- 1 teaspoon dried oregano

Prepare the focaccia dough following the instructions on page 60. • Preheat the oven to 400°F (200°C/gas 6). • Oil an 8 x 12-inch (20 x 30 cm) baking pan. • Bake the bell peppers in the oven until dark and charred all over, 20–30 minutes. • Place the hot bell peppers in a brown paper bag. Close the bag and let rest for 10 minutes. Peel and seed the bell peppers. Rinse well, dry, and slice thinly. • Turn the dough out onto a lightly floured surface and knead for 5 minutes. • Divide into 2 equal portions and press one portion into the prepared pan using your fingertips. Prick with a fork. • Cover with the peppers, garlic, and Gorgonzola. Season with salt and pepper and drizzle with 2 tablespoons of oil. • Roll out the remaining dough in a rectangle large enough to cover the pan. Cover the filling with the dough. • Press the cherry tomatoes into the dough at regular intervals. Sprinkle with the oregano and drizzle with the remaining oil. • Bake until the focaccia is golden brown, 25–30 minutes. • Serve hot or at room temperature.

Serves: 4 • Prep: 45 min + 2 hr 30 min to rise • Cooking: 1 hr • Level: 1

AROMATIC FOCACCIA WITH HAM AND OLIVES

Focaccia aromatica con prosciutto e olive

- 1 quantity basic dough (see page 60)
- 1/4 cup (60 ml) extra-virgin olive oil
- 4 oz (125 g) ham, very finely chopped
- 1 small onion, very finely chopped
- 4 sage leaves, very finely chopped
- 1 tablespoon finely chopped rosemary
- 1 tablespoon finely chopped thyme
- 12 green olives
- 1 tablespoon coarse sea salt

Prepare the focaccia dough following the instructions on page 60. Gradually work 2 tablespoons of the oil into the dough as you knead. Let rise until doubled in volume, about 2 hours. • Turn the dough out onto a lightly floured work surface and knead for 5–10 minutes, incorporating the ham, onion, sage, rosemary, and thyme, as you work. • Oil a 12-inch (30-cm) pizza or quiche pan. • Press the dough into the prepared pan using your fingertips. • Let rise for 30 minutes. • Preheat the oven to 400°F (200°C/gas 6). • Top the focaccia with the olives, pressing them into the dough. Drizzle with the remaining oil and sprinkle with the coarse salt. • Bake until risen and golden brown, 25–30 minutes. • Serve hot or at room temperature.

Serves: 4 • Prep: 30 min + 2 hr 30 min to rise • Cooking: 25–30 min • Level: 1

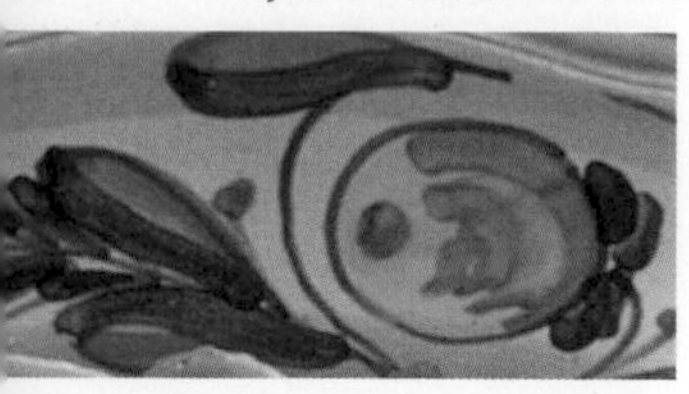

Baby focaccias with tomato and ham

Focaccine con pomodoro e prosciutto

- 1 quantity basic dough (see page 60)
- 1/4 cup (60 ml) extra-virgin olive oil
- 4 oz (125 g) sliced prosciutto (Parma ham), cut into ribbons
- 1 small onion, finely sliced
- 1 tablespoon salt-cured capers, rinsed and coarsely chopped
- 3 medium tomatoes, peeled and chopped
- 2 tablespoons finely chopped parsley
- 2 tablespoons finely chopped basil

Prepare the focaccia dough following the instructions on page 60. Gradually work 1 tablespoon of the oil into the dough as you knead. • Divide the dough into walnut-size balls and place, well-spaced, on a lightly floured work surface. Cover with a cloth and let rise until doubled in size, about 1 hour. • Preheat the oven to 375°F (190°C/gas 5). • Oil a baking sheet. • Roll out each ball of dough on a floured work surface into a disk about 4 inches (10 cm) in diameter. • Place the disks on the baking sheet. • Bake until golden brown, 12–15 minutes. • While the focaccias are in the oven, heat 1 tablespoon of the remaining oil in a frying pan over medium heat. Add the prosciutto, onion, and capers and sauté until the onion is tender, 3–4 minutes. • Add the tomatoes, parsley, and basil. Simmer until the tomato begins to break down, about 5 minutes. • Stir in the remaining oil. • Place the hot focaccias on a serving dish and spread each one with a little of the sauce. • Serve at once.

Serves: 4 • Prep: 35 min + 1 hr to rise • Cooking: 15–20 min
Level: 1

Focaccia with zucchini

Focaccia con zucchine

Prepare the dough following the instructions on page 60, working 2 tablespoons of the oil into the dough as you knead. • Oil a large rectangular baking pan (a 10 x 15-inch/25 x 38-cm jelly-roll pan is ideal). • Preheat the oven to 425°F (225°C/gas 7). • Place the risen dough on a lightly floured work surface and knead for 2–3 minutes. • Place the dough in the prepared pan and use your fingertips to spread it evenly over the bottom. • Cover with the zucchini and drizzle with the remaining oil. Season with salt and pepper. • Bake until the zucchini are tender and the dough is browned, about 25 minutes.

Serves: 4 • Prep: 35 min + 1 hr 30 min to rise • Cooking: 25 min • Level: 1

- 1 quantity basic dough (see page 60)
- 1/2 cup (125 ml) extra-virgin olive oil
- 1 1/2 lb (750 g) zucchini (courgettes), thinly sliced lengthwise
- salt and freshly ground black pepper

Baby focaccia with tomato and ham

Baby focaccia with salami and beans

Focaccia with tuna and mozzarella

Focaccia con tonno e mozzarella

- 1 quantity basic dough (see page 60)
- 1/3 cup (90 ml) extra-virgin olive oil
- 2 large onions, finely sliced
- 1 1/2 cups (150 g) black olives, pitted and coarsely chopped
- salt
- 6 oz (180 g) tuna preserved in oil, drained and crumbled
- 4 oz (125 g) fresh mozzarella cheese, drained and cut into small cubes

Prepare the focaccia dough following the instructions on page 60. Gradually work 3 tablespoons of the oil into the dough as you knead. Let rise in a warm place until doubled in volume, about 2 hours. • Heat 2 tablespoons of the remaining oil in a large frying pan over medium heat. Add the onions and sauté until transparent, 3–4 minutes. • Add the olives and sauté for 5 minutes. Season with salt and remove from the heat. Add the tuna and mix well. • Preheat the oven to 425°F (220°C/gas 7). Oil a 12-inch (30-cm) pizza or quiche pan. • Turn the dough out onto a floured work surface and knead for 5 minutes. • Press two-thirds of the dough into the prepared pan using your fingertips. • Spread with the tuna mixture and top with the mozzarella. • Roll out the remaining dough until large enough to cover the pan. Cover the filling with the dough and seal the edges. Brush with the remaining oil. • Bake until golden brown, about 30 minutes. • Serve hot.

Serves: 4 • Prep: 50 min + 2 hr 30 min to rise • Cooking: 40 min • Level: 1

Baby focaccias with salami and beans

Focaccia con salame e fave

- 1 oz (30 g) fresh yeast or 2 (1/4-oz/7-g) packages active dry yeast
- 1/4 cup (50 g) sugar
- 3/4 cup (200 ml) lukewarm milk + extra, to brush
- 3 1/3 cups (500 g) all-purpose (plain) flour
- salt
- 4 oz (125 g) fresh or frozen fava (broad) beans
- 1/3 cup (50 g) coarsely grated Fontina or Cheddar cheese
- 2 oz (60 g) salami, diced
- 1/2 cup (125 g) butter, cut into pieces
- 1 large egg, lightly beaten

Use the first 5 ingredients to prepare the focaccia dough following the instructions on page 60. Cover and let rise until doubled in volume, about 2 hours. • Cook the beans in a large pot of boiling water until tender, about 5 minutes. Drain well. • Oil a baking sheet. • Place the dough on a lightly floured work surface and knead, gradually adding the beans, cheese, salami, and butter as you work. • Divide the dough into egg-size balls. Arrange on the prepared baking sheet, leaving plenty of space between each ball. Let rise for 30 minutes. • Preheat the oven to 350°F (180°C/gas 4). • Brush the focaccias with the extra milk. • Bake until risen and golden brown, about 20 minutes. • Serve hot or at room temperature.

Serves: 4–6 • Prep: 35 min + 2 hr 30 min to rise • Cooking: 20 min • Level: 1

PIZZA

According to legend, pizza was invented in the beautiful southern city of Naples. In a certain sense this is true, or at least what we now know as a typical pizza certainly comes from Naples: a bread base spread with tomato, melted mozzarella cheese, and a drizzle of extra-virgin olive oil, usually further enriched with any number of other ingredients such as olives, garlic, capers, oregano, anchovies, mushrooms, ham, and salami. *Pizza Napoletana* (see page 60) and *Pizza Margherita* (see page 60)—which both have an almost infinite number of variations—are the two classic recipes in this tradition. Neapolitan pizza-makers made these pizzas famous throughout the world during the 19th century when several million Italians left their homeland for the Americas and Australia, among other places. But originally, the word "pizza" was a generic term for any savory or sweet focaccia and there are an enormous number of traditional pizzas from many other regions and a host of modern inventions based on the simple idea of combining a bread base with a delicious topping.

Pizza Margherita with black olives (see page 76)

Pizza with tomatoes and black olives

NEAPOLITAN PIZZA

Pizza Napoletana

- 1 quantity basic dough (see page 60)
- 1 (14-oz/400-g) can tomatoes, with juice, chopped
- 5 oz (150 g) fresh mozzarella cheese, drained and sliced
- 4–6 anchovy fillets preserved in oil, drained and coarsely chopped
- salt and freshly ground black pepper
- 1/4 cup (60 ml) extra-virgin olive oil
- 1/2 teaspoon dried oregano

Prepare the pizza dough following the instructions on page 60. • Preheat the oven to 425°F (220°C/gas 7). • Oil a 12-inch (30-cm) pizza pan. • Knead the risen dough briefly on a lightly floured work surface then spread in the prepared pan using your fingertips. • Spread with the tomatoes. Add the anchovies and season with salt and pepper. Drizzle with the oil and sprinkle with oregano. • Bake for 15 minutes. Top with the mozzarella and bake until the base is crisp and golden brown and the mozzarella is melted, 5–10 minutes. • Serve hot or at room temperature.

Serves: 2–4 • Prep: 30 min + 1 hr 30 min to rise • Cooking: 20–25 min • Level: 1

TOMATO AND GARLIC PIZZA

Pizza marinara

This simple pizza is a classic. For a heartier dish, try adding a handful of arugula (rocket), some sliced cherry tomatoes, and a slice or two of prosciutto (Parma ham) to the cooked pizza.

- 1 quantity basic dough (see page 60)
- 1 (14-oz/400-g) can tomatoes, with juice, chopped
- 2 cloves garlic, thinly sliced
- 1 dried teaspoon oregano
- salt and freshly ground black pepper
- 3 tablespoons extra-virgin olive oil

Prepare the pizza dough following the instructions on page 60. • Preheat the oven to 425°F (220°C/gas 7). • Oil a 12-inch (30-cm) pizza pan. • Knead the risen dough for 1 minute on a lightly floured work surface then spread in the prepared pan using your fingertips. • Spread the tomatoes and garlic evenly over the top. Sprinkle with the oregano, salt, and pepper and drizzle with 1 tablespoon of the oil. • Bake until golden brown, 20–25 minutes. • Drizzle with the remaining oil and serve hot.

Serves: 2–4 • Prep: 30 min + 1 hr 30 min to rise • Cooking: 20–25 min • Level: 1

PIZZA WITH ONION AND PESTO

Pizza con cipolla e pesto

- 1 quantity basic dough (see page 60)
- 1 quantity pesto (see page 130)
- 1 (14-oz/400-g) can tomatoes, with juice, chopped
- salt
- 4 small white onions, finely sliced

Prepare the pizza dough following the instructions on page 60. • Preheat the oven to 425°F (220°C/gas 7). • Oil two 8-inch (20-cm) pizza pans. • Prepare the pesto. It should be smooth and fairly dense. • Roll out the pizza dough on a lightly floured work surface into two 8-inch (20-cm) disks. Place in the prepared pans. • Spread evenly with the tomatoes. Season with salt. • Bake for 10 minutes. Remove from the oven and add the onions, sprinkling them evenly over the two pizzas. • Bake until the base is crisp and the onions are lightly browned, 10–15 minutes. Remove from the oven and dot with the pesto. • Serve hot.

Serves: 2–4 • Prep: 30 min + 1 hr 30 min to rise • Cooking: 20–25 min • Level: 1

PIZZA WITH TOMATOES AND BLACK OLIVES

Pizza con le olive nere

- 1 quantity basic dough (see page 60)
- 1/3 cup (90 ml) extra-virgin olive oil
- 1 large onion, finely sliced
- 1 (14-oz/400-g) can tomatoes, with juice, chopped
- 1 tablespoon capers preserved in brine, drained and chopped
- 1 cup (100 g) black olives, pitted
- 4 oz (125 g) freshly grated pecorino cheese
- salt and freshly ground black pepper

Prepare the pizza dough following the instructions on page 60. • Preheat the oven to 425°F (220°C/gas 7). • Oil a 12-inch (30-cm) pizza pan. • Heat half the oil in a frying pan over medium heat. Add the onion and sauté until transparent, 3–4 minutes. Remove from the heat. • Knead the risen pizza dough briefly on a lightly floured work surface then press it into the prepared pan using your fingertips. • Spread with the tomatoes and top with the onion, capers, olives, and pecorino. Season with salt and pepper and drizzle with the remaining oil. • Bake until the base is crisp and golden brown, 20–25 minutes. • Serve hot or at room temperature.

Serves: 2–4 • Prep: 30 min + 1 hr 30 min to rise • Cooking: 20–25 min • Level: 1

Pizza Margherita

Pizza Margherita

- 1 quantity basic dough (see page 60)
- 1 (14-oz/400-g) can tomatoes, with juice, chopped
- 6 oz (180 g) fresh mozzarella cheese, drained and thinly sliced
- 2 tablespoons freshly grated Parmesan cheese
- salt
- 3 tablespoons extra-virgin olive oil
- 10 leaves fresh basil, torn

This is one of the classic pizzas and for many people it is synonymous with pizza. According to legend, it was invented by the Neapolitan pizzaiolo *Raffaele Esposito in 1889 in honor of the Italian queen Margherita. If liked, add a handful of black olives.*

Prepare the pizza dough following the instructions on page 60. • Preheat the oven to 425°F (220°C/gas 7). • Oil a 12-inch (30-cm) pizza pan. • Knead the risen dough briefly on a floured work surface then press into the pan using your fingertips. • Spread with the tomatoes, mozzarella, and Parmesan. Season with salt and drizzle with 1 tablespoon of oil. • Bake until the crust is golden brown, 15–20 minutes. • Garnish with the basil, drizzle with the remaining oil, and serve hot.

Serves: 2–4 • Prep: 30 min + 1 hr 30 min to rise • Cooking: 15–20 min • Level: 1

Pizza Margherita with Arugula

Pizza Margherita estiva

Prepare the pizza. Add the garlic to the pizza together with the tomato. • When the pizza is cooked, sprinkle with the arugula and Parmesan. Drizzle with a little extra olive oil and serve hot.

Serves: 2–4 • Prep: 30 min + 1 hr 30 min to rise • Cooking: 15–20 min • Level: 1

- 1 Pizza Margherita (see recipe at left)
- 3 cloves garlic, sliced
- 1 small bunch arugula (rocket), coarsely chopped
- 2 oz (60 g) Parmesan cheese, flaked

Pizza Margherita

Pizza with eggplant and tomatoes

Pizza with zucchini flowers

Pizza ai fiori di zucca

- 1 quantity basic dough (see page 60)
- 2 tablespoons extra-virgin olive oil
- 6 oz (180 g) fresh, water buffalo mozzarella cheese, thinly sliced
- 4–6 large zucchini flowers, rinsed and dried
- 10–12 cherry tomatoes, cut in half
- salt and freshly ground black or white pepper

This pizza should only be made in early summer when zucchini flowers are in season. Use real water buffalo mozzarella, the freshest cherry tomatoes, and the best cold pressed olive oil for a gourmet pizza experience.

Prepare the pizza dough following the instructions on page 60. • Preheat the oven to 425°F (220°C/gas 7). • Oil a 14-inch (35-cm) pizza pan. • Knead the risen pizza dough briefly on a lightly floured work surface then press it into the prepared pan using your fingertips. • Drizzle with half the oil and cover with the mozzarella. • Bake for 15 minutes. Top with the zucchini flowers and cherry tomatoes and drizzle with the remaining oil. • Bake until the base is crisp and golden brown, 5–10 minutes. • Serve hot or at room temperature.

Serves: 2–4 • Prep: 30 min + 1 hr 30 min to rise • Cooking: 20–25 min • Level: 1

Pizza with eggplant and tomatoes

Pizza con melanzane e pomodorini

- 1 quantity basic dough (see page 60)
- 1 large eggplant (aubergine), thinly sliced
- salt
- 1/3 cup (90 ml) extra-virgin olive oil
- 1/2 teaspoon red pepper flakes
- 1 clove garlic, finely chopped
- 1 cup (250 g) canned tomatoes, with juice, chopped
- 5 oz (150 g) fresh mozzarella cheese, drained and thinly sliced
- handful black olives, pitted
- 8 oz (250 g) cherry tomatoes, cut in half

Prepare the pizza dough following the instructions on page 60. • Oil a 12-inch (30-cm) pizza pan. • Place the eggplant in a colander and sprinkle with salt. Let rest for 10 minutes. Rinse and drain well. Arrange the eggplant on a plate. Drizzle with half the oil. Sprinkle with the red pepper flakes and the garlic. Let rest for 30 minutes. • Preheat the oven to 400°F (200°C/gas 6). • Preheat a grill pan or griddle over high heat. Grill the eggplant until tender, 3–5 minutes each side. • Knead the risen pizza dough briefly on a lightly floured work surface then press it into the prepared pan using your fingertips. • Spread with the canned tomatoes. Season with salt. Add the eggplant and olives and drizzle with the remaining oil. Bake for 20 minutes. • Add the mozzarella and bake until the base is crisp and golden brown, 5–10 minutes. • Top with the cherry tomatoes and serve hot.

Serves: 2–4 • Prep: 25 min + 1 hr 30 min to rise • Cooking: 25–30 min • Level: 1

Four cheese pizza

Pizza with seafood

Pizza ai frutti di mare

- 1 quantity basic dough (see page 60)
- 12 oz (350 g) mixed frozen seafood, thawed
- 1/4 cup (60 ml) extra-virgin olive oil
- salt
- 8 oz (250 g) mussels in shell, cleaned
- 1 (14-oz/400-g) can tomatoes, with juice, chopped
- 3 cloves garlic, finely chopped
- freshly ground black pepper

Prepare the pizza dough following the instructions on page 60. • Preheat the oven to 425°F (220°C/gas 7). • Oil a 12-inch (30-cm) pizza pan. • Place the mixed seafood in a bowl. Add the oil and season with salt. Mix well and let rest for 1 hour. • Place the mussels in a large saucepan over high heat. Cook until they open, 5–7 minutes. Remove from the heat. • Shell the mussels, discarding any that did not open. • Knead the risen pizza dough briefly on a lightly floured work surface then press it into the prepared pan using your fingertips. • Spread with the tomatoes and sprinkle with the garlic. • Drain the mixed seafood reserving the oil. Drizzle the pizza with the reserved oil and season with salt and pepper. • Bake for 15 minutes. Remove from the oven and top with the mixed seafood and mussels. Bake until the seafood is cooked and the base is crisp and golden brown, 10–15 minutes. • Serve hot.

Serves: 2–4 • Prep: 30 min + 2 hr to rise and rest • Cooking: 20–25 min • Level: 1

Italian riviera pizza

Pizza della riviera

This is a variation on the French pissaladière, *from Provence, served along the italian Riviera in neighboring Liguria. For an authentic touch, use the tiny, highly flavored Taggiasche olives that come from this region.*

- 1 quantity basic dough (see page 60)
- 1/3 cup (90 ml) extra-virgin olive oil
- 1/4 cup (60 ml) milk
- 14 oz (400 g) onions, sliced
- salt and freshly ground black pepper
- 1/2 teaspoon ground cinnamon
- 1 teaspoon sugar
- 14 oz (400 g) tomatoes, peeled and sliced
- 8 anchovy fillets, chopped
- 1 cups (100 g) small black olives
- 1 clove garlic, finely sliced
- 2 tablespoons freshly grated Parmesan cheese
- 1 teaspoon dried oregano

Prepare the pizza dough following the instructions on page 60. • Oil a 14-inch (35-cm) pizza pan. • Place the risen dough in the pan and use your fingertips to spread it evenly over the bottom. • Heat half the oil with the milk in a large frying pan over medium heat. Add the onions and simmer until the onions are very soft and the liquid has evaporated, about 15 minutes. • Season with salt and pepper. Add the cinnamon and sugar. • Spread the onions over the dough. Top with the tomatoes. Sprinkle with the anchovies, olives, garlic, Parmesan, and oregano. Drizzle with the remaining oil and let rise for 30 more minutes. • Preheat the oven to 400°F (200°C/gas 6). • Bake for about 30 minutes, or until golden brown. • Serve hot.

Serves: 2–4 • Prep: 15 min + 2 hr to rise • Cooking: 45 min Level: 2

Four cheese pizza

Pizza ai quattro formaggi

- 1 quantity basic dough (see page 60)
- 4 oz (120 g) fresh mozzarella cheese, drained and diced
- 1/4 cup (30 g) freshly grated Parmesan cheese
- 4 oz (125 g) Gorgonzola cheese, diced
- 2 oz (60 g) Emmental cheese, thinly sliced
- 1 tablespoon extra-virgin olive oil
- freshly ground white pepper
- 1 tablespoon finely chopped oregano

Try this pizza with a whole-wheat (wholemeal) crust, by simply replacing half the all-purpose (plain) flour in the basic dough recipe with whole-wheat flour. It may take a little longer to double in bulk during the rising time; allow 2 hours.

Prepare the pizza dough following the instructions on page 60. • Preheat the oven to 425°F (220°C/gas 7). • Oil a 12-inch (30-cm) pizza pan. • Knead the risen dough briefly on a lightly floured work surface then spread in the prepared pan using your fingertips. • Spread the dough with the cheeses, drizzle with the oil, and season with pepper. • Bake until golden brown, 20–25 minutes. • Serve hot.

Serves: 2–4 • Prep: 30 min + 1 hr 30 min to rise • Cooking: 20–25 min • Level: 1

Spicy salami and black olive pizza

Pizza with mushrooms

Pizza coi funghi

- 1 quantity basic dough (see page 60)
- 2 tablespoons butter
- 1 clove garlic, lightly crushed but whole
- 12 oz (350 g) button mushrooms, sliced
- salt
- 1 (14-oz/400-g) can tomatoes, with juice, chopped
- 4 oz (125 g) fresh mozzarella cheese, drained and cut into small cubes
- $^1/_3$ cup (50 g) freshly grated Parmesan cheese
- freshly ground black pepper
- 2 tablespoons extra-virgin olive oil
- 1 tablespoon finely chopped parsley

Prepare the pizza dough following the instructions on page 60. • Preheat the oven to 425°F (220°C/gas 7). • Oil a 14-inch (35-cm) pizza pan. • Melt the butter in a large frying pan over medium heat. Add the garlic, mushrooms, and salt. Sauté until the mushrooms are tender, 5–7 minutes. Remove from the heat. Discard the garlic. • Knead the risen pizza dough briefly on a lightly floured work surface then press it into the prepared pan using your fingertips. • Spread with the tomatoes and top with the mushrooms. Add the mozzarella and Parmesan. Season with salt and pepper. Drizzle with the oil and bake until the crust is crisp and golden brown, 20–25 minutes. • Sprinkle with parsley and serve hot or at room temperature.

Serves: 2–4 • Prep: 20 min + 1 hr 30 min to rise • Cooking: 25–30 min • Level: 1

Pizza with bell peppers

Pizza coi peperoni

Prepare the pizza dough following the instructions on page 60. • Preheat the oven to 400°F (200°C/gas 6). • Oil a 12-inch (30-cm) pizza pan. • Place the risen dough on a lightly floured work surfacc and, gradually incorporating 3 tablespoons of the oil, knead until the dough is smooth and elastic, 5 minutes. • Press the dough into the prepared pan using your fingertips. • Spread the dough with the tomatoes. Top with the onions, bell peppers, garlic, and basil. Season with salt and pepper. Drizzle with the remaining oil. • Bake until the topping is cooked and the base is crisp and golden brown, 25–30 minutes. • Serve hot or at room temperature.

Serves: 2–4 • Prep: 45 min + 1 hr 30 min to rise • Cooking: 20–25 min • Level: 1

- 1 quantity basic dough (see page 60)
- 12 oz (350 g) ripe tomatoes, peeled and thinly sliced
- $^1/_4$ cup (60 ml) extra-virgin olive oil
- 2 small white onions, finely sliced
- 1 medium yellow bell pepper (capsicum), seeded and finely sliced
- 1 medium red bell pepper (capsicum), seeded and finely sliced
- 2 cloves garlic, finely chopped
- 2 tablespoons finely chopped basil
- salt and freshly ground black pepper

Pizza with mixed toppings

Pizza capricciosa

- 1 quantity basic dough (see page 60)
- 1 cup (250 g) canned tomatoes, with juice
- 2 oz (60 g) ham, chopped
- 4 salt-cured anchovy fillets, chopped
- 6 oz (180 g) fresh mozzarella cheese, drained and diced
- 2 oz (60 g) artichokes in oil, drained and chopped
- 2 oz (60 g) black olives
- 2 oz (60 g) button mushrooms preserved in oil, cut in half
- 2 cloves garlic, sliced
- 1 teaspoon dried oregano
- 3 tablespoons extra-virgin olive oil

Prepare the pizza dough following the instructions on page 60. • Preheat the oven to 425°F (220°C/gas 7). • Oil a 12-inch (30-cm) pizza pan. • Knead the risen dough for 1 minute on a lightly floured work surface. Press into the pan using your fingertips. • Spread with the tomatoes, ham, anchovies, mozzarella, artichokes, olives, mushrooms, and garlic. Sprinkle with oregano and drizzle with 1 tablespoon of oil. • Bake until the crust is crisp and golden brown, 15–20 minutes. • Drizzle with the remaining oil and serve hot.

Serves: 1–2 • Prep: 30 min + 1 hr 30 min to rise • Cooking: 15–20 min • Level: 1

Spicy salami and black olive pizza

Pizza con olive e salamino piccante

Prepare the pizza dough following the instructions on page 60. • Preheat the oven to 400°F (200°C/gas 6). • Oil an 8 x 12-inch (20 x 30-cm) rectangular pizza pan. • Knead the risen dough briefly on a lightly floured work surface then press it into the prepared pan using your fingertips. • Arrange the salami, olives, tomatoes, and onions on top of the dough. Season with salt and pepper. Drizzle with the oil and sprinkle with oregano. • Bake until the base is crisp and golden brown, 25–30 minutes. • Serve hot.

Serves: 2–4 • Prep: 30 min + 1 hr 30 min to rise • Cooking: 25–30 min • Level: 1

- 1 quantity basic dough (see page 60)
- 6 oz (180 g) spicy salami, thinly sliced
- 12 black olives, pitted
- 10 cherry tomatoes, sliced
- 4 baby onions, thinly sliced
- salt and freshly ground black pepper
- $^1/_4$ cup (60 ml) extra-virgin olive oil
- 1 teaspoon dried oregano

Four-seasons pizza

Pizza quattro stagioni

- 1 quantity basic dough (see page 60)
- 12 oz (350 g) mussels, in shell
- 5 oz (150 g) white mushrooms, sliced
- 3 tablespoons extra-virgin olive oil
- salt
- 1 cup (250 g) canned tomatoes, with juice, chopped
- 3 oz (90 g) artichokes in oil, drained and cut in half
- 3 oz (90 g) pitted black olives
- 2 salt-cured anchovy fillets, chopped
- 1 clove garlic, thinly sliced

Prepare the pizza dough following the instructions on page 60. • Soak the mussels in a large bowl of water for 1 hour. Scrub off their beards and rinse well in cold water • Preheat the oven to 425°F (220°C/gas 7). • Oil a 12-inch (30-cm) pizza pan. • Heat 1 tablespoon of oil in a medium saucepan over medium-high heat and sauté until tender, for 3–4 minutes. Season with salt and set aside. • Place the mussels in a large frying pan over high heat, shaking the pan frequently. When open, discard the shells o all but 4 mussels. Strain the liquid they hav produced and set aside with the mussels in a bowl. • Knead the risen dough for 1 minute on a lightly floured work surface. Press into the pan using your fingertips. • Spread with the tomatoes and season with salt. • Imagin the pizza divided into 4 equal parts: garnish one quarter with the mushrooms, one quarter with the artichokes, one quarter with the olives and anchovies, and the final quarter with the garlic. • Bake until the crus is crisp and golden brown, 15–20 minutes. • Arrange the mussels on the part garnished with tomato and garlic. Drizzle the pizza with the remaining oil and serve hot.

Serves: 2–4 • Prep: 45 min + 1 hr 30 min to rise • Cooking: 25–30 min • Level: 1

Pizza

Onion calzones

Calzone alla cipolla

- 2 quantities basic dough (see page 60)
- $1\frac{1}{2}$ lb (750 g) onions, thinly sliced
- $\frac{1}{3}$ cup (90 ml) extra-virgin olive oil
- 1 (14-oz/400-g) can tomatoes, with juice
- 6 oz (250 g) black olives, pitted and halved
- 8 anchovy fillets, crumbled
- 2 tablespoons capers
- 8 leaves fresh basil, torn
- salt
- 6 oz (180 g) pecorino cheese, diced

Prepare the pizza dough following the instructions on page 60. • Heat $\frac{1}{4}$ cup (60 ml) of oil in a large frying pan and sauté the onions until softened, about 10 minutes. • Add the tomatoes, olives, anchovies, capers, basil, and salt. Simmer over medium-low heat for 10 minutes. Remove from the heat. • Let cool a little then add the pecorino. • Preheat the oven to 425°F (220°C/gas 7). • Oil a baking sheet. • Knead the risen pizza dough briefly on a floured work surface then divide into 4 equal portions. • Roll the dough into disks about 9 inches (23 cm) in diameter. • Spread a quarter of the filling on one half of each disk, leaving a 1-inch (2.5-cm) border around the edges. Fold the other half of the dough over the top, pressing down on the edges to seal. • Brush with the remaining oil and place on the baking sheet. • Bake until puffed and golden brown, 25 minutes. • Serve hot

Serves: 4 • Prep: 35 min + 1 hr 30 min to rise • Cooking: 25 min • Level: 1

Fried pizzas

Panzerotti

- 2 quantities basic dough (see page 60)

Filling

- 14 oz (400 g) fresh mozzarella, sliced
- 6 tomatoes, sliced
- 8 anchovy fillets, chopped
- 2 tablespoons finely chopped parsley
- salt and freshly ground black pepper
- 2 cups (500 ml) oil, for frying

Prepare the pizza dough following the instructions on page 60. • Knead the risen pizza dough briefly on a floured work surface then divide into 6 equal portions. • Roll the dough into 8 inch (20 cm) disks. • Cover half of each disk with slices of mozzarella and tomato, leaving a 1-inch (2.5-cm) border around the edges. Sprinkle with anchovies, parsley, salt, and pepper. Fold the other half of the dough over the top, pressing down on the edges to seal. • Heat the oil to very hot in a large frying pan and fry the pizzas two at a time until golden brown. • Serve hot.

Serves: 6 • Prep: 25 min + 1 hr 30 min to rise • Cooking: 30 min • Level: 2

Impanadas

Impanadas

The filling for impanadas varies from region to region and from season to season. Many recipes call for cold cuts, artichokes, peas or olives. They can also be made using lamb, sausage or even eel.

Filling

- 2 large firm ripe tomatoes, peeled and chopped
- 6 tablespoons freshly chopped parsley
- 2 tablespoons freshly chopped basil
- 1 clove garlic, finely chopped
- 8 oz (250 g) lean ground (minced) beef
- 8 oz (250 g) lean ground (minced) pork
- pinch of saffron strands
- 2 oz (60 g) lard, chopped
- salt and freshly ground black pepper

Pastry

- $2\frac{2}{3}$ cups (400 g) all-purpose (plain) flour
- $\frac{1}{3}$ cup (80 g) lard, chopped
- 1 egg, lightly beaten
- salt
- $\frac{1}{2}$ cup (125 ml) water

- 1 large egg yolk, lightly beaten

Place the tomatoes in a large bowl with the parsley, basil, and garlic. • Add the beef, pork, saffron, and lard. Season with salt and pepper and mix well. Cover and chill in the refrigerator for 30 minutes. • Pastry: Preheat the oven to 350°F (180°C/gas 4). • Place the flour in a mound on a work surface and make a well in the center. Add the lard, egg, and a pinch of salt. Mix well, adding enough water to make a stiff dough. • Knead on a lightly floured surface until smooth and elastic, 10 minutes. • Roll out the dough on a lightly floured surface until it is $\frac{1}{4}$-inch (5-mm) thick. • Cut the dough into 4 inch (10 cm) disks using a bowl or a large cookie cutter. • Place spoonfuls of the filling in the center of half the disks. Cover each one with one of the remaining disks. Seal the pastry around the edges, pinching it together with your fingers. • Arrange the impanadas on an oiled baking sheet. • Beat the egg yolk in a small bowl with a tablespoon of water. Brush the impanadas with this mixture. • Bake for until cooked through and lightly browned, 30–35 minutes. • Serve hot or at room temperature.

Serves: 4 • Prep: 40 min + 30 min to chill the filling • Cooking: 40 min • Level: 2

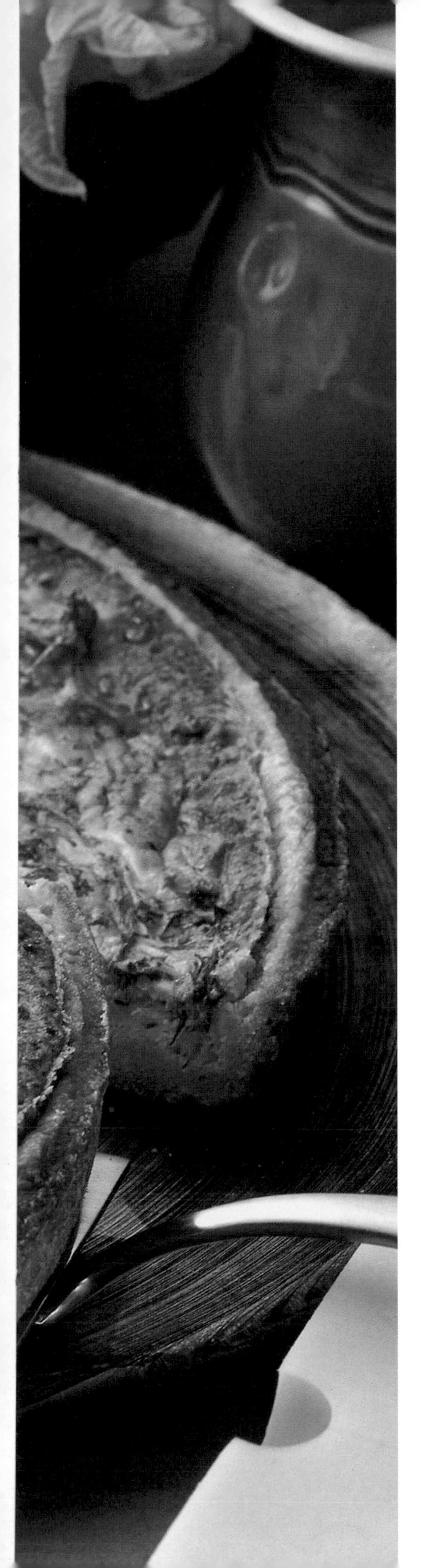

SAVORY PIES

Savory pies and quiche-like preparations, called *torte salate* in Italian, are a classic snack food or appetizer and there is a huge variety of fillings and toppings to choose from. In this chapter we have included 16 traditional and modern dishes. Some of the *torte salate* have bread dough bases while others have a short pastry crust. Serve these savory pies hot straight from the oven or at room temperature for lunch or to hungry children as a nutritious after-school snack. They can be prepared ahead of time and also make excellent buffet and party dishes and great food for a picnic spread.

Zucchini flower quiche (see page 91)

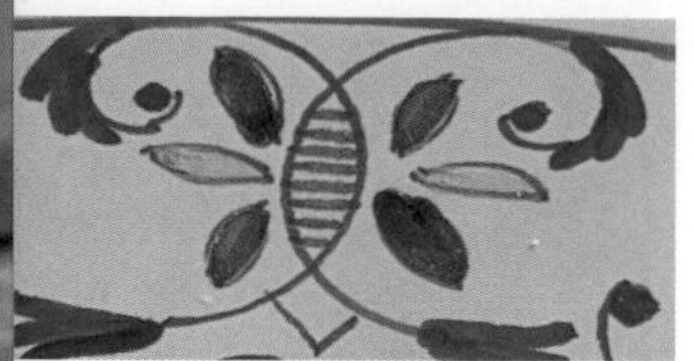

Cherry tomato quiche

CHERRY TOMATO QUICHE

Torta ai pomodorini

- 1 quantity Quick Pastry (see page 91)

Filling
- 15–20 cherry tomatoes
- 4 large eggs
- 1/2 cup (125 ml) heavy (double) cream
- 1/2 cup (125 g) fresh ricotta cheese, drained
- 6 tablespoons freshly grated Parmesan cheese
- salt and freshly ground black pepper
- 4–6 leaves fresh basil, finely chopped
- 1/2 teaspoon dried oregano

Prepare the quick pastry. Shape into a ball and wrap in plastic wrap (cling film). Refrigerate for 30 minutes. • Preheat the oven to 350°F (180°C/gas 4). • Butter a 10-inch (25-cm) springform pan or pie plate. • Filling: Cut the cherry tomatoes in half and gently squeeze out as many seeds as possible. • Beat the eggs, cream, ricotta, and Parmesan in a large bowl. Season with salt and pepper. Stir in the basil and oregano. • Roll the pastry out on a lightly floured work surface to 1/4 inch (5 mm) thick. Line the prepared pan with the pastry. Pour the egg and cheese mixture into the crust. • Add the tomatoes one by one, cut side down, pressing them into the filling slightly. • Bake until the pastry is golden brown and the filling has set, 30–40 minutes. Serve hot or at room temperature.

Serves: 4–6 • Prep: 30 min + 30 min to chill the dough
Cooking: 45 min • Level: 2

APULIAN POTATO PIE

Torta di patate alla pugliese

- 2 lb (1 kg) potatoes, peeled and cut in small cubes
- 14 oz (400 g) frozen puff pastry, thawed
- 1/2 cup (125 g) butter, melted
- 1 cup (250 ml) milk
- 3 oz (90 g) pancetta or bacon, cut into cubes
- 1 large egg + 1 large egg yolk
- 1/2 cup (50 g) freshly grated Parmesan cheese
- salt and freshly ground black pepper

Boil the potatoes in salted water until tender, about 10 minutes. Drain well and mash until smooth. • Preheat the oven to 325°F (170°C/gas 3). • Butter a 10-inch (26-cm) springform pan. Line with waxed paper. Butter the paper. • Roll the dough out into a disk large enough to line the base and sides of the pan and to overlap sufficiently to enclose the filling. • Sauté the pancetta in a small frying pan until crisp, 5 minutes. • Mix the potatoes, butter, milk, pancetta, egg, egg yolk, Parmesan, salt, and pepper in a large bowl. Spoon the filling into the pan. Fold the edges of the pastry over the filling. • Bake until golden brown, 35–45 minutes. Serve hot or at room temperature.

Serves: 4–6 • Prep: 15 min • Cooking: 50–55 min • Level: 1

EMILIAN SWISS CHARD PIE

Erbazzone emiliano

Filling
- 2 1/2 lb (1.2 kg) Swiss chard (silver beet) or spinach leaves
- 5 oz (150 g) chopped pancetta
- 2 tablespoons finely chopped parsley
- 1 clove garlic, finely chopped
- 6 scallions (green onions), finely chopped
- 2 tablespoons butter
- 3/4 cup (90 g) freshly grated Parmesan cheese
- salt and freshly ground pepper

Dough
- 3 cups (450 g) all-purpose flour
- 1 teaspoon salt
- 1/4 cup (60 g) lard, melted
- about 1 cup (250 ml) lukewarm water

Filling: Rinse the Swiss chard or spinach leaves under cold running water, but do not dry. Cook for a few minutes with just the water left clinging to the leaves. Squeeze out as much moisture as possible and chop coarsely. • Sauté the pancetta, parsley, garlic, and scallions in a large frying pan with 1 tablespoon of butter for 5 minutes. • Set 1 tablespoon of this mixture aside. Leave the rest in the pan and add the Swiss chard or spinach, Parmesan, salt, and pepper. Sauté for 2–3 minutes and remove from the heat. • Preheat the oven to 400°F (200°C/gas 6). • Butter a 10-inch (26-cm) springform pan or pie plate. • Dough: Sift the flour and salt into a large bowl. Pour in the lard and stir it into the flour, adding a little warm water at intervals, to form a fairly firm dough. • Transfer to a lightly floured work surface and knead the dough until smooth and elastic, about 5 minutes. • Divide into two portions, one twice as large as the other, and roll out to 1/4 inch (5 mm) thick. Use the larger one to line the base and sides of the prepared pan. It should overlap the edges a little. • Spoon the filling into the crust. Cover with the other disk of pastry, sealing the edges well. • Spread the reserved fried mixture over the top. • Bake until the pastry is golden brown and the filling has set, 30–40 minutes. Serve hot or at room temperature.

Serves: 4–6 • Prep: 35 min • Cooking: 35 min • Level: 2

Ri

Filling
- 2 cups (500 ml) water
- 1 3/4 cups (450 ml) milk
- salt and freshly ground black pepper
- 1 1/2 cups (300 g) short-grain rice
- 1 lb (500 g) pumpkin
- 6 tablespoons freshly grated Parmesan cheese
- 1/2 cup (125 g) fresh ricotta cheese, drained
- 1 egg
- 1 1/2 tablespoons butter

Dough
- 1 1/2 cups (225 g) all-purpose (plain) flour
- 1/2 teaspoon salt
- 1/4 cup (60 ml) extra-virgin olive oil
- 4–6 tablespoons warm water

Vegetable and fresh garlic soup

Vegetable and fresh garlic soup

Zuppa di verdura all'agliata

- 12 oz (350 g) tomatoes
- 1/4 cup (60 ml) extra virgin olive oil
- 1 medium onion, finely sliced
- 12 oz (350 g) Savoy cabbage, shredded
- 10 lettuce leaves, shredded
- 10 Swiss chard (silver beet) leaves, shredded
- 1 stalk celery, finely sliced
- 4 medium potatoes, peeled and thinly sliced
- 2 large carrots, thinly sliced
- 4 cups (1 liter) vegetable stock, homemade (see page 112), or bouillon cube
- freshly ground black pepper
- 1/3 cup (90 g) butter
- 4 large slices crusty white bread
- 1 1/2 cups (250 g) frozen peas
- 5 cloves garlic, very finely chopped
- 3 tablespoons finely chopped parsley
- 1/4 cup (30 g) freshly grated Parmesan cheese

Blanch the tomatoes in boiling water for 2 minutes. Drain and peel them. Chop coarsely. • Heat the oil in a large saucepan over low heat. Add the onion and sauté until softened, 3–4 minutes. • Add the cabbage, lettuce, Swiss chard, celery, carrots, potatoes, and tomatoes. Mix well and simmer until the vegetables begin to soften, about 10 minutes. • Add the stock and season with pepper. Bring to a boil, cover, and simmer until the vegetables are very tender, about 20 minutes. • Melt the butter in a large frying pan over medium heat. Add the bread and fry until golden brown on both sides, about 5 minutes. Drain on paper towels. • Add the peas to the soup and simmer for 5 minutes. Add the garlic and parsley, and mix well. Check the seasoning. • Arrange the fried bread in serving bowls. Ladle the soup over the top. Sprinkle with the cheese and serve hot.

Serves: 4 • Prep: 15 min • Cooking: 45 min • Level: 2

Chicken stock

Brodo di pollo

- 1 chicken, about 4 lb (2 kg)
- 2 large carrots
- 1 large onion, stuck with 4 cloves
- 2 large stalks celery
- 4 small tomatoes
- 5 sprigs parsley
- 1–2 teaspoons salt
- 3 quarts (3 liters) water

Free-range hens make the tastiest stock, although they take a little longer to cook. Chicken stock freezes well.

Place the chicken, vegetables, parsley, and salt in a large pot with the water and bring to a boil. Cover and simmer over low heat for 2–3 hours. • Filter the stock, discarding the vegetables. The chicken can be used to make chicken salad. • As the stock cools, fat will form on top; it should be discarded.

Makes: about 8 cups (2 liters) • Prep: 10 min • Cooking: 2 hr • Level: 1

Beef stock

Brodo di carne

Stock is easy to make at home and while bouillon cubes are convenient the stock made using them never tastes quite as good. Stock freezes well, so make a large quantity and freeze for future use.

Place all the vegetables, the meat, bones, and salt in a large pot with the water. Bring to a boil over high heat. Reduce heat to low and simmer for about 2 hours. • Remove the bones and vegetables and discard. (The meat can be served with freshly boiled vegetables, or try it in the delicious recipe—Boiled beef with onions—on page 294). • As the stock cools, fat will form on top and can be scooped off and discarded.

Makes: about 8 cups (2 liters) • Prep: 10 min • Cooking: 2 hr • Level: 1

- 1 large carrot
- 1 medium onion
- 1 large stalk celery
- 4 small tomatoes
- 5 sprigs parsley
- 10 leaves basil
- 2 lb (1 kg) lean boiling beef + 2 lb (1 kg) beef bones
- 1–2 teaspoons salt
- 3 quarts (3 liters) water

Pearl barley soup

Zuppa di orzo

Put the vegetables, pancetta, and stock in a large pot over medium heat and bring to a boil. • Rinse the pearl barley under cold running water and add to the boiling stock. Cover the pot and simmer for 1 hour, stirring occasionally. • When the barley is tender, season with salt and pepper and remove from heat. Drizzle with the oil, cover, and let rest for 5 minutes before serving.

Serves: 4 • Prep: 20 min • Cooking: 1 hr • Level: 1

- 1 large carrot, diced
- 1 large zucchini (courgette), diced
- 1 large potato, diced
- 1 leek (white part only), thinly sliced
- 2 small celery hearts, sliced
- 1 medium onion, thinly sliced
- 1 oz (30 g) spinach, coarsely chopped
- 2 tablespoons finely chopped parsley
- 1/2 cup (100 g) pancetta, diced
- 5 cups (1.25 liters) boiling beef stock, homemade (see recipe above), or bouillon cube
- 1 cup (200 g) pearl barley
- salt and freshly ground black pepper
- 1/4 cup (60 ml) extra-virgin olive oil

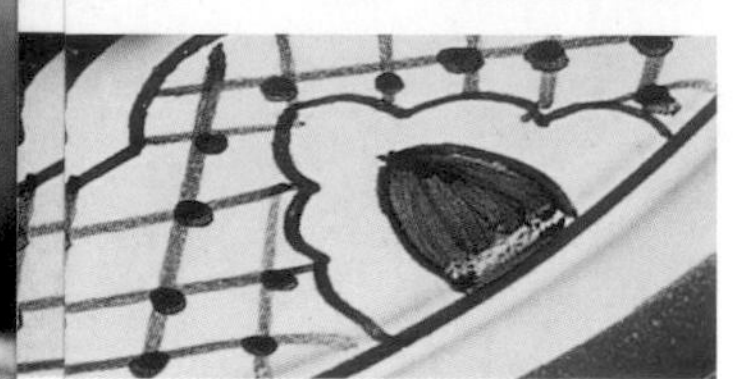

Vegetable stock

Brodo vegetale

- $\frac{1}{4}$ cup (60 ml) extra-virgin olive oil
- 2 large onions, chopped
- 2 large carrots, chopped
- 2 leeks, chopped
- 2 stalks celery, chopped
- 4 tomatoes, cut in half
- 6 sprigs parsley
- 1 tablespoon black peppercorns
- 2 bay leaves
- 4 quarts (4 liters) cold water
- salt

Heat the oil in a large saucepan over low heat. Add the onions, carrots, leeks, celery, tomatoes, parsley, peppercorns, and bay leaves and sauté for 10 minutes. • Pour in the water and season with salt. Bring to a boil and simmer for 1 hour. Skim off any foam as it forms. • Strain the stock.

Makes: about 3 quarts (3 liters) • Prep: 10 min • Cooking: 1 hr 15 min • Level: 1

Garbanzo bean soup

Zuppa di ceci e verdure

- 4 quarts (4 liters) water, + more as needed
- 2 cups (300 g) dried garbanzo beans (chickpeas), soaked overnight
- salt
- 1 lb (500 g) cardoons or celery stalks, tough strings removed and coarsely chopped
- 1 oz (30 g) dried mushrooms, soaked in warm water for 15 minutes
- 2 Italian sausages, crumbled
- $\frac{1}{3}$ cup (90 ml) extra-virgin olive oil
- 1 teaspoon all-purpose (plain) flour
- freshly ground black pepper
- 12 oz (350 g) small dried soup pasta, such as ditalini

Bring the water with the beans to a boil in a large saucepan over medium-low heat. Skim off the froth. Simmer over low heat until the beans are very soft, about 1 hour 30 minutes. • Season with salt and remove from the heat (there should still be plenty of cooking water). Drain, reserving the cooking water. • Cook the cardoons in salted boiling water until tender, 25–30 minutes. • Drain and set aside. • Sauté the mushrooms and sausage in the oil in a large saucepan over medium heat until the sausage is browned all over, about 10 minutes. • Sprinkle with the flour and season with salt and pepper. Pour in 4 cups (1 liter) of the reserved cooking water. Cover and simmer over medium heat for 30 minutes. • Stir in the cooked garbanzo beans and cardoons. • Add the pasta and cook until al dente, 5–7 minutes. • Serve hot.

Serves: 6 • Prep: 40 min + overnight to soak the beans Cooking: 2 hr 30 min • Level: 1

Florentine vegetable and bread soup

La ribollita

This is a traditional recipe from Florence where ribollita is served often throughout the winter months. In Tuscany, the Savoy cabbage is substituted with the local black or Tuscan kale, although this is not always easy to find outside of the region.

- 2 cups (400 g) dried cannellini beans, soaked overnight and drained
- 8 cup (2 liters) water
- salt
- 4 oz (125 g) cotenna (pork skin with layer of fat attached) or same quantity pancetta of bacon
- $\frac{2}{3}$ cup (150 ml) extra-virgin olive oil
- 2 oz (60 g) pancetta, sliced into strips
- 1 large onion, finely sliced
- 3 large carrots, finely sliced
- 2 medium leeks, finely sliced
- 1 stalk celery, finely chopped
- 4 tablespoons finely chopped basil
- 4 tablespoons finely chopped parsley
- $\frac{1}{2}$ Savoy cabbage, shredded
- $\frac{1}{2}$ red cabbage, shredded
- 1 (14-oz/400-g) can tomatoes, with juice
- freshly ground black pepper
- 8–10 slices firm-textured bread

Place the beans in a large saucepan with the water. Bring to a boil and simmer over low heat until the beans are tender, about 1 hour. • Transfer half the beans to a food processor and chop to make a smooth purée. Return the purée to the pan and mix well. Season with salt and remove from the heat. • Scrape the pork skin to remove any hairs. Place in a small saucepan and cover with water. Bring to a boil over medium heat. Simmer for 10 minutes and then drain. Slice the pork skin into thin strips. • Heat $\frac{1}{3}$ cup (90 ml) of the oil in a large saucepan over medium heat. Add the pork skin, pancetta, onion, carrots, leeks, celery, basil, and parsley. Sauté until the vegetables begin to soften, about 5 minutes. Add the cabbage and sauté until wilted, about 5 minutes. Be careful not to let the cabbage brown. • Add the tomatoes and basil. Season with salt and pepper. Simmer for 10 minutes and then add the bean mixture. Simmer over very low heat for 1 hour. • Toast the bread until golden brown all over. Arrange a layer of the bread in the bottom of an earthenware pot. Ladle some of the soup over the bread and then add another layer of bread. Repeat until all the ingredients are in the pot. Cover the pot and set aside for at least 2 hours. Leave overnight, if liked. • Preheat the oven to 325°F (160°C/gas 3). • Heat the soup in the oven until warmed through, 15–20 minutes. • Drizzle with the remaining oil and serve hot.

Serves: 6–8 • Prep: 30 min + 12 h to soak the beans + time to rest the soup • Cooking: 2 hr 30 min • Level: 2

Zucchini soup

Minestra di zucchine

- 1/4 cup (60 ml) extra-virgin olive oil
- 2 scallions (green onions), finely chopped
- 8 zucchini (courgettes), cleaned and diced
- salt and freshly ground black pepper
- 6 cups (1.5 liters) boiling beef stock, homemade (see page 104) or bouillon cube
- 2 eggs, lightly beaten
- 1 tablespoon finely chopped parsley
- 1 tablespoon finely chopped basil
- 1/4 cup (30 g) freshly grated Parmesan cheese
- 4 slices firm-textured bread, toasted and cut in cubes

Heat the oil in a heavy-bottomed saucepan and sauté the scallions until softened, 2–3 minutes. • Add the zucchini and sauté for 5 more minutes. Season with salt and pepper. • Add the stock and simmer over medium-low heat or until the zucchini are tender, about 10 minutes. • Add the eggs, parsley, and basil and stir rapidly. Serve hot, with the toasted bread passed separately.

Serves: 4 • Prep: 10 min • Cooking: 20 min • Level: 1

Spelt soup

Minestra di farro

Spelt has been cultivated in Italy since the rise of Rome, but went out of fashion during the 19th and 20th centuries. Recently, as we have begun to rediscover our regional traditions and to look for healthy alternatives to processed foods, spelt has made a comeback.

- 1 raw salted ham bone (with some ham still on the bone)
- 8 cups (2 liters water)
- 1 onion, cut into quarters
- 1 carrot, coarsely chopped
- 1 stalk celery, coarsely chopped
- 1 firm-ripe tomato, cut in half
- 4 sprigs fresh parsley
- 1/4 teaspoon whole black peppercorns
- salt
- 2 cups (200 g) crushed spelt (farro)
- 3/4 cup (90 g) freshly grated pecorino cheese

Place the ham bone in a large saucepan and pour in the water. Add the onion, carrot, celery, tomato, parsley, and peppercorns. Bring to a boil over low heat and simmer until the vegetables are very tender, about 45 minutes. • Use a slotted spoon to remove the vegetables and process them in a food processor or blender until puréed. • Remove the meat from the bone and return the meat to the saucepan. Add the puréed vegetables. Season with salt and bring to a boil. • Add the spelt and simmer, stirring occasionally, until the spelt is tender, about 30 minutes. • Sprinkle with the pecorino and serve hot.

Serves: 4 • Prep: 40 min • Cooking: 1 hr 15 min • Level: 1

Cream of pumpkin soup

Crema di zucca

- 2 lb (1 kg) pumpkin, peeled and cut in pieces
- 4 carrots, sliced
- 4 leeks, cleaned and sliced (white part only)
- 3 stalks celery sliced
- 2 cloves garlic
- 4 cups (1 liter) boiling beef stock, homemade (see page 104) or bouillon cube
- 1/2 cup (125 ml) heavy (double) cream
- salt and freshly ground white pepper
- 1/2 cup (60 g) freshly grated Parmesan cheese
- croutons or squares of toasted bread

Place the pumpkin, carrots, leeks, celery, and garlic in a large saucepan and add the stock. Cover and simmer, stirring occasionally, until tender, about 30 minutes. • Chop in a blender or food processor to obtain a smooth, fairly dense purée. • Set over medium heat for 1–2 minutes. • Stir in the cream and season with salt and pepper. • Let stand for 1 minute, sprinkle with the Parmesan, and serve hot.

Serves: 4 • Prep: 30 min • Cooking: 30 min • Level: 1

White wine soup

Zuppa di vino bianco

- 3 cups (750 ml) dry white wine (Sauvignon or Pinot Grigio)
- 2 tablespoons sugar
- 1/2 teaspoon ground cinnamon
- 1/2 teaspoon freshly grated nutmeg
- 1/4 cup (60 g) butter
- 3 tablespoons all-purpose (plain) flour
- 3 cups (750 g) milk
- salt and freshly ground black pepper
- 6 egg yolks
- 1/4 cup (30 g) freshly grated Parmesan cheese

Bring the wine to a boil in a medium saucepan and stir in the sugar, cinnamon, and nutmeg. • Melt the butter in a large, heavy-bottomed pan and stir in the flour. Gradually add the milk and stir to make a creamy sauce. Season with salt and pepper. • Pour the hot wine into the sauce and stir until smooth. • Stir the egg yolks in just before removing from heat. Sprinkle with the Parmesan and serve.

Serves: 4 • Prep: 10 min • Cooking: 20 min • Level: 1

- 1 oz
  mus
- 1 ta
  cho
- 2 cl
  fine
- $\frac{1}{4}$ c
  virg
- $1\frac{1}{2}$
  mus
  and
- $\frac{1}{2}$ c
  whi
- 6 cu
  stoc
  (see
  bou
- 1 tal
  (pla
- salt
  blac
- 4 sli
  brea

- 8 th
  text
- 2 cl
- 8 oz
  Gru
- salt
  blag
- 5 cu
  boi
  hor
  104

SPAGHETTI, PENNE & CO.

In this chapter we have gathered more than 50 classic and modern recipes for dried long and short pasta shapes, from spaghetti, bucatini, and linguine, to penne, fusilli, and farfalle, among others. The wonderful thing about dried pasta is that it is so quick and easy to prepare; a family meal can be made in minutes by simply garnishing the cooked pasta with sliced fresh tomatoes, some mozzarella cheese, fresh basil, and garlic and drizzling it all with extra-virgin olive oil. Dishes like these not only look good but they are also good for you. Among the classics, we have included *La carbonara* (Spaghetti with pancetta and egg, see page 126), Linguine with pesto, potatoes, and green beans (see page 130), and Bucatini with Amatriciana sauce (see page 138). There are also two good recipes for basic pasta sauces—Tomato sauce and Meat sauce (both on page 132).

Spaghetti with mozzarella and tomato (see page 124)

Spaghetti with tomato and lemon

Spaghetti with Garlic, Oil, and Chile Peppers

Spaghetti, aglio, olio e peperoncino

- 1 lb (500 g) spaghetti
- 4 cloves garlic, finely chopped
- 2 dried chile peppers, finely chopped
- $1/2$ cup (125 ml) extra-virgin olive oil
- 2 tablespoons finely chopped fresh parsley or other fresh herbs, as liked (optional)

This classic spaghetti dish is famous in Italy as the preferred midnight snack for revelers when they get home late from a night on the town. Quick, easy and nourishing, it is also a favorite with students.

Cook the pasta in a large pot of salted boiling water until al dente. • While the pasta is cooking, sauté the garlic and chile peppers in the oil in a large frying pan over medium heat until the garlic is pale gold, 2–3 minutes. • Drain the pasta and add to the frying pan. • Toss over high heat for 1 minute, sprinkle with the herbs, if using, and serve hot.

Serves: 4–6 • Prep: 5 min • Cooking: 15 min • Level: 1

Spaghetti with Tomato and Mozzarella

Spaghetti con pomodorini e mozzarella

Prepare this dish during the summer months when cherry tomatoes are at their succulent best.

Cook the pasta in a large pot of salted, boiling water until al dente. • Drain and toss with the tomatoes, mozzarella, basil, mint, garlic, and oil in a large bowl. Season with salt and pepper. • Garnish with the basil leaves and serve hot.

Serves: 4–6 • Prep: 10 min • Cooking: 15 min • Level: 1

- 1 lb (500 g) spaghetti
- 2 lb (1 kg) cherry tomatoes, cut in half
- 8 oz (250 g) fresh mozzarella cheese, drained and cut into small cubes
- 2 tablespoons finely chopped basil
- 1 tablespoon finely chopped mint
- 1 clove garlic, finely chopped
- $1/2$ cup (125 ml) extra-virgin olive oil
- salt and freshly ground black pepper
- fresh basil leaves, to garnish

Spaghetti with Garlic and Bread

Spaghetti con la mollica

- 1 lb (500 g) spaghetti
- $1/2$ cup (125 ml) extra-virgin olive oil
- 4 cloves garlic, finely chopped
- 2 cups (100 g) fine dry bread crumbs
- 2 tablespoons finely chopped fresh oregano or 2 teaspoons dried oregano
- freshly ground black pepper

Cook the pasta in a large pot of salted boiling water until al dente. • While the spaghetti is cooking, heat the oil in a large frying pan over medium heat. Add the garlic and sauté for 1 minute. • Add the bread crumbs and oregano and sauté until the bread crumbs have browned, about 3 minutes. Remove from the heat. • Drain the pasta and add to the pan with the sauce. • Toss over medium heat until the sauce sticks to the pasta, 1–2 minutes. • Season with pepper and serve hot.

Serves: 4–6 • Prep: 10 min • Cooking: 15 min • Level: 1

Spaghetti with Tomato and Lemon

Spaghetti al limone

Blanch the tomatoes in boiling water for 2 minutes. Drain and peel them. Chop coarsely. • Cook the pasta in a large pot of salted boiling water until al dente. • Drain well and transfer to a large serving dish. • Add the tomatoes, basil, oil, lemon juice, and garlic. Season with salt and pepper. Toss well. • Garnish with basil and serve hot.

Serves: 4–6 • Prep: 10 min • Cooking: 15 min • Level: 1

- 2 lb (1 kg) ripe tomatoes
- 1 lb (500 g) spaghetti
- 4 tablespoons finely chopped basil + extra leaves, to garnish
- $1/3$ cup (90 ml) extra-virgin olive oil
- freshly squeezed juice of 1 lemon
- 2 cloves garlic, finely chopped
- salt and freshly ground black pepper

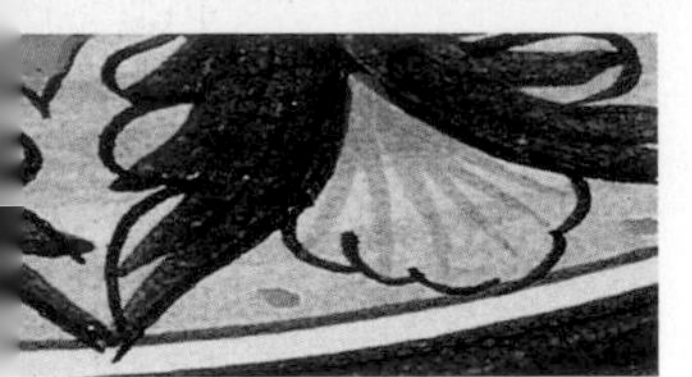

Spaghetti with Pancetta and Egg

Spaghetti alla carbonara

- 1 onion, finely chopped
- 1/4 cup (60 ml) extra-virgin olive oil
- 1 1/3 cups (150 g) diced bacon
- 6 large eggs
- 1/3 cup (90 ml) heavy (double) cream
- salt and freshly ground black pepper
- 3/4 cup (100 g) freshly grated Parmesan cheese
- 1 lb (500 g) spaghetti

La carbonara *is a classic Roman sauce. The trick is to toss the pasta very quickly with the egg until it is just cooked and serve as quickly as possible.*

Cook the pasta in a large pot of salted boiling water until al dente. • Sauté the onion in the oil in a small saucepan over medium heat until lightly browned, 2–3 minutes. • Add the pancetta and sauté until crisp, about 5 minutes. Remove from the heat and set aside. • Beat the eggs and cream in a large bowl. Season with salt and pepper and sprinkle with the Parmesan. • Drain the pasta and add to the pancetta. Return to high heat, add the egg mixture, and toss the briefly so that the eggs cook lightly but are still creamy. • Serve immediately.

Serves: 4–6 • Prep: 15 min • Cooking: 15 min • Level: 1

Spaghetti with Vegetable Sauce

Spaghetti alle verdure

Heat the oil in a large frying pan over medium heat. Add the onions, celery, carrots, peas, and zucchini. Season with salt and pepper. Sauté until the vegetables are softened, about 5 minutes. • Add the tomatoes and mix well. Cover and simmer over low heat until the tomatoes have reduced, about 20 minutes. • Meanwhile, cook the pasta in a large pot of salted boiling water until al dente. • Drain and add to the frying pan. Toss over high heat for 1 minute. • Sprinkle with the Parmesan and serve hot.

Serves: 4–6 • Prep: 10 min • Cooking: 20 min • Level: 1

- 1/4 cup (60 ml) extra-virgin olive oil
- 2 large onions, finely sliced
- 6 celery stalks, finely chopped
- 2 medium carrots, finely chopped
- 1 cup (150 g) frozen peas
- 2 medium zucchini (courgettes), cut into small pieces
- salt and freshly ground black pepper
- 1 (14-oz/400-g) can tomatoes, with juice
- 1 lb (500 g) whole-wheat (wholemeal) spaghetti
- 1/2 cup (60 g) freshly grated Parmesan cheese

Spaghetti with Pecorino

Spaghetti cacio e pepe

- 1 lb (500 g) spaghetti
- 1 1/4 cups (150 g) freshly grated aged pecorino cheese
- 1 teaspoon freshly ground black pepper
- salt
- 1/2 cup (125 ml) water

Cook the pasta in a large pot of salted boiling water until al dente. • Mix the pecorino and pepper in a large bowl. Dilute with the water. • Drain the pasta, reserving a little cooking water, and add to the bowl with the pecorino. Add a little of the cooking water and extra black pepper to taste. Do not add too much water or the cheese will melt into strings instead of making a creamy sauce.

Serves 4–6 • Prep: 5 min • Cooking: 15 min • Level: 1

Spaghetti with Zucchini

Spaghetti con zucchini

Rinse the zucchini under cold running water. Cut into rounds or slice lengthwise. • Heat the oil in a large deep frying pan until very hot. Fry the zucchini in 2 or 3 batches until golden brown, 5–7 minutes per batch. Drain on paper towels. Season with salt. • Meanwhile, cook the pasta in a large pot of salted boiling water until al dente. • Drain and place in a heated serving dish. Sprinkle with the pecorino. Top with the fried zucchini and basil. Add a little cooking water if the sauce is too dry. • Toss well and serve hot.

Serves: 4–6 • Prep: 15 min • Cooking: 25 min • Level: 1

- 1 lb (500 g) zucchini (courgettes)
- 2 cups (500 ml) oil, for frying
- salt
- 1 lb (500 g) spaghetti
- 1/2 cup (60 g) freshly grated pecorino cheese
- 10 leaves fresh basil, torn

Spaghetti with olives and anchovies

SPAGHETTI WITH OLIVES AND ANCHOVIES

Spaghetti alla puttanesca

- 1/3 cup (90 ml) extra-virgin olive oil
- 1 red onion, finely chopped
- 1–2 dried chile peppers, crumbled
- 3 cloves garlic, finely chopped
- 4 salt-cured anchovy fillets
- 1½ lb (750 g) ripe tomatoes, peeled and finely chopped
- 1 cup (100 g) black olives
- 1 tablespoon salt-cured capers, chopped
- 1 lb (500 g) spaghetti
- 1 tablespoon finely chopped parsley

Another classic Roman sauce. Feel free to make it as hot and spicy as you like.

Heat the oil in a large frying pan over medium heat. Add the onion, garlic, chile peppers and sauté until softened, about 5 minutes. • Add the anchovies and sauté over low heat, crushing the anchovies with a fork until they have dissolved into the oil, about 5 minutes. • Stir in the tomatoes and simmer until reduced, about 15 minutes. • Add the olives and capers and simmer for 5 more minutes. • While the sauce is simmering, cook the pasta in a large pot of salted boiling water until al dente. • Drain and add to the sauce. Sprinkle with the parsley, toss gently, and serve hot.

Serves: 4–6 • Prep: 20 min • Cooking: 30 min • Level: 1

BAVETTE WITH MUSHROOMS

Bavette coi funghi

- 1¼ lb (600 g) mixed mushrooms (porcini, white, champignons)
- 1 onion, finely chopped
- 1/3 cup (90 ml) extra-virgin olive oil
- salt
- 2 cloves garlic, finely chopped
- 1 dried chile pepper, crumbled
- 1/3 cup (90 ml) dry white wine
- 16 cherry tomatoes, coarsely chopped
- 1 tablespoon finely chopped basil
- 1 tablespoon finely chopped parsley
- 1 lb (500 g) bavette

Clean the mushrooms very carefully and cut the larger ones into small pieces. • Sweat the onion in the oil in a frying pan over low heat for 20 minutes. Season with salt and add the garlic and chile. • Increase the heat and pour in the wine. • Add the mushrooms and sauté over high heat for 5 minutes. • Stir in the tomatoes, basil, and parsley. Season with salt and simmer until the mushrooms are tender and the sauce reduced, about 20 minutes. • Cook the pasta in a large pan of salted, boiling water until al dente. • Drain and add to the sauce. Toss well and serve hot.

Serves: 4–6 • Prep: 30 min • Cooking: 45 min • Level: 1

SPAGHETTI WITH MUSHROOMS AND OLIVES

Spaghetti alla disperata

- 2 tablespoons dried porcini mushrooms, soaked for 15 minutes in warm water
- 1 oz (30 g) salt-cured capers
- 1 large onion, finely chopped
- 1/3 cup (90 ml) extra-virgin olive oil
- 2 large firm-ripe tomatoes, peeled and cut into small cubes
- 16 green olives, pitted
- 6 salt-cured anchovy fillets
- ½ teaspoon dried oregano
- salt and freshly ground white pepper
- 1 lb (500 g) spaghetti
- ½ cup (60 g) freshly grated pecorino cheese

Drain the mushrooms, reserving the soaking liquid, and chop finely. Strain the soaking liquid. • Rinse the capers under cold running water and transfer to a small saucepan. Add enough water to cover and place over medium heat. Bring to a boil, drain the capers, rinse them again, and pat dry on paper towels. • Sauté the onion in the oil in a small saucepan over medium heat until softened, 3–4 minutes. • Add the mushrooms and tomato and simmer for 8–10 minutes, adding 2–3 tablespoons of the strained soaking water from the mushrooms. • Finely chop the olives, capers, and anchovies. Add to the sauce and season with oregano, salt, and pepper. Simmer over low heat for 5 minutes. The sauce should not come to a boil. It should remain fairly liquid. Add more of the liquid from the mushrooms, if needed. • Meanwhile, cook the pasta in a large pot of salted boiling water until al dente. • Drain and sprinkle with pecorino. Top with the sauce, toss gently, and serve hot.

Serves: 4–6 • Prep: 20 min + 15 min to soak the mushrooms
Cooking: 20 min • Level: 1

Linguine with pesto, potatoes, and green beans

Linguine with pesto, potatoes, and green beans

Linguine con pesto, patate e fagiolini

- 14 oz (400 g) green beans, cut in short lengths
- 1 lb (500 g) linguine
- 6–8 small new potatoes, cut into small cubes

Pesto

- 1 large bunch fresh basil leaves
- 2 cloves garlic
- 3 tablespoons pine nuts
- ½ cup (125 ml) extra-virgin olive oil
- salt and freshly ground black pepper
- 6 tablespoons freshly grated pecorino cheese

This recipe comes from Genoa, on the Italian Riviera, in the northwest. Genoa is the hometown of pesto, which has become a classic sauce in modern cuisines.

Cook the green beans in a large pot of salted boiling water until almost tender, 4–5 minutes. Drain and set aside. • Pesto: Chop the basil, garlic, and pine nuts in a food processor. Gradually add the oil as you chop. • Transfer to a small bowl. Stir in the cheese and season with salt and pepper. • Cook the linguine in a large pot of salted boiling water for 5 minutes. Add the potatoes and cook until the pasta is al dente and the potatoes are tender, about 7–8 minutes more. • Drain well, reserving 3 tablespoons of the cooking liquid. Place the pasta and potatoes in a heated serving bowl. • Add the reserved cooking liquid to the pesto. Pour the pesto into the pasta and potatoes, add the green beans, and toss well. • Season with pepper. Serve hot.

Serves: 4–6 • Prep: 15 min • Cooking: 20 min • Level: 1

Spaghetti with fried eggplant and tomato

Spaghetti alla Norma

This recipe comes from Sicily and is named after Bellini's masterpiece, the opera Norma.

Place the eggplant slices in a colander and sprinkle with the coarse sea salt. Let drain for 1 hour. • Heat the oil in a large deep frying pan until very hot. • Shake the salt off the eggplant and fry in small batches until golden brown, 5–7 minutes per batch. Drain on paper towels. • Stir the tomatoes, onion, garlic, basil, oil, sugar, and salt in a medium saucepan. Cover and simmer over medium heat until the tomatoes have broken down, about 15 minutes. • Uncover and simmer over low heat until the sauce is reduced, about 30 minutes. Transfer to a food processor and chop until smooth. • Cook the pasta in a large pot of salted boiling water until al dente. • Drain and add to the sauce. Toss well. Top with the fried eggplant and sprinkle with the cheese. Serve hot.

Serves: 4–6 • Prep: 25 min + 1 hr to drain • Cooking: 1 hr 10 min • Level: 1

- 1 large eggplant (aubergine), weighing about 1 lb (500 g), thinly sliced
- 2 tablespoons coarse sea salt
- 1 cup (250 ml) olive oil, for frying
- 2 lb (1 kg) firm-ripe tomatoes, peeled and coarsely chopped
- 1 red onion, thinly sliced
- 2 cloves garlic, finely chopped
- leaves from 1 small bunch fresh basil, torn
- 2 tablespoons extra-virgin olive oil
- ½ teaspoon sugar
- salt
- 1 lb (500 g) spaghetti or bucatini
- ½ cup (60 g) freshly grated pecorino cheese

Spaghetti with sun-dried tomatoes

Spaghetti con pomodori secchi

- ¼ cup (60 ml) extra-virgin olive oil
- 3 cloves garlic, thinly sliced
- 3 oz (90 g) sun-dried tomatoes, soaked in warm water for 15 minutes, drained and coarsely chopped
- 1 (14-oz/400-g) can tomatoes, with juice
- 1 lb (500 g) spaghetti
- 12 oz (350 g) green beans, cut in short lengths
- salt and freshly ground black pepper

Heat the oil in a large frying pan over medium heat. Add the garlic and sun-dried tomatoes and sauté until the garlic is pale gold, about 3 minutes • Add the canned tomatoes and simmer until the sauce is thick, about 10 minutes. • Meanwhile, cook the pasta in a large pot of salted boiling water for 5 minutes. Add the green beans and cook until the pasta is al dente and the beans are tender. • Drain well and add to the frying pan with the sauce. Season with salt and pepper. Toss gently over high heat for 1 minute. • Serve hot

Serves: 4–6 • Prep: 25 min • Cooking: 20 min • Level: 1

Spaghetti with tuna and tomatoes

Spaghetti al tonno

Cook the spaghetti in a large pot of salted, boiling water until al dente. • Sauté the garlic and parsley in the oil over medium-low heat for 2 minutes. • Add the tomatoes, season with salt, and simmer until heated through, 4–5 minutes. • Add the tuna, stir well, and turn off the heat immediately. • Drain the pasta well and place in a heated serving dish. Toss gently with the sauce and serve hot.

Serves: 4–6 • Prep: 10 min • Cooking: 15 min • Level: 1

- 1 lb (500 g) spaghetti
- 2 cloves garlic, finely chopped
- 3 tablespoons finely chopped parsley
- ½ cup (125 ml) extra-virgin olive oil
- 16–20 cherry tomatoes, cut in half
- salt
- 12 oz (2350 g) canned tuna, flaked

Spaghetti with Tuna, Porcini Mushrooms, and Pancetta

Spaghetti alla carrettiera con tonno

- 1 oz (30 g) dried mushrooms
- 1/3 cup (90 ml) extra-virgin olive oil
- scant 2/3 cup (75 g) chopped pancetta (or bacon)
- 2 cloves garlic, finely chopped
- 2 dried chile peppers, crumbled
- 4 large tomatoes, peeled and chopped
- 4 oz (125 g) canned tuna, drained and crumbled
- salt and freshly ground black pepper
- 1 lb (500 g) spaghetti
- 2 tablespoons finely chopped parsley

The carrettieri *(cart-drivers) were the men who drove the horse-drawn carts that carried the wine into central Rome from the vineyards of the Castelli Romani in the Alban Hills. There are many versions of this hearty Roman pasta sauce.*

Soak the mushrooms in ½ cup (125 ml) of warm water for 15 minutes. Drain well, reserving the liquid. Chop the drained mushrooms finely. • Heat the oil in a large frying pan over medium heat. Add the pancetta, garlic, and chile peppers. Sauté until the garlic is pale golden brown, 2–3 minutes. • Add the mushrooms and tomatoes and sauté until reduced, about 10 minutes. Add a little of the reserved soaking liquid and let it evaporate. • Stir in the tuna. Mix well and season with salt. Lower the heat and simmer for 5 minutes. • Meanwhile, cook the pasta in a large pot of salted boiling water until al dente. Drain well and transfer to the frying pan with the sauce. Add a little more of the mushroom liquid if the sauce is too thick. • Toss over high heat for 1 minute and season with pepper. • Garnish with the parsley and serve hot.

Serves: 4–6 • Prep: 15 min + 15 min to drain • Cooking: 30 min • Level: 1

Spaghetti with Bell Peppers and Pancetta

Spaghetti con peperoni e pancetta

- 1/3 cup (90 ml) extra-virgin olive oil
- 1 cup (100 g) chopped pancetta (or bacon)
- 1 large onion, finely chopped
- 1 clove garlic, finely chopped
- 2 tablespoons finely chopped parsley
- 6 basil leaves, torn
- 2 red bell peppers (capsicums), seeded and finely sliced
- 2 yellow bell peppers (capsicums), seeded and finely sliced
- 1 (14-oz/400-g) can tomatoes, with juice
- 1 red chile pepper, seeded and chopped
- 1 teaspoon dried oregano
- salt
- 2 tablespoons salt-cured capers, rinsed and drained
- handful green olives, pitted and coarsely chopped
- 1 lb (500 g) spaghetti
- 1/4 cup (30 g) freshly grated pecorino or Parmesan cheese

Heat the oil in a large frying pan over medium heat. Add the pancetta and sauté until lightly browned, about 3 minutes. • Add the onion, garlic, parsley, basil, and bell peppers. Sauté until the peppers and the onions are softened, about 10 minutes. • Stir in the tomatoes, chile pepper, and oregano, and season with salt. Mix well, cover, and simmer over low heat until the tomatoes have broken down, about 25 minutes. • Add the capers and olives. Mix well and cook for 2 minutes. • Meanwhile, cook the pasta in a large pot of salted boiling water until al dente. • Drain and add to the frying pan. Toss over high heat for 1 minute. • Sprinkle with the cheese and serve hot.

Serves: 4–6 • Prep: 25 min • Cooking: 40 min • Level: 1

Seafood spaghetti en papillote

Ziti with sardines

Ziti con le sarde

- 3 quarts (3 liters) water
- 1 tablespoon coarse sea salt
- 1 large bulb fennel, cleaned and cut in quarters
- 12 oz (350 g) fresh or frozen (thawed) sardines
- 1 medium onion, finely chopped
- 1/3 cup (90 ml) extra-virgin olive oil
- 4–6 salt-cured anchovy fillets
- 2 tablespoons small, seedless white raisins
- 3 tablespoons pine nuts
- 1/4 cup (40 g) toasted almonds, chopped
- freshly ground black pepper
- 1/4 teaspoon saffron, dissolved in 2 tablespoons hot water
- 1 lb (500 g) ziti pasta
- 2/3 cup (100 g) fine dry bread crumbs, toasted in a hot oven

Bring the water to a boil in a large saucepan and add the salt and fennel. Simmer for 15 minutes, then drain, reserving the water to cook the pasta. • Squeeze the fennel to remove excess moisture and chop coarsely. • Remove any scales from the sardines and gently pull off their heads. Use kitchen scissors to cut down their bellies and lay them out flat. • Sauté the onion in the oil, then add the anchovies, crushing them with a fork so that they dissolve in the oil. • Add the sardines, raisins, pine nuts, and almonds. Season with salt and pepper. • Simmer over medium-low heat for 10 minutes, then add the fennel and saffron. Stir gently to avoid breaking up the fish. Reduce the heat to low, cover, and simmer for 10 minutes. • Preheat the oven to 425°F (220°C/gas 7). • Bring the fennel-flavored water to a boil, add the pasta, and cook until al dente. Drain and toss with the sardines and sauce. • Place in an oiled ovenproof dish and sprinkle with the bread crumbs. • Bake for 10 minutes. Serve hot.

Serves: 4–6 · Prep: 30 min · Cooking: 50 min · Level: 3

Spaghetti with lobster

Spaghetti con l'aragosta

- 1 onion, finely chopped
- 1/4 cup (60 ml) extra-virgin olive oil
- 2 tablespoons finely chopped parsley
- 8 oz (250 g) peeled tomatoes, pressed through a fine mesh strainer (passata)
- salt
- 12 oz (350 g) lobster meat, cut into large chunks (meat from 1 lobster, weighing 1 1/2 lb/750 g)
- 12 oz (350 g) spaghetti

Sauté the onion in the oil in a large frying pan over medium heat until softened, 3 minutes. • Add half the parsley and the tomatoes. Simmer over low heat for 15–20 minutes. • Season with salt and add the lobster meat. Simmer for 5 minutes. • Meanwhile, cook the pasta in a large pot of salted boiling water until al dente. Drain and add to the pan. • Sprinkle with the remaining parsley and serve hot.

Serves: 4 • Prep: 45 min • Cooking: 35 min • Level: 2

Seafood spaghetti en papillote

Spaghetti al cartoccio con frutti di mare

En papillote *is a French cooking term for the Italian* al cartoccio *that involves wrapping a food (usually fish with a vegetable garnish) in parchment paper or aluminum foil and baking it in a hot oven. The package is usually opened at the table so that diners can enjoy the escaping aromas.*

- 1 1/2 lb (750 g) clams, in shell
- 1 1/2 lb (750 g) mussels, in shell
- 14 oz (400 g) small squid, cleaned
- 2 cloves garlic, finely chopped
- 1 dried chile pepper, crumbled
- 2 tablespoons finely chopped parsley
- 1/3 cup (90 ml) extra-virgin olive oil
- 1/2 cup (125 ml) dry white wine
- 1 1/2 lb (750 g) firm-ripe tomatoes, peeled and chopped
- 12 oz (350 g) shelled crayfish
- 1 lb (500 g) spaghetti
- salt

Soak the clams and mussels in separate bowls of cold water for 1 hour. Drain and set aside. • Remove the mottled skin from the squid and cut the bodies into small chunks. Cut the tentacles in half. • Preheat the oven to 350°F (180°C/gas 4). • Sauté the garlic, chile, and parsley in the oil in a small saucepan over high heat until the garlic is pale gold, about 3 minutes. • Pour in the wine and let it evaporate. • Add the tomatoes and simmer for 10 minutes. • Add the squid, clams, mussels, and crayfish. Cover and simmer over medium heat until the clams and mussels open up. • Remove from the heat and discard any clams or mussels that haven't opened. Shell half the shellfish. • Meanwhile, cook the spaghetti in salted boiling water for half the time indicated on the package. • Drain and add to the seafood sauce. • Cut 4–6 large pieces of aluminum foil or parchment paper and fold each one in half to double the thickness. • Divide the pasta into 4–6 portions and place in the center of the pieces of foil or paper, adding 3 tablespoons of cooking water from the pasta to each portion. Close, sealing well. There should be a small air pocket in each of the packages. • Bake until puffed up slightly, 12–15 minutes. • Serve the packages on the table; diners can open and eat directly from them.

Serves: 4–6 • Prep: 30 min + 1 hr to soak • Cooking: 40 min Level: 2

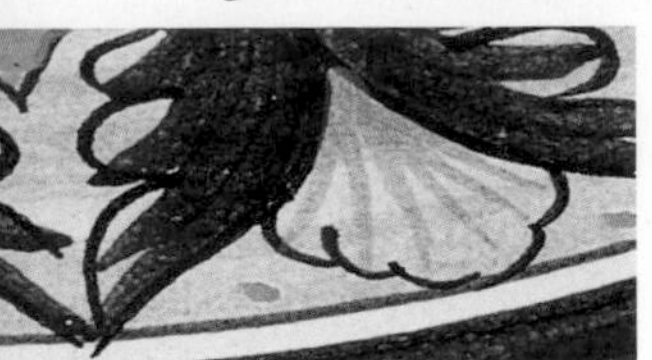

Bucatini with amatriciana sauce

Bucatini all'amatriciana

- 8 oz (250 g) pancetta, cut into thin strips
- 2 lb (1 kg) ripe tomatoes, peeled and chopped
- 1 medium onion, finely chopped
- 1 small red chile pepper, seeded and chopped
- salt and freshly ground black pepper
- 1 lb (500 g) bucatini

Amatrice, a small town in the rolling hills of Lazio, is the hometown of this pasta sauce. It has become a favorite in Rome and every summer a festival is held both in Amatrice and in the beautiful Roman piazza Campo de'Fiori to celebrate.

Sauté the pancetta in a large frying pan over medium heat until lightly browned, about 5 minutes. • Add the onion and sauté until softened, about 3 minutes. • Add the tomatoes and chile pepper. Mix well and season with salt and pepper. • Partially cover and simmer over low heat until the tomatoes are well reduced, about 30 minutes. • Cook the pasta in a large pot of salted boiling water until al dente. • Drain well and then add to the sauce. Toss over high heat for 1 minute and serve hot.

Serves: 4–6 • Prep: 15 min • Cooking: 40 min • Level: 1

Linguine with seafood sauce

Linguine ai frutti di mare

- 1 lb (500 g) squid or cuttlefish, cleaned
- 2 cloves garlic, finely chopped
- 1/2 cup (125 ml) extra-virgin olive oil
- 6 jumbo shrimp or king prawns
- 6 crayfish, shelled, leaving the head on
- 6 shrimp (prawns), shelled
- 1 lb (500 g) linguine
- 1/2 cup (125 ml) dry white wine
- salt
- 6 cups (1.5 liters) fish stock, boiling

Cut the squid bodies into small chunks and slice the tentacles in half. • Heat the oil in a large frying pan over high heat. Add the garlic and sauté until pale gold, 1–2 minutes. • Add the squid, jumbo shrimp, crayfish, and shrimp and cook over medium heat for 5 minutes. • Cook the pasta for half the time indicated on the package in a large pot of salted boiling water. • Drain and add to the sauce. • Pour in the wine, season with salt, and cook, gradually adding the boiling fish stock and stirring often until the pasta is cooked al dente, 5–10 minutes. Serve hot.

Serves: 4–6 • Prep: 15 min • Cooking: 25 min • Level: 2

Spaghetti with mussels

Pasta alle cozze

- 4 lb (2 kg) mussels, in shell
- 3/4 cup (180 ml) dry white wine
- 4 cloves garlic, finely chopped
- 1 fresh red chile pepper, finely chopped
- 1 tablespoon finely chopped fresh parsley
- 1/3 cup (90 ml) extra-virgin olive oil
- 3 lb (1.5 kg) firm-ripe tomatoes, peeled and coarsely chopped
- salt
- 1 lb (500 g) spaghetti

Soak the mussels in a large bowl of cold salted water for 1 hour. Rinse and drain well. • Pour 1/2 cup (125 ml) of the wine into a large saucepan and place the mussels in the pan. Cover and cook over high heat, shaking the pan occasionally until they all open up. Discard any that do not open. • Let the mussels cool a little then remove most of the mollusks from the shells. Leave some mussels in the shells to garnish. • Sauté the garlic, chile, and parsley in the oil in a large frying pan over medium heat until the garlic is pale gold, 2–3 minutes. • Increase the heat, pour in the remaining 1/4 cup (60 ml) wine and let it evaporate. • Stir in the tomatoes, season with salt, and simmer over low heat for, 15–20 minutes. • Add the shelled mussels and simmer for 2–3 minutes more. • Meanwhile, cook the pasta in a large pot of salted boiling water until al dente. • Drain and transfer to a serving pan with the sauce. Toss well. Garnish with the mussels in their shells and serve hot.

Serves: 4 • Prep: 30 min + 1 hr to soak the mussels
Cooking: 30 min • Level: 1

Penne with spicy tomato sauce

Penne with Spicy Tomato Sauce

Penne all'arrabbiata

- 5 oz (150 g) pancetta (or bacon), cut into small strips
- 1/3 cup (90 ml) extra-virgin olive oil
- 2 fresh red chile peppers, seeded and finely sliced
- 3 cloves garlic, finely chopped
- 2 (14-oz/400-g) cans tomatoes, with juice
- salt
- 1 tablespoon finely chopped parsley
- 1 lb (500 g) penne
- 1/4 cup (30 g) freshly grated pecorino cheese

Arrabbiata, *which means "angry," in Italian, is a common pasta sauce in central Italy. The angry element is provided by the chile pepper.*

Sauté the pancetta in the oil in a frying pan over medium heat until crisp and lightly browned, 5 minutes. • Remove from the heat and transfer the pancetta to a plate, keeping it warm. • In the same oil, sauté the chile pepper and garlic until the garlic is pale gold, 2–3 minutes. • Stir in the tomatoes and season with salt. Add the parsley and simmer until the tomatoes have broken down, 15 minutes. • Add the pancetta and simmer for 3 minutes. • Meanwhile, cook the pasta in a large pot of salted boiling water until al dente. Drain and add to the sauce. Sprinkle with the pecorino, toss well, and serve hot.

Serves: 4–6 • Prep: 30 min • Cooking: 45 min • Level: 1

Penne with Gorgonzola and Peas

Penne al gorgonzola e piselli

- 1 tablespoon butter
- 12 oz (350 g) creamy Gorgonzola cheese, crumbled
- 2/3 cup (150 ml) heavy (double) cream
- salt and freshly ground white pepper
- 1 cup (150 g) frozen peas
- 1 lb (500 g) penne
- 1/2 cup (60 g) freshly grated Parmesan cheese

Heat the butter and Gorgonzola with the cream in a double boiler over barely simmering water until the cheese has melted. Season lightly salt and a generous grinding of pepper. • Cook the peas in a small pan of lightly salted water until tender, 5 minutes. Drain well. • Cook the pasta in a large pot of salted boiling water until al dente. • Drain and place in a heated serving bowl. Add the peas and cheese mixture and toss well. Sprinkle with the Parmesan and serve hot.

Serves: 4–6 • Prep: 10 min • Cooking: 25 min • Level: 1

Penne with Fresh Ricotta Cheese

Penne alla ricotta

- 1 lb (500 g) penne
- 1 cup (250 ml) whole milk, heated
- 14 oz (400 g) very fresh ricotta cheese, drained
- 1 tablespoon sugar
- 1 teaspoon ground cinnamon
- salt and freshly ground white pepper
- 1 tablespoon finely chopped marjoram

Cook the penne in a large pot of salted, boiling water until al dente. • Combine the hot milk with the ricotta, sugar, cinnamon, salt, pepper, and marjoram. Beat with a fork until smooth and creamy. • Drain the pasta and place in a heated serving dish. Toss with the sauce and serve hot.

Serves: 4–6 • Prep: 10 min • Cooking: 15 min • Level: 1

Rigatoni with Onion Sauce

Rigatoni con salsa di cipolle

- 2/3 cup (150 g) butter or diced pork lard
- 3 large onions, finely chopped
- 1/4 cup (60 ml) dry white wine
- 1 lb (500 g) rigatoni
- salt and freshly ground black pepper
- 6 tablespoons freshly grated pecorino cheese

Melt the butter in a small saucepan over low heat. Add the onion and simmer until caramelized, about 30 minutes. • Increase the heat, pour in the wine, and let it evaporate, about 5 minutes. • Meanwhile, cook the pasta in a large pot of salted boiling water until al dente. • Drain and add to the pan with the sauce. Season with salt and pepper. Sprinkle with pecorino, toss well, and serve hot.

Serves 4–6 • Prep: 15 min • Cooking: 35 min • Level: 2

SICILIAN MACARONI

Maccheroni alla siciliana

- 2 salt-cured anchovies, rinsed
- 2 tablespoons salt-cured capers, rinsed
- 1/3 cup (40 g) green olives
- 2 cloves garlic, lightly crushed but whole
- 1/3 cup (90 ml) extra-virgin olive oil
- 2 eggplants (aubergines), cut into cubes
- 1 1/2 lb (750 g) peeled tomatoes, finely chopped
- 2 yellow bell peppers (capsicums), seeded and cut into thin strips
- salt and freshly ground black pepper
- Leaves from 1 bunch fresh basil, torn
- 1 lb (500 g) smooth or ridged macaroni
- 1/2 cup (60 g) freshly grated peppered pecorino cheese

Chop the anchovies finely with the capers. • Pit the olives and crush them slightly. • Sauté the garlic in the oil in a large frying pan over medium heat until pale gold, about 3 minutes. • Discard the garlic and add the eggplant to the oil. Sauté for 15 minutes. • Add the tomatoes and bell peppers and season with salt and pepper. Simmer until the bell peppers are tender, 15 minutes. • Add the olives, capers and anchovies, and basil. • Meanwhile. cook the pasta in a large pot of salted boiling water until al dente. Drain and add to the pan with the sauce. Sprinkle with the pecorino and serve hot.

Serves 4–6 • Prep: 15 min • Cooking: 40 min • Level: 1

PENNETTE WITH CRAB MEAT

Pennette al granchio

Roughly chop the crab sticks. • Pour the oil into a large frying pan and sauté the garlic and parsley over medium-low heat for 1 minute. • Add the crab sticks and orange zest. Mix well and simmer for 1 minute. Pour in the cognac and cook until it has evaporated. • Add the orange juice. Season with salt and a generous grinding of pepper. Simmer until the liquid has evaporated. • After about 10 minutes add the cream and simmer for 2–3 minutes. • Meanwhile, cook the pasta in a large pot of salted, boiling water until al dente. Drain and transfer to the pan with the sauce.Toss gently for 1–2 minutes. Serve hot.

Serves: 4–6 • Prep: 15 min • Cooking: 25 min • Level: 1

- 16 crab sticks, fresh or frozen
- 1/3 cup (90 ml) extra-virgin olive oil
- 2 cloves garlic, finely chopped
- 2 tablespoons finely chopped parsley
- 1 tablespoon orange zest, cut in julienne strips
- 1/2 cup (125 ml) cognac
- 1/2 cup (125 ml) fresh orange juice
- salt and freshly ground black pepper
- 1/2 cup (125 ml) heavy (double) cream
- 1 lb (500 g) pennette (small penne)

PENNE WITH CREAMY MEAT SAUCE

Penne strascicate

Cook the pasta in a large pot of salted boiling water until not quite al dente. • Drain and set aside. • Melt half the butter in a large frying pan and add the meat sauce. Cook until it begins to bubble. • Add the pasta and finish cooking until al dente, mixing in the cream. • Sprinkle with Parmesan and remove from the heat. • Dot with the remaining butter, letting it melt into the pasta, and serve hot.

Serves 4 • Prep: 10 min + time to make sauce • Cooking: 10 min • Level: 1

- 1 lb (500 g) dried penne
- 1/3 cup (90 g) butter
- 3 cups (750 g) meat sauce (storebought or homemade – see meat sauce, page 132)
- 1/2 cup (125 ml) heavy (double) cream
- 1/4 cup (30 g) freshly grated Parmesan cheese

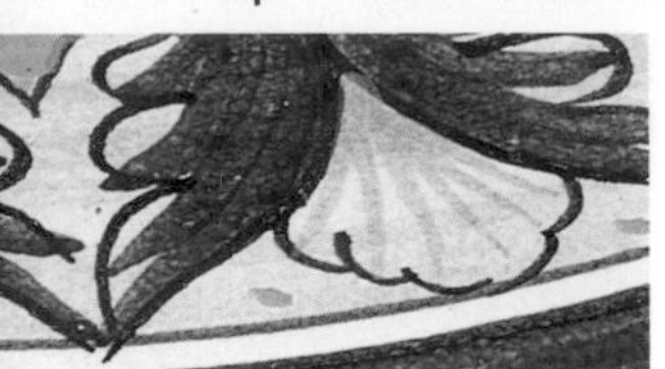

Trofie with spicy fava bean sauce

Malloreddus with sausage

Malloreddus con salsiccia

- $1/4$ cup (60 ml) extra-virgin olive oil
- 14 oz (400 g) Italian pork sausages, skinned and crumbled
- 1 large onion, finely chopped
- 3 cloves garlic, finely chopped
- 8 basil leaves, torn + extra to garnish
- $1\frac{1}{2}$ lb (750 g) fresh tomatoes, peeled and chopped
- salt and freshly ground black pepper
- $1/3$ cup (45 g) freshly grated pecorino cheese
- 1 lb (500 g) malloreddus

Malloreddus pasta is a specialty of Sardinia. Substitute with another small, short pasta if preferred.

Heat the oil in a large frying pan over medium heat. Add the sausages, onion, garlic, and torn basil and sauté until the onion turns pale gold, 4–5 minutes. • Add the tomatoes and season with salt and pepper. Simmer for until the sauce thickens and reduces, 25–30 minutes. • Meanwhile, cook the malloreddus in a large pan of salted, boiling water until al dente. • Drain well and add to the pan with the sauce. Sprinkle with the pecorino and toss gently. Garnish with the extra basil and serve hot.

Serves: 4–6 • Prep: 10 min • Cooking: 45 min • Level: 1

Trofie with spicy fava bean sauce

Trofie piccanti alle fave

Cook the Catalogna chicory in a large pan of salted, boiling water for 5 minutes, then add the pasta. • In the meantime, heat $1/4$ cup (60 ml) of oil in a large frying pan and sauté the garlic until pale golden brown. • Add the fava beans and chile pepper. Season with salt and pepper, cover, and simmer over medium-high heat until the beans are tender, about 10 minutes. • Drain the pasta and chicory and add them to the pan with the fava bean sauce. • Add the tomatoes and drizzle with the remaining oil. Season with a little more salt and pepper, if liked. • Toss gently over medium heat for 2–3 minutes. Serve hot.

Serves: 4–6 • Prep: 15 min • Cooking: 25 min • Level: 1

- 12 oz (350 g) Catalogna chicory, coarsely chopped
- 1 lb (500 g) trofie or other short dried pasta
- $1/3$ cup (90 ml) extra-virgin olive oil
- 3 cloves garlic, finely chopped
- 12 oz (300 g) frozen fava (broad) beans
- 1 dried chile pepper, crumbled
- salt and freshly ground black pepper
- 16–20 cherry tomatoes, diced

Malloreddus with lamb sauce

Malloreddus al sugo di agnello

- $1/3$ cup (90 ml) extra-virgin olive oil
- 1 onion, finely chopped
- 4 cloves garlic, finely chopped
- 2 tablespoons finely chopped rosemary
- 2 lb (1 kg) lamb, cut from the leg and finely chopped with a knife
- salt and freshly ground black pepper
- 1 lb (500 g) peeled and chopped tomatoes
- 1 lb (500 g) malloreddus
- 4 oz (125 g) freshly grated pecorino cheese

Heat the oil in a heavy-bottomed saucepan and sauté the onion, garlic, and rosemary until softened, about 5 minutes. • Add the lamb, season with salt and pepper, and sauté until nicely browned, 7–10 minutes. • Add the tomatoes, cover the pan and simmer over low heat for at least 2 hours. • Cook the malloreddus in a large pan of salted, boiling water until al dente. • Drain and add to the pan with the sauce. Toss well, sprinkle with the pecorino, and serve hot.

Serves: 4–6 • Prep: 25 min • Cooking: 2 hr 15 min • Level: 1

Farfalle with shrimp and zucchini

Farfalle con gamberetti e zucchini

Remove the zucchini flowers and rinse carefully under cold running water. Clean the zucchini and slice thinly lengthwise. • Sauté the onion in the butter in a large frying pan over medium heat until softened, 3–4 minutes. • Meanwhile, cook the pasta in a large pot of salted, boiling water until al dente. • Add the zucchini to the onions and season with salt and pepper. Cover and simmer over medium heat for 10 minutes, stirring often. • Add the shrimp and zucchini flowers and cook for 5 minutes. • Mix in the cream and cook until heated through. • Drain the pasta and add to the pan with the sauce. Sprinkle with the parsley and toss well. Serve hot.

Serves: 4–6 • Prep: 20 min • Cooking: 30 min • Level: 1

- 14 oz (400 g) zucchini (courgettes) with flowers attached
- 1 onion, finely chopped
- $1/4$ cup (60 g) butter
- 1 lb (500 g) farfalle
- salt and freshly ground black pepper
- 14 oz (400 g) shrimp (prawns)
- $1/2$ cup (125 ml) heavy (double) cream
- 2 tablespoons finely chopped parsley

Cannelloni with tomatoes and cheese

Cannelloni with tomatoes and cheese

Cannelloni con pomodori e formaggio

- 2 cups (500 ml) fresh ricotta cheese, drained
- $1\frac{1}{4}$ cups (150 g) freshly grated pecorino cheese
- 1 tablespoon finely chopped basil
- 1 egg + 1 egg yolk
- salt and freshly ground black pepper
- 2 lb (1 kg) tomatoes
- $\frac{1}{2}$ cup (125 ml) extra-virgin olive oil
- 10 oz (300 g) cannelloni pasta
- 5 oz (150 g) mozzarella, diced

Preheat the oven to 350°F (180°C/gas 4). • Butter a baking dish. • Mix the ricotta, half the pecorino, half the basil, and the egg and egg yolk in a large bowl. Season with salt and pepper and mix well. • Cut the tomatoes in half horizontally. Arrange half of them in the prepared baking dish. Drizzle with 2 tablespoons of oil and season with salt, pepper, and the remaining basil. Sprinkle with 2 tablespoons of pecorino. • Spoon the ricotta mixture into the cannelloni. Arrange the cannelloni on top of the tomatoes, one next to the other. Season with salt and pepper and drizzle with 2 tablespoons oil. Sprinkle with 2 tablespoons of pecorino. • Place the mozzarella on top of the cannelloni. Cover with the remaining halved tomatoes, cut-side down. Drizzle with the remaining oil and season with salt and pepper. Cover with aluminum foil and bake for 20 minutes. • Remove the foil and sprinkle with the remaining pecorino. Bake until golden brown, about 20 minutes. Serve hot.

Serves: 4–6 • Prep: 45 min • Cooking: 40 min • Level: 2

Baked pasta with cheese

Pasta al forno con formaggio

- 1 lb (500 g) short hollow dried pasta, such as macaroni or penne
- 2 teaspoons extra-virgin olive oil

Béchamel Sauce

- $\frac{1}{2}$ cup (125 g) butter, cut up
- $\frac{2}{3}$ cup (100 g) all-purpose (plain) flour
- 2 cups (500 ml) milk
- salt and freshly ground white pepper
- $\frac{1}{4}$ teaspoon freshly grated nutmeg

- $1\frac{1}{4}$ cups (150 g) freshly grated pecorino cheese
- 5 oz (150 g) Caciocavallo or ricotta salata cheese, thinly sliced

Preheat the oven to 400°F (200°C/gas 6). • Butter a large baking dish. • Cook the pasta in a large pot of salted boiling water with a drop of the oil for half the time indicated on the package. • Drain, running under cold water to stop the cooking process, and transfer to a serving bowl. Drizzle with the remaining oil to prevent sticking. • Béchamel Sauce: Melt $\frac{1}{3}$ cup (90 ml) of the butter in a small saucepan over medium heat and add the flour. Simmer for 3–4 minutes. Remove from the heat and add the milk all at once. Stir thoroughly, return to the heat, and bring to a boil, stirring constantly. As soon as the sauce comes to a boil, lower the heat, and season with salt, pepper, and nutmeg. Simmer over low heat for 10 minutes, stirring constantly. • Mix the pasta into the Béchamel sauce with nearly all of the pecorino. • Arrange a layer of pasta in the baking dish and cover with the Caciocavallo. Top with the remaining pasta and sprinkle with pecorino. Top with the remaining 2 tablespoons of butter. • Bake until the top is golden brown, 40–45 minutes. • Serve hot.

Serves 6 • Prep: 30 min • Cooking: 40–45 min • Level: 2

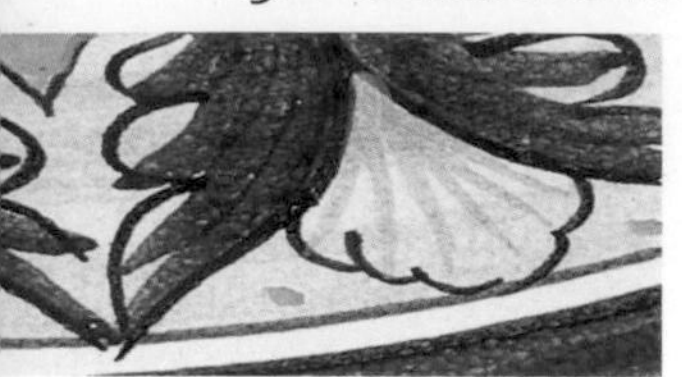

Baked macaroni with black truffles

BAKED MACARONI WITH BLACK TRUFFLES

Maccheroni al forno con tartufi neri

- 1 small onion, finely sliced
- 4 oz (125 g) ground (minced) beef
- generous 1/3 cup (100 g) butter
- 1/3 cup (90 ml) water
- salt and freshly ground black pepper
- 5 oz (150 g) turkey breast, diced
- 5 oz (150 g) chicken livers, diced
- 1 small black truffle, finely grated
- 1 3/4 cups (200 g) diced ham
- 1/2 cup (125 ml) heavy (double) cream
- 12 oz (350 g) large macaroni
- 3/4 cup (90 g) freshly grated Gruyère cheese

Sauté the onion and beef in 2 tablespoons of butter in a large frying pan over medium heat until the onion has softened and the meat is browned, about 5 minutes. • Add the water and lower the heat. Season with salt and pepper. Simmer for 10 minutes. Set aside. • Put the turkey, chicken livers, black truffle, and ham in the bowl of a food processor and blend until smooth. Mix in 2 tablespoons of cream and season with salt and pepper. • Preheat the oven to 400°F (200°C/gas 6). • Oil a large baking dish. • Cook the pasta in a large pot of salted boiling water until just al dente. • Drain well. Use a teaspoon to fill each piece of pasta with the meat purée. • Arrange the filled pasta in the prepared dish. Cover with the ground beef mixture and dot with the remaining butter. Drizzle with the remaining cream and sprinkle with the Gruyère. • Bake until lightly browned, about 15 minutes. • Serve hot.

Serves: 4–6 • Prep: 25 min • Cooking: 40 min • Level: 2

BAKED RIGATONI PASTA

Rigatoni ripieni al forno

Sauté the onion in the oil in a large frying pan over medium until softened, about 3 minutes. Season with salt. • Pierce the sausages and blanch in boiling water for 3 minutes. Drain, remove the casings, and crumble the meat. • Add the sausage meat, salami, and beef to the onion. Simmer over medium-low heat for 30 minutes, adding some stock if the mixture starts to stick to the pan. • Add the eggs and season with salt and pepper. • Cook the pasta for half the time on the package. Drain and let cool. • Preheat the oven to 350°F (180°C/gas 4). Butter a baking dish and sprinkle with bread crumbs. • Use a teaspoon to fill the pasta with the meat sauce. • Arrange the pasta in the baking dish. Spoon the tomato sauce over the top and sprinkle with the pecorino. • Bake until golden brown, 35–40 minutes. Serve hot.

Serves: 6–8 • Prep: 1 hr • Cooking: 80 min • Level: 2

- 1 large onion, finely chopped
- 1/4 cup (60 ml) extra-virgin olive oil
- salt and freshly ground black pepper
- 2 Italian sausages
- 1 cup (150 g) diced salami
- 1 lb (500 g) ground (minced) beef
- 1 cup (250 ml) beef stock (optional), homemade (see page 104), or bouillon cube
- 3 hard-boiled eggs, crumbled
- 1 lb (500 g) large rigatoni pasta
- 4 cups (1 liter) store-bought tomato sauce (or see recipe page 132)
- 1 cup (125 g) freshly grated aged pecorino cheese

BAKED PASTA WITH PEAS AND MEAT SAUCE

Pasta al forno con piselli e ragu

- 5 tablespoons extra-virgin olive oil
- 1 onion, finely chopped
- 8 oz (250 g) beef, cut into small cubes
- 8 oz (250 g) pork, cut into small cubes
- 1 cup (250 g) dry red wine
- 1 lb (500 g) peeled and chopped tomatoes
- 2 cups (500 ml) hot water
- salt

Heat 1/4 cup (60 ml) of oil in a large frying pan and sauté half the onion until softened, about 3 minutes. • Add the beef and pork and cook until browned all over, 5–7 minutes. • Pour in the wine and let it evaporate. • Stir in the tomatoes and water. Season with salt. Cover and simmer over low heat for 1 hour. • Heat the remaining oil in a large frying pan and sauté the remaining onion until softened. Stir in the peas. Cover and simmer for 15 minutes. • Cook the pasta in a large pan of salted, boiling water until just al dente. • Drain and add to the meat sauce. Sprinkle with pecorino. • Preheat the oven to 425°F (220°C/gas 7). • Butter a 10-in (25-cm) springform pan and sprinkle it with half the bread crumbs. Spoon in half the pasta and top with the ricotta salata and cooked peas. Cover with the remaining pasta, smoothing the top. Sprinkle with the remaining bread crumbs and drizzle with the remaining oil. • Bake for 20 minutes. • Let rest for 5 minutes before serving.

Serves: 4–6 • Prep: 40 min • Cooking: 1 hr 30 min • Level: 2

- 2 cups (300 g) frozen peas, thawed
- 1 lb (500 g) anellini (small pasta rings)
- 10 oz (300 g) freshly grated pecorino cheese
- 3/4 cup (100 g) dry bread crumbs
- 2/3 cup (150 g) ricotta salata (or aged pecorino) cheese, cut into small cubes

TAGLIATELLE, RAVIOLI & CO.

Making fresh and filled pasta at home is not difficult, especially if you have a pasta machine to help you to roll and cut the dough. However, for best results, be sure to knead the dough by hand rather than in a machine. Pasta machines that mix and knead the dough will almost always produce an inferior product; after all, it is the warmth and skill of the human hand that adds that extra "something" to homemade pasta. That said, making pasta at home requires a little practice and quite a lot of time, so you may sometimes prefer to buy fresh or filled pasta from a good Italian delicatessen or supermarket. This chapter begins with a basic fresh pasta recipe (see page 156), but also has about 30 recipes for fresh or filled pasta sauces that can be served with either homemade or storebought pasta. There are also about a dozen recipes for those special Italian regional pasta types each with their own delicious sauce that can only be made at home.

Genoese herb ravioli in tomato sauce (see page 178)

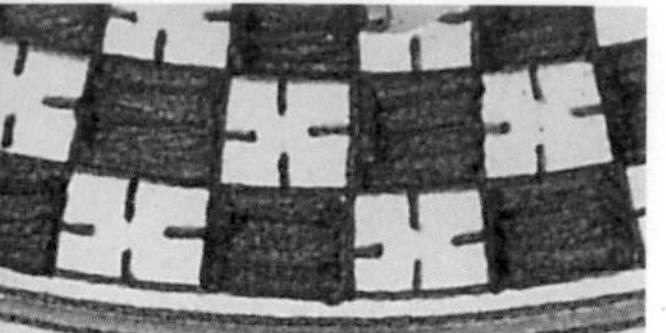

Tagliatelle with roasted tomato sauce

Homemade pasta

Pasta fatta in casa

Plain pasta
- 3 cups (450 g) all-purpose (plain) flour
- 4 large eggs

Spinach or tomato pasta
- $2\frac{1}{2}$ cups (375 g) all-purpose (plain) flour
- 3 large eggs
- 2 oz (60 g) spinach purée or tomato concentrate (paste)

Sift the flour and salt into a mound on a clean work surface. Make a hollow in the center and break the eggs into it. Using a fork, gradually mix the eggs into the flour. • If making spinach or tomato pasta, add the spinach purée or tomato concentrate now. Continue until all the flour is incorporated. When the dough is too thick to mix with a fork, use your hands to shape it into a smooth ball. • Knead the dough by pushing downward and forward on the ball of pasta with the heel of your palm. Fold the dough in half, give it a quarter-turn, and repeat. Knead for about 10 minutes. • Set aside for 15–20 minutes to rest. • To roll and cut the pasta by hand: place a rolling pin on the ball and roll outward from the center. When about $\frac{1}{4}$ inch (6 mm) thick, curl the far edge of the dough around the pin and gently stretch it as you roll it onto the pin. Unroll and repeat until the dough is almost transparent. • Fold the sheet of dough loosely into a flat roll. Use a sharp knife to cut into $\frac{1}{8}$-inch (3-mm) slices for tagliolini, $\frac{1}{4}$-inch (5-mm) slices for fettuccine, $\frac{1}{2}$-inch (1-cm) slices for tagliatelle, or $\frac{3}{4}$-inch (2-cm) slices for pappardelle. To make lasagna, cut into 3 x 12-inch (8 x 30-cm) sheets. To make maltagliati, cut into diamond shapes. Paglia e fieno is made with one half quantity each of plain fettuccine and spinach fettuccine. • To roll and cut the pasta using a pasta machine: divide the dough into 4–6 pieces and flatten by hand. Set the machine with its rollers at the widest and run each piece through. Reduce by one notch and repeat. Continue until all the pasta has been rolled at the thinnest setting. Cut into sheets about 12 inches (30 cm) long. Attach the cutters to the machine and set at the desired width. Lay the cut pasta on clean cloths for 2 hours to rest.

Serves: 4 • Prep: 1 hr + 2 hr 20 min to rest • Level: 2

Tagliatelle with mushrooms

Tagliatelle con funghi

- 1 quantity tagliatelle (see recipe left) or 14 oz (400 g) fresh storebought tagliatelle
- $\frac{1}{2}$ cup (125 ml) extra-virgin olive oil
- 2 cloves garlic, finely chopped
- 3 tablespoons finely chopped parsley
- 12 oz (350 g) white mushrooms, chopped
- 1 cup (100 g) pitted black olives
- 8 leaves fresh mint, torn
- salt and freshly ground black pepper
- $\frac{1}{3}$ cup (90 ml) boiling water

If using homemade pasta, prepare it following the instructions to the left. • Bring a large pan of salted water to a boil over high heat. • Heat the oil in a large frying pan over medium heat. Sauté the garlic and parsley until the garlic turns pale gold, 2–3 minutes. • Add the mushrooms and simmer until almost tender, 5–10 minutes. • Stir in the olives, mint, salt, pepper, and boiling water. Simmer for 5 minutes. • Cook the pasta in the boiling water until al dente, 3–4 minutes. • Drain and place in a heated serving dish. Toss gently with the sauce and serve hot.

Serves: 4 • Prep: 10 min + time to make pasta • Cooking: 20 min • Level: 1

Tagliatelle with roasted tomato sauce

Tagliatelle con salsa di pomodori arrostiti

- 1 quantity tagliatelle (see recipe left) or 14 oz (400 g) fresh storebought tagliatelle
- 2 lb (1 kg) firm-ripe tomatoes
- 2 cloves garlic, finely chopped
- $\frac{1}{3}$ cup (90 ml) extra-virgin olive oil
- 1 tablespoon finely chopped parsley
- salt

If using homemade pasta, prepare it following the instructions on this page. • Bring a large pan of salted water to a boil over high heat. • Preheat the oven to 400°F (200°C/gas 6). • Cut the tomatoes in half and remove the seeds. Place the tomato shells upside-down on a baking sheet. • Bake until the tomatoes have lost their excess water and the skins are burnt, 20 minutes. • Let cool a little. Slip off the skins and mash the flesh in a large bowl. • Stir in the garlic, oil, parsley, and salt. • Cook the pasta in the salted boiling water until al dente. • Drain well and place in a heated serving dish. Add the sauce, toss well, and serve hot.

Serves: 4 • Prep: 15 min + 1 hr to make pasta • Cooking: 30 min • Level: 2

Fettuccine with walnut sauce

Fettuccine with walnut sauce

Fettuccine con salsa alle noci

- 1 quantity fettuccine (see page 156) or 14 oz (400 g) fresh storebought fettuccine
- 2 cups (250 g) freshly shelled walnuts
- 1 teaspoon sugar
- 1/3 cup (90 g) fresh bread crumbs
- 1/2 teaspoon freshly grated nutmeg
- 1/4 cup (60 ml) extra-virgin olive oil
- 1/2 cup (60 g) freshly grated Parmesan cheese

Walnut sauce for pasta is typical of Liguria, but some delicious walnut based pasta sauces are also served in Tuscany and Umbria.

If using homemade pasta, prepare it following the instructions on page 156. • Bring a large pan of salted water to a boil over high heat. • Chop the walnuts very finely in a food processor. Place in a bowl and add the sugar, bread crumbs, nutmeg, and oil. Mix well. The sauce should be the consistency of a thick coarse paste. • Cook the pasta in the boiling water until al dente, 3–4 minutes. • Drain well and transfer to a large serving dish. Add the walnut sauce and toss gently. Sprinkle with the cheese and serve hot.

Serves: 4 • Prep: 15 min + time to make pasta • Cooking: 5 min • Level: 1

Tagliolini with mascarpone cheese

Tagliolini al mascarpone

- 1 quantity tagliolini (see page 156) or 14 oz (400 g) fresh storebought tagliolini
- 1 cup (250 g) mascarpone cheese
- 3 very fresh large egg yolks
- 1/2 cup (60 g) freshly grated Parmesan cheese
- salt
- 1/4 teaspoon freshly grated nutmeg

If using homemade pasta, prepare it following the instructions on page 156. • Bring a large pan of salted water to a boil over high heat. • Mix the mascarpone and egg yolks in a large bowl. Place over barely simmering water and cook until the egg mixture registers 160°F (80°C) on an instant-read thermometer. Remove from the heat and plunge into a pan of cold water. • Add the Parmesan and season with salt and nutmeg. • Cook the tagliolini in the boiling water until al dente, 2–3 minutes. • Pour a little of the pasta water into the serving dish to warm it, then pour off the water. • Drain the pasta and transfer to the serving dish. • Stir the mascarpone mixture into the tagliolini, diluting with a few tablespoons of cooking water. Serve hot.

Serves: 4 • Prep: 10 min + time to make pasta • Cooking: 10 min • Level: 1

Tagliatelle with truffles

Tagliatelle coi tartufi

- 1 quantity tagliatelle (see page 156) or 14 oz (400 g) fresh storebought tagliatelle
- 6 tablespoons freshly grated Parmesan cheese
- 1/2 cup (125 g) butter
- 1 sprig fresh rosemary (or 1 sprig fresh sage)
- 2 oz (60 g) freshly grated white truffle

White truffles grow in many parts of northern Italy. As expensive as they are rare, their pungent perfume adds an unforgettable touch to pasta dishes.

If using homemade pasta, prepare it following the instructions on page 156. • Bring a large pan of salted water to a boil over high heat. • Cook the pasta in the boiling water until al dente, 3–4 minutes. • Drain the pasta and transfer to a heated serving dish. Sprinkle with the Parmesan. • While the pasta is cooking, heat the butter and rosemary until the butter turns a pale, golden brown. • Drizzle the hot butter over the tagliatelle and toss gently. • Top with the fresh truffle and serve hot.

Serves: 4 • Prep: 15 min + time to make pasta • Cooking: 5 min • Level: 1

Tagliolini with Treviso radicchio

Tagliolini al radicchio rosso di treviso

- 1 quantity tagliolini (see page 156) or 14 oz (400 g) fresh storebought tagliolini
- 1/3 cup (90 g) butter
- 1 red onion, finely chopped
- 4 oz (125 g) diced pancetta
- salt and freshly ground black pepper
- 14 oz (400 g) Treviso radicchio, finely shredded
- 1 cup (250) ml dry red wine

Treviso radicchio is a type of red chicory that comes from the Veneto region. It has a strong, almost bitter flavor that goes beautifully with fresh pasta.

If using homemade pasta, prepare it following the instructions on page 156. • Bring a large pan of salted water to a boil over high heat. • Melt the butter in a large frying pan over medium heat. Add the onion and sauté until softened, 3–4 minutes. • Add the pancetta and sauté until browned, about 5 minutes. • Add the radicchio and season with salt and pepper. Pour in the wine and cook until it evaporates. • Cook the pasta in the boiling water until al dente, 2–3 minutes. Drain and add to the pan. Toss gently and serve hot.

Serves: 4 • Prep: 15 min + time to make pasta • Cooking: 15 min • Level: 2

Tagliatelle with cream and ham

Tagliatelle con panna e prosciutto

- 1 quantity tagliatelle (see page 156) or 14 oz (400 g) fresh storebought tagliatelle
- 4 oz (125 g) ham, cut into thin strips
- 1/4 cup (60 g) butter
- generous 3/4 cup (200 ml) heavy (double) cream
- salt and freshly ground white pepper
- 1/4 teaspoon freshly grated nutmeg
- 1/2 cup (60 g) freshly grated Parmesan cheese

If using homemade pasta, prepare it following the instructions on page 156. • Bring a large pan of salted water to a boil over high heat. • Melt the butter in a large frying pan over medium heat. Add the ham and sauté until crisp, about 5 minutes. • Pour in the cream and simmer until thickened, about 5 minutes. • Season with salt, pepper, and nutmeg. • Cook the pasta in the boiling water until al dente, 3–4 minutes. • Drain and add to the pan with the sauce. Toss gently until the pasta is well flavored with the sauce. • Sprinkle with the Parmesan and serve hot.

Serves: 4 • Prep: 10 min + time to make pasta • Cooking: 15 min • Level: 1

Tagliatelle with peas and pancetta

Tagliatelle con piselli e pancetta

- 1 quantity tagliatelle (see page 156) or 14 oz (400 g) fresh storebought tagliatelle
- 1 onion, finely chopped
- 1/3 cup (90 g) butter
- 1/2 cup (60 g) diced pancetta or bacon
- 1 clove garlic, finely chopped
- 2 cups (300 g) frozen peas
- salt and freshly ground white pepper
- 1/4 teaspoon sugar
- 2 cups (500 ml) hot water
- 6 tablespoons freshly grated Parmesan cheese
- 1 tablespoon finely chopped parsley

If using homemade pasta, prepare it following the instructions on page 156. • Bring a large pan of salted water to a boil over high heat. • Melt 1/4 cup (60 g) of the butter in a large frying pan over medium heat. Add the onion and sauté until softened, 3–4 minutes. • Add the pancetta and garlic and sauté until the garlic is pale gold, 3–4 minutes. • Add the peas and season with salt, pepper, and sugar. • Pour in the water, cover, and simmer over low heat for 10 minutes. • Uncover and simmer until the sauce has reduced by half, about 10 minutes. • Cook the pasta in the boiling water until al dente, 3–4 minutes. • Drain and add to the sauce. Toss with the remaining butter, Parmesan, and parsley and serve hot.

Serves: 4 • Prep: 15 min + time to make pasta • Cooking: 30 min • Level: 1

Tagliatelle with peas and pancetta

Tagliatelle with cherry tomatoes

Tagliatelle coi pomodorini

- 1 quantity tagliatelle (see page 156) or 14 oz (400 g) fresh storebought tagliatelle
- 1/4 cup (60 ml) extra-virgin olive oil
- 4 salt-cured anchovy fillets
- 14 oz (400 g) cherry tomatoes
- 1 clove garlic, finely chopped
- 1 tablespoon finely chopped parsley
- 1 tablespoon finely chopped basil
- 1 spicy red or green chile pepper (optional)
- 8 oz (250 g) bocconcini (mozzarella cheese balls)
- salt and freshly ground black pepper

If using homemade pasta, prepare it following the instructions on page 156. • Bring a large pan of salted water to a boil over high heat. • Heat the oil in a small saucepan and add the anchovies. Mash with a fork until dissolved in the oil. Remove from the heat. • Cut the tomatoes in halves or quarters and combine in a bowl with the garlic, parsley, basil, and chile pepper, if using. • Cook the pasta in the boiling water until al dente, 3–4 minutes. • Drain and transfer to a serving bowl. Add the tomato mixture and bocconcini, then pour the flavored oil over the top. Season with salt and pepper. • Toss gently and serve hot.

Serves: 4 • Prep: 25 min + time to make pasta • Cooking: 5 min • Level: 1

Paglia e fieno with Gorgonzola

Paglia e fieno al gorgonzola

- 1/2 quantity plain tagliatelle and 1/2 quantity spinach tagliatelle (see page 156) or 14 oz (400 g) storebought paglia e fieno pasta
- 1/4 cup (60 g) butter
- 8 oz (250 g) Gorgonzola cheese, cut into small cubes
- 2/3 cup (180 ml) heavy (double) cream (or milk)
- salt and freshly ground white pepper
- 6 tablespoons freshly grated Parmesan cheese (optional)

If using homemade pasta, prepare it following the instructions on page 156. • Bring a large pan of salted water to a boil over high heat. • Melt the butter in a saucepan and add the Gorgonzola and cream. Season with salt and pepper. Simmer over low heat, stirring constantly, until the cheese has melted. • Cook both types of pasta together in the boiling water until al dente, 3–4 minutes. • Drain and transfer to a heated serving bowl. Add the Gorgonzola sauce and toss gently. • Sprinkle with the Parmesan, if using, and serve hot.

Serves: 4 • Prep: 10 min + time to make pasta • Cooking: 10 min • Level: 1

Tagliatelle with cherry tomatoes

Roman fettuccine

Pappardelle with duck sauce

Pappardelle al sugo d'anatra

- 1 quantity pappardelle (see page 156) or 14 oz (400 g) fresh storebought pappardelle
- 1 large onion, finely chopped
- 1 bay leaf
- 4 leaves sage, finely chopped
- 1/2 carrot, finely chopped
- 1 tablespoon finely chopped parsley
- 2 celery leaves, finely chopped (optional)
- 3 oz (90 g) ham, chopped
- 5 tablespoons extra-virgin olive oil
- 1 duck (about 3 lb/ 1.5 kg), cleaned and cut in 4–8 pieces
- 2/3 cup (150 ml) dry red wine
- 1 lb (500 g) firm-ripe tomatoes, chopped
- salt and freshly ground black pepper
- 1 cup (250 ml) beef stock, homemade (see page 104) or bouillon cube
- 1/2 cup (60 g) freshly grated Parmesan cheese

If using homemade pasta, prepare it following the instructions on page 156. • Heat in the oil in a large saucepan over medium-low heat. Sauté the onion, bay leaf, sage, carrot, parsley, celery leaves (if using), and ham for 15 minutes. • Add the duck and sauté over high heat until well browned, about 10 minutes. • Pour in the wine and simmer over low heat for 15 minutes. • Stir in the tomatoes and season with salt and pepper. Pour in the stock, cover, and simmer for 1 hour. • Bone the duck and cut the meat into small chunks. Return the meat to the sauce and simmer for 15 minutes. • Cook the pasta in a large pot of salted boiling water until al dente, 3–5 minutes. • Drain and add to the sauce. Sprinkle with Parmesan, toss gently, and serve hot.

Serves: 4 • Prep: 30 min + time to make pasta • Cooking: 2 hr • Level: 2

Roman fettuccine

Fettuccine alla romana

- 1 quantity fettuccine (see page 156) or 14 oz (400 g) fresh storebought fettuccine
- 1 red onion, finely chopped
- 1 small carrot, finely chopped
- 1 small stalk celery, finely chopped
- 1/4 cup (60 ml) extra-virgin olive oil
- 8 oz (250 g) lean ground (minced) beef
- 1/3 cup (90 ml) dry red wine
- 4 oz (125 g) chicken livers, trimmed and diced
- 1 1/4 cups (310 g) tomato passata (purée)
- 1/2 oz (15 g) dried porcini mushrooms, soaked in warm water for 15 minutes and finely chopped
- 1 bay leaf
- salt and freshly ground black pepper
- 1 cup (125 g) freshly grated Parmesan cheese
- 1/4 cup (60 g) butter

If using homemade pasta, prepare it following the instructions on page 156. • Heat the oil in a large saucepan over medium heat. Add the onion, carrot, and celery and sauté until the onion is lightly browned, 5 minutes. • Stir in the beef and sauté until browned all over, about 5 minutes. • Pour in the wine and cook until it has evaporated, about 4 minutes. • Add the chicken livers and simmer over low heat for 15 minutes. • Add the tomatoes, mushrooms, and bay leaf and season with salt and pepper. Cover and simmer over low heat for about 1 hour. • Cook the pasta in a large pot of salted boiling water until al dente, 3–4 minutes. • Drain and add to the sauce. Sprinkle with the Parmesan, dot with the butter, toss well, and serve hot.

Serves: 4 • Prep: 30 min + time to make pasta • Cooking: 1 hr 30 min • Level: 2

Sicilian pappardelle

Pappardelle alla siciliana

- 1 quantity pappardelle (see page 156) or 14 oz (400 g) fresh storebought pappardelle
- 6 oz (180 g) ground (minced) pork
- 6 oz (180 g) ground (minced) veal
- 1/4 cup (60 ml) extra-virgin olive oil
- 2 tablespoons tomato concentrate (paste)
- 1/2 cup (125 ml) dry white or dry red wine
- 1 (14-oz/400-g) can tomatoes, with juice
- salt and freshly ground black pepper
- 3 oz (90 g) ricotta salata cheese
- 8 oz (250 g) fresh ricotta cheese, drained
- 1/2 cup (60 g) freshly grated pecorino cheese

If using homemade pasta, prepare it following the instructions on page 156. • Heat the oil in a large frying pan over medium heat. Add the pork and veal and sauté until browned, 5–8 minutes. • Add the tomato paste mixed with the wine. Simmer for 4–5 minutes, then add the tomatoes and season with salt and pepper. Partially cover the pan and simmer over low heat for 40 minutes. • Cook the pappardelle in a large pot of salted, boiling water until al dente, 3–5 minutes. • While the pasta is cooking, use a fork to break the ricotta salata into small, crumbly pieces. • When the pasta is nearly done, mix the fresh ricotta with 2 tablespoons of the cooking water in a large, heated serving dish. • Drain the pasta and toss carefully with the fresh ricotta and meat sauce. • Sprinkle with the ricotta salata and pecorino and serve hot.

Serves: 4 • Prep: 10 min + time to make pasta • Cooking: 1 hr • Level: 1

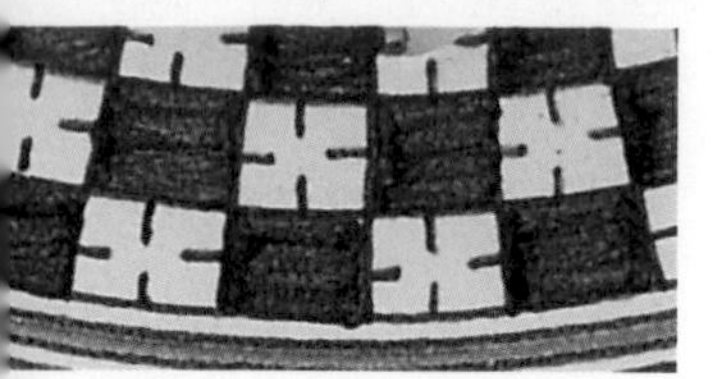

Baked pumpkin Pappardelle

Pappardelle with wild game sauce

Pappardelle con la lepre

- 1 quantity pappardelle (see page 156) or 14 oz (400 g) fresh storebought pappardelle
- 1 hare or rabbit, cleaned and cut into 6 + giblets (liver, heart, and spleen)
- 1 carrot, coarsely chopped
- 1 stalk celery, coarsely chopped
- 1 onion, coarsely chopped
- 3 cloves garlic, crushed but whole
- 1/3 cup (90 ml) white wine vinegar
- 4 cups (1 liter) dry white wine + more as needed
- 5 tablespoons extra-virgin olive oil
- 1 bunch fresh sage
- 1 twig rosemary
- 2 cups (500 ml) beef stock, homemade (see page 104) or bouillon cube
- 3 tablespoons salt-cured capers, rinsed
- salt and freshly ground black pepper
- 1 cup (100 g) black olives, pitted

If using homemade pasta, prepare it following the instructions on page 156. • Place the hare (without the giblets) in a bowl with the carrot, celery, onion, 2 cloves of garlic, and 1/4 cup (60 ml) of vinegar. Pour in enough wine to cover. Place in the refrigerator to marinate for 12 hours. • Remove the hare and pat dry on paper towels. • Chop the vegetables finely and reserve the marinade. • Sauté the vegetables in the oil in a Dutch oven or heavy saucepan over medium heat until lightly golden, 5–7 minutes. • Add the sage, rosemary, and hare and sauté over high heat until browned all over, about 10 minutes. • Pour in 1/4 cup (60 ml) of the reserved marinade. Add 1/2 cup (125 ml) of stock, the giblets, and 2 tablespoons of capers. Season with salt and pepper. Partially cover and simmer for about 1 hour, adding more stock if the sauce becomes too dry. • Remove the larger pieces of hare, place on a chopping board, and bone them. Transfer the boned meat to a food processor or blender and add the drippings, giblets, the remaining garlic, and the remaining capers. Process until finely chopped. • Return the processed mixture to the saucepan with the small pieces of hare. Pour in the remaining vinegar and thicken with some stock if needed. • Stir in the olives and cook for 5 minutes more. • Cook the pasta in a large pot of salted boiling water until al dente, 3–5 minutes. • Drain the pasta and add to the sauce. Toss gently and serve hot.

Serves: 4–6 • Prep: 1 hr + 12 hr to marinate + time to make pasta • Cooking: 1 hr 45 min • Level: 2

Baked pumpkin pappardelle

Pappardelle al forno con la zucca

- 1 quantity pappardelle (see page 156) or 14 oz (400 g) fresh storebought pappardelle
- 1 cup (125 g) diced pancetta or bacon
- 1 clove garlic, lightly crushed but whole
- 1/4 cup (60 ml) extra-virgin olive oil
- 8 oz (250 g) pumpkin flesh, thinly sliced
- 1/2 cup (125 ml) dry white wine
- 1 tablespoon finely chopped parsley
- freshly ground black pepper
- 8 oz (250 g) Fontina cheese, grated
- 1 tablespoon butter
- 4 tablespoons freshly grated Parmesan cheese

If using homemade pasta, prepare it following the instructions on page 156. • Preheat the oven to 400°F (200°C/gas 6). • Oil a large baking dish. • Sauté the pancetta and garlic in the oil in a large frying pan over medium heat until pale gold. • Add the pumpkin and wine and simmer for 10 minutes. • Cook the pasta in a large pot of salted boiling water until al dente, 3–5 minutes. • Drain and add to the pumpkin. Simmer over medium heat for 2 minutes. • Add the parsley and season with pepper. Discard the garlic. • Transfer the mixture to the prepared dish. Top with the Fontina and butter. Sprinkle with the Parmesan. • Bake until lightly browned, 10–15 minutes. • Serve hot.

Serves: 4–6 • Prep: 10 min + time to make pasta • Cooking: 35 min • Level: 1

Pappardelle with bell peppers

Pappardelle ai peperoni e pancetta

- 1 quantity pappardelle (see page 156) or 14 oz (400 g) fresh storebought pappardelle
- 1/4 cup (60 ml)extra-virgin olive oil
- 1 onion, finely chopped
- 1 stalk celery, finely chopped
- 1 carrot, finely chopped
- 1 cup (125 g) diced pancetta or bacon
- 1 lb (500 g) yellow bell peppers (capsicums), cut into thin strips
- salt and freshly ground black pepper
- 2 tablespoons butter, cut up
- 1 cup (125 g) freshly grated Parmesan cheese
- 1 small bunch parsley, finely chopped

If using homemade pasta, prepare it following the instructions on page 156. • Bring a large pan of salted water to a boil over high heat. • Heat the oil in a large saucepan over medium heat. Add the onion, celery, and carrot and sauté until softened, about 5 minutes. • Add the pancetta and sauté until crisp, about 5 minutes. • Add the bell peppers and cover the pan. Simmer over medium heat until softened, about 10 minutes. Season with salt and pepper. • Cook the pasta in the boiling water until al dente, 3–5 minutes. • Drain and transfer to serving dishes. Top with the bell pepper sauce. Melt the butter over the top and sprinkle with the Parmesan and parsley. Serve hot.

Serves: 4 • Prep: 20 min + time to prepare pasta • Cooking: 20 min • Level: 1

Orecchiette

Orecchiette

- $1^1/_3$ cups (200 g) semolina flour
- $1^1/_3$ cups (200 g) all-purpose (plain) flour ù
- $^1/_2$ teaspoon salt
- 1 tablespoon extra-virgin olive oil
- lukewarm water

Orecchiette, or "little ears," pasta are a specialty of Puglia and neighboring regions in the south of Italy. Sift both types of flour and the salt onto a work surface and make a well in the center. Mix in the oil and enough water to make a smooth dough. Knead until smooth and elastic, 15–20 minutes. • Shape the dough into thin cylinders and cut them into $^1/_2$-inch (1-cm) lengths. Make the orecchiette by pressing down on each piece of pasta with a knife with a rounded blade. Place each piece on your finger and mold into a small shell or ear shape • Arrange the orecchiette on a clean cloth sprinkled with semolina and let dry for at least 30 minutes before cooking.

Serves: 4 • Prep: 1 hr + time to dry • Level: 3

Orecchiette with meat ragù

Orecchiette col ragù

- 1 quantity orecchiette, —see recipe on this page—or 1 lb (500 g) storebought orecchiette
- $^1/_3$ cup (90 ml) extra-virgin olive oil
- 2 large onions, finely chopped
- 1 lb (500 g) lean ground (minced) beef, lamb, or pork
- 1 lb (500 g) tomatoes, peeled and chopped
- 2 stalks celery, finely chopped
- 2 tablespoons freshly chopped basil
- salt and freshly ground black pepper
- $^1/_2$ cup (60 g) freshly grated pecorino or Parmesan cheese

If using homemade pasta, prepare it following the instructions on this page. • Heat the oil in a large saucepan over medium heat. Add the onions and sauté until softened, 3–4 minutes. • Add the meat and sauté until browned all over, about 5 minutes. • Add the tomatoes, celery, and basil. Season with salt and pepper. Cover and simmer over low heat for about 1 hour. • Cook the pasta in a large pot of salted boiling water until al dente. Drain well and then add to the sauce. • Toss well over high heat for 1 minute. Sprinkle with the pecorino or Parmesan and serve hot.

Serves: 4–6 • Prep: 10 min + time to make pasta • Cooking: 1 hr 10 min • Level: 2

Orecchiette with broccoli

Orecchiette con i broccoli

- 1 quantity orecchiette, —see recipe on this page—or 1 lb (500 g) storebought orecchiette
- 1 lb (500 g) fresh broccoli, cut into florets, stem cut in small dice
- 4 cloves garlic, finely chopped
- $^1/_4$ cup (60 ml) extra-virgin olive oil
- 1 red chile pepper, thinly sliced
- salt
- 1 cup (125 g) freshly grated pecorino cheese

If using homemade pasta, prepare it following the instructions on this page. • Boil the broccoli stem and florets in a large pot of salted water until tender, 5–7 minutes. • Drain well, reserving the water to cook the pasta. • In a large frying pan, sauté the garlic in the oil until pale golden brown, 3 minutes. • Add the broccoli and chile pepper, season with salt, and simmer over low heat for 5 minutes. • Meanwhile, bring the water used to cook the broccoli back to the boil, add the pasta, and cook until al dente. • Drain well, and add to the broccoli in the pan. • Toss over high heat for 1–2 minutes. Remove from heat, sprinkle with the pecorino and serve hot.

Serves: 4 • Prep: 15 min + time to make pasta • Cooking: 40 min • Level: 1

Orecchiette with turnip greens

Orecchiette alle cime di rapa

- 1 quantity orecchiette, —see recipe on this page—or 1 lb (500 g) storebought orecchiette
- 2 lb (1 kg) turnip greens, coarsely chopped
- 4 cloves garlic, lightly crushed but whole
- $^1/_3$ cup (90 ml) extra-virgin olive oil
- 6 salt-cured anchovy fillets
- salt

If using homemade pasta, prepare it following the instructions on this page. • Cook the turnip greens in salted boiling water until tender, 12–15 minutes. • Use a slotted spoon to remove the greens, reserving the cooking water. • Heat the oil in a large frying pan over medium heat. Sauté the garlic until pale gold, 3–5 minutes. • Turn the heat down to low and add the anchovies. Stir until they dissolve into the oil, 5–10 minutes. • Add the greens and sauté until well mixed, about 5 minutes. Season with salt. • Bring the cooking water from the greens back to a boil. Add the orecchiette and cook until al dente. • Drain and add to the sauce. • Toss well and serve hot.

Serves: 4 • Prep: 15 min + time to make pasta • Cooking: 40 min • Level: 1

Milk pasta with cherry tomatoes

Pizzoccheri with potatoes and savoy cabbage

Pizzoccheri valtellinesi

Pasta Dough

- 2 cups (300 g) buckwheat flour
- 1 cup (150 g) all-purpose (plain) flour
- 1/2 teaspoon salt
- 3/4 cup (180 ml) lukewarm water + more as needed

Sauce

- 6 medium potatoes, peeled and cut into small chunks
- 1/2 head Savoy cabbage, finely shredded
- 2/3 cup (150 g) butter
- 3 cloves garlic, lightly crushed but whole
- 1 sprig fresh sage
- salt and freshly ground black pepper
- 1 cup (125 g) freshly grated Parmesan cheese
- 5 oz (150 g) Bitto cheese, flaked or Fontina cheese, grated

Pizzoccheri are a specialty of Valtellina, in Lombardy. They are quite complicated to make, but well worth the effort. Factory-made, dried pizzoccheri are now available in specialty stores.

Pasta Dough: Sift the buckwheat and all-purpose flours and salt onto a work surface and make a well in the center. Mix in enough water to make a smooth dough. Knead until smooth and elastic, 15–20 minutes. Shape the dough into a ball, wrap in plastic wrap (cling film), and let rest for 30 minutes. • Roll out the dough on a lightly floured surface to a 1/4-inch (5-mm) thick. The dough will be very fragile. Cut into 1/2-inch (1-cm) strips, then into 2-inch (5-cm) rectangles. Let stand until ready to cook. • Sauce: Cook the potatoes and cabbage in salted boiling water for 15 minutes. • Melt the butter in a small saucepan with the garlic, sage, and a little salt for 1 minute then discard the garlic and sage. • Add the pasta to the potatoes and cabbage and cook until the pasta is al dente and the vegetables are tender, about 5 minutes. • Drain the pasta and vegetables. • Layer the pasta and vegetables in a serving bowl with the Parmesan, Bitto, and the melted butter. Season with pepper and serve hot.

Serves: 6 • Prep: 90 min + 30 min to rest the dough
Cooking: 25 min • Level: 3

Milk pasta with cherry tomatoes

Garganelli con salsiccia e piselli

Pasta Dough

- 1 1/3 cups (200 g) all-purpose (plain) flour
- 1 1/3 cups (200 g) durum wheat flour
- 1 tablespoon extra-virgin olive oil
- about 2/3 cup (180 ml) warm milk

Sauce

- 4 tablespoons fine dry bread crumbs
- 3 cloves garlic, finely chopped
- 2 tablespoons finely chopped parsley
- 1 tablespoon finely chopped oregano
- 8 leaves fresh basil, torn
- pinch of sugar
- 1/3 cup (90 ml) extra-virgin olive oil
- 1 1/2 lb (750 g) cherry tomatoes
- salt and freshly ground black pepper

Prepare the pasta dough following the instructions on page 156, using both flours, the oil, and enough milk to obtain a fairly firm dough. Knead for 15 minutes, then wrap in plastic wrap (cling film) and let rest for 30 minutes. • Divide the dough into 4 pieces and roll them through a pasta machine one notch at a time down to the second thinnest setting. Cut into 1-inch (2.5-cm) squares. Dry the sheets of pasta on a lightly floured cloth for 30 minutes. • Sauce: Preheat the oven to 350°F (180°C/gas 4). • Mix the bread crumbs, garlic, parsley, oregano, and half the basil in a small bowl. Add the sugar and half the oil. • Place the tomatoes in a large, shallow baking dish, cut-side up. Sprinkle with salt and the herb mixture and bake in the oven for 40 minutes. • Cook the pasta in a large pan of salted boiling water until al dente, 3–4 minutes. • Drain the pasta and place in a heated serving dish. Spoon the tomatoes and their cooking liquid over the top. Drizzle with the remaining oil and sprinkle with the remaining basil and a generous grinding of pepper. Toss gently. • Serve hot.

Serves: 6 • Prep: 1 hr + 30 min to rest the dough • Cooking: 1 hr • Level: 2

Classic baked lasagne

Lasagne al forno alla ferrarese

- 1 quantity lasagna (see page 156) or 14 oz (400 g) fresh storebought lasagna
- 1 tablespoon extra-virgin olive oil

Meat Sauce
- 1/3 cup (90 g) butter
- 8 oz (250 g) prosciutto, finely chopped
- 1 medium onion, finely chopped
- 1 medium carrot, finely chopped
- 1 small stalk celery, finely chopped
- 12 oz (350 g) lean ground (minced) beef
- 1/3 cup (90 ml) dry white wine
- 1 large tomato, peeled and chopped
- about 1/2 cup (125 ml) beef stock, homemade (see page 104) or bouillon cube
- salt

Béchamel Sauce
- 1/4 cup (60 g) butter
- 1/3 cup (50 g) all-purpose (plain) flour
- 2 cups (500 ml) milk
- salt and freshly ground black pepper

- scant 1 1/4 cups (150 g) freshly grated Parmesan
- 2 tablespoons butter

If using homemade pasta, prepare it following the instructions on page 156. • Meat Sauce: Melt the butter in a medium saucepan over medium heat. Add the prosciutto, onion, carrot, and celery. Sauté until the vegetables have softened, about 5 minutes. • Add the beef and sauté until lightly browned, about 5 minutes. • Add the wine and simmer until it evaporates. Add the tomato and stock. Mix well and season with salt. Cover and simmer over low heat for 2 hours. Stir the sauce from time to time and add a little more stock if it begins to stick to the pan. • Béchamel Sauce: Melt the butter in a large saucepan over medium heat. Add the flour and stir until smooth. Remove from the heat and add the milk all at once, mixing well to prevent lumps from forming. Return the saucepan to the heat and simmer, stirring constantly, until thickened and cooked, 5–7 minutes. Season with salt and pepper. • Preheat the oven to 400°F (200°C/ gas 6). • Blanch the lasagne sheets in small batches in a large pan of salted boiling water with 1 tablespoon of oil. Scoop out with a slotted spoon, squeeze gently, and let dry on a clean cloth. • Butter a large ovenproof dish and cover with a little of the Béchamel. Place a layer of lasagna on top. Spoon a little of the meat sauce over the lasagna and then add a layer of the Béchamel sauce. Sprinkle with a little of the Parmesan. Add another layer of pasta and repeat until all the ingredients are in the dish. Sprinkle with the Parmesan and dot with the remaining butter. • Bake until golden brown and bubbling, about 20 minutes. Let rest for 5 minutes. Serve hot.

Serves: 4–6 • Prep: 50 min + time to make the pasta Cooking: 2 hr 45 min • Level: 2

Stuffed pasta roll

Rotolo di pasta ripieno

- 1 quantity plain pasta dough (see page 156)
- 2 lb (1 kg) spinach leaves
- generous 3/4 cup (200 g) butter
- 3/4 cup (90 g) freshly grated Parmesan cheese
- 8 oz (250 g) fresh mushrooms, thinly sliced
- 8 oz (250 g) trimmed chicken livers
- 4 oz (125 g) fresh Italian sausage meat
- 8 oz (250 g) ground (minced) lean beef
- salt

Prepare the pasta dough. • Roll it out to a thin, rectangular sheet measuring 12 x 16 inches (30 x 40-cm). Cover with a clean cloth. • Cook the spinach in a little salted water until tender, about 5 minutes. Squeeze out excess moisture and chop coarsely. • Sauté the spinach in 2 tablespoons of butter and stir in 1 tablespoon of Parmesan. • Sauté the mushrooms in 2 tablespoons of butter for 5 minutes. • Poach the chicken livers in a little water. Drain and chop finely. • Melt 1 tablespoon of butter in a saucepan and fry the sausage meat over a low heat with the chopped chicken livers and ground veal. Season with salt and cook for 10 minutes, moistening with a little water if necessary. • Spread the mixture over the sheet of pasta dough, stopping just short of the edges. Cover with with an even layer of spinach. • Roll up lengthwise to form a long sausage. • Wrap tightly in a piece of cheesecloth (muslin) and tie the gathered ends of the cloth with string. • Place the roll in barely simmering water in an oval casserole dish and simmer for 50 minutes. • Remove from the water and set aside to cool a little before untying and removing the cloth. • Slice and sprinkle with the remaining Parmesan. Drizzle with the remaining butter and serve hot.

Serves: 4–6 • Prep: 1 hr time to make pasta • Cooking: 1 hr 30 min • Level: 3

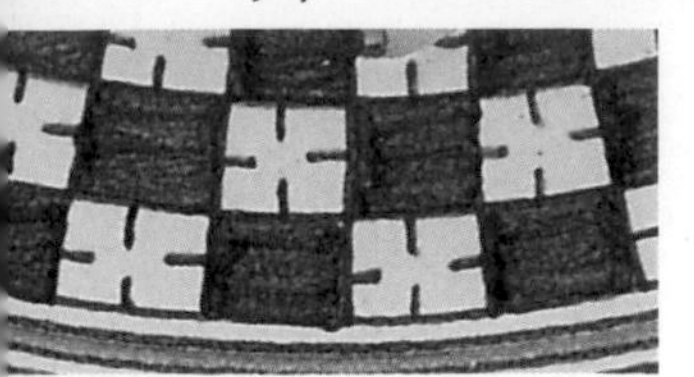

Seafood Lasagne

Neapolitan lasagne

Lasagne alla napoletana

- 1 quantity lasagna (see page 156) or 14 oz (400 g) fresh storebought lasagna
- 12 oz (350 g) ground (minced) beef
- 1 cup (60 g) fresh bread crumbs
- 1/2 cup (60 g) freshly grated Parmesan cheese
- 2 tablespoons finely chopped parsley
- 1 clove garlic, finely chopped
- 1/8 teaspoon nutmeg
- 1/8 teaspoon salt
- 1/2 cup (125 ml) extra-virgin olive oil
- 2 cups (500 g) tomato sauce (see page 132)
- 3/4 cup (180 g) fresh ricotta cheese, drained
- salt
- 1 tablespoon hot water
- 8 oz (250 g) fresh mozzarella cheese, thinly sliced
- 3/4 cup (90 g) diced ham
- 2 hard-boiled eggs, thinly sliced

If using homemade pasta, prepare it following the instructions on page 156. • Mix the beef, bread crumbs, Parmesan, parsley, garlic, nutmeg, and salt in a large bowl. Shape into small meatballs. • Heat the oil in a large frying pan and fry the meatballs until browned and cooked through, 7–10 minutes. • Drain the oil from frying pan, leaving the meatballs in it, and pour in the tomato sauce. Cook for 2 minutes, then remove the meatballs with a slotted spoon and set aside. • Smear a thin layer of the sauce over the bottom of a large baking dish. • Preheat the oven to 350°F (180°C/gas 4). • Mix the ricotta with the water and season with salt. • Blanch the lasagne sheets in small batches in a large pan of salted boiling water with 1 tablespoon of oil. Scoop out with a slotted spoon, squeeze gently, and let dry on a clean cloth. • Place a layer in the baking dish. • Spread with a layer of ricotta, tomato sauce, mozzarella, and eggs. Cover with pasta and a layer of meatballs and ham. Cover with pasta and repeat until all the ingredients are in the dish, finishing with a layer of ricotta. • Bake for 30 minutes, or until golden brown. • Serve hot.

Serves: 6 • Prep: 1 hr • Cooking: 1 hr • Level: 3

Seafood lasagne

Lasagne di pesce

- 1 quantity lasagna (see page 156) or 14 oz (400 g) fresh storebought lasagna
- 5 tablespoons extra-virgin olive oil
- 2 cloves garlic, finely chopped
- 2 tablespoons finely chopped parsley
- 1/2 cup (125 ml) dry white wine
- 12 oz (350 g) squid, cleaned and chopped
- 12 oz (350 g) shrimp (prawn) tails, shelled and deveined
- 12 oz (350 g) mixed clams and mussels, shelled
- 14 oz (400 g) firm-textured fish fillets, chopped
- salt and freshly ground white pepper
- 1/3 cup (90 g) butter
- 1/2 cup (75 g) all-purpose (plain) flour
- 4 cups (1 liter) fish stock, homemade (see page 193) or bouillon cube

If using homemade pasta, prepare it following the instructions on page 156. • Blanch the lasagne sheets in small batches in a large pan of salted boiling water with 1 tablespoon of oil. Scoop out with a slotted spoon, squeeze gently, and let dry on a clean cloth. • Heat the remaining oil in a large frying pan and sauté the garlic and half the parsley until the garlic is pale gold, 3 minutes. • Pour in the wine and simmer until it evaporates. • Add the squid and sauté over high heat for 5 minutes. Add the shrimps, shellfish, and fish. Season with salt and pepper and simmer over medium heat for 5 minutes. Add the remaining parsley and remove from the heat. • Preheat the oven to 350°F (180°C/gas 4). • Butter a large baking dish. • Melt the butter in a medium saucepan and stir in the flour. Pour in the stock and simmer for 10 minutes, stirring often. • Arrange a layer of pasta in the bottom of the dish. Spread with a layer of fish sauce and cover with a layer of fish cream. Repeat until all the ingredients are in the dish. • Bake until golden brown, 20–30 minutes. • Let rest for 10 minutes before serving.

Serves: 6 • Prep: 40 min + time to make pasta • Cooking: 1 hr • Level: 3

Lasagne with spring vegetables

Lasagne di verdura

- 1 quantity lasagna (see page 156) or 14 oz (400 g) fresh storebought lasagna
- 1 tablespoon extra-virgin olive oil
- 1 quantity pesto (see page 130)
- 1 quantity Béchamel sauce (see page 172)
- 2 lb (1 kg) firm-ripe tomatoes, peeled and coarsely chopped
- 1 lb (500 g) cooked potatoes, cut in cubes
- 14 oz (400 g) green beans, cooked and cut in short lengths
- 12 oz (350 g) mozzarella cheese, thinly sliced
- salt and freshly ground white pepper
- 3/4 cup (90 g) freshly grated Parmesan cheese

If using homemade pasta, prepare it following the instructions on page 156. • Blanch the lasagne sheets in small batches in a large pan of salted boiling water with 1 tablespoon of oil. Scoop out with a slotted spoon, squeeze gently, and let dry on a clean cloth. • Preheat the oven to 350°F (180°C /gas 4). • Butter a large baking dish. • Stir the pesto into the Béchamel. • Mix the tomatoes, potatoes, green beans, and mozzarella in a large bowl. • Spread the bottom of the baking dish with a layer of the Béchamel mixture. Cover with a layer of pasta followed by a layer of vegetables and mozzarella. Season with salt and pepper and sprinkle with Parmesan. Repeat until all the ingredients are in the dish, finishing with a layer of Béchamel. Sprinkle with the Parmesan. • Bake until golden brown, 20–30 minutes. • Let rest for 10 minutes before serving.

Serves: 6 • Prep: 45 min + time to make pasta • Cooking: 1 hr • Level: 3

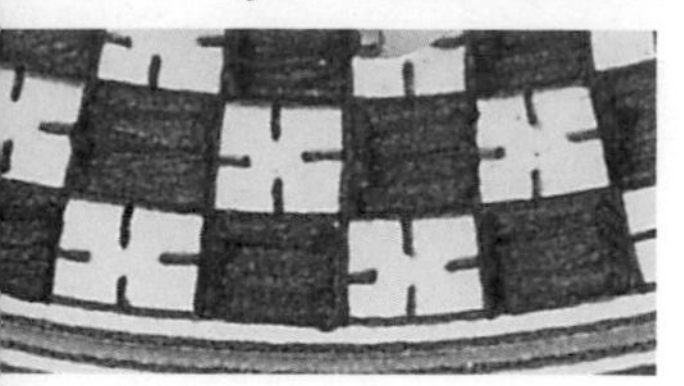

Potato ravioli with pesto

Genoese herb ravioli in tomato sauce

Ravioli verdi alla genovese

- 1 quantity plain pasta dough (see page 156)
- 1 quantity of homemade tomato sauce or homemade meat sauce (see page 132)
- generous 1/3 cup (100 g) butter
- 1 large onion, finely chopped
- 12 oz (350 g) diced beef
- 1/2 cup (125 ml) beef stock, homemade (see page 104) or bouillon cube
- 1 lb (500 g) fresh spinach leaves
- 8 oz (250 g) Swiss chard (silver beet)
- salt
- 3 tablespoons finely chopped parsley
- 1/2 tablespoon finely chopped basil
- 1/2 tablespoon finely chopped chervil
- 2 large egg yolks
- 1 cup (120 g) freshly grated Parmesan cheese
- freshly ground black pepper

Prepare the pasta dough. • Prepare the tomato or meat sauce. • Melt half the butter in a large frying pan over medium heat. Add the onion and sauté until pale golden brown, about 5 minutes. • Add the meat and sauté until it is lightly browned, 5–7 minutes. Add the stock, cover, and simmer until the meat is tender, about 20 minutes. Remove from the heat and let cool slightly. • Place the spinach and Swiss chard in a large saucepan with a little salted water over medium heat. Cook until tender and wilted, 5–7 minutes. • Drain well, squeezing gently to remove excess liquid. Chop the cooked vegetables very finely. • Remove the meat form the frying pan and chop finely in a food processor. • Melt the remaining butter in the frying pan over low heat. Transfer the chopped vegetables to the frying pan and sauté for 2 minutes. • Stir in the parsley, basil, and chervil. • Transfer the mixture to a large bowl. Add the chopped meat, egg yolks, and half the Parmesan and season with pepper. Mix well. • Roll out the dough on a lightly floured surface until paper thin. Cut the pasta into long sheets about 4-inches (10-cm) wide. Place heaped teaspoons of the filling down the center of the sheets of pasta at intervals of about 2 inches (5 cm). Moisten the edges of the dough and fold over to seal, pressing down gently between the mounds of filling. Use a fluted pastry cutter to cut between the mounds. • Lay the pasta on a lightly floured cloth. • Cook the pasta in small batches in a large pot of salted boiling water for 2–3 minutes. • Use a slotted spoon to transfer to a heated serving dish. Arrange in layers. • Spoon some of the hot meat or tomato sauce over each layer and sprinkle with a little Parmesan. Sprinkle with the remaining Parmesan and serve hot.

Serves: 4–6 • Prep: 1 hr + time to make pasta • Cooking: 45 min + time to cook sauce • Level: 3

Potato ravioli with pesto

Ravioli di patate con pesto

- 1 quantity plain pasta dough (see page 156)
- 1 quantity pesto (see page 130)

Filling

- 2 lb (1 kg) potatoes, peeled
- 1/2 cup (125) ml dry white wine
- 1 cup (250 ml) water
- 5 oz (150 g) Italian sausage meat
- 2 2/3 cups (400 g) all-purpose (plain) flour
- 1/2 cup(125 ml) milk
- 2 tablespoons freshly grated Parmesan cheese
- 3 eggs
- 1 teaspoon marjoram

Prepare the pasta dough. • Prepare the pesto. • Filling: Boil the potatoes in a large pot of salted, boiling water until tender, about 25 minutes. • Drain and mash in a large bowl. • Bring the wine and water to a boil in a small saucepan. • Add the sausage meat and simmer for about 5 minutes to remove the fat. • Drain and add to the potatoes. Mix in the flour, milk, Parmesan, eggs, and marjoram. • Roll the dough out on a lightly floured surface until very thin. Cut into 1½ x 3-inch (4 x 8-cm) rectangles. • Put a teaspoonful of the filling on each rectangle, fold each one in half, and seal, pinching the edges together. • Cook the pasta in small batches in a large pot of salted, boiling water until al dente.Use a slotted spoon to drain the pasta and toss gently with the pesto. Serve immediately.

Serves: 4–6 • Prep: 45 min + time to make pasta • Cooking: 35 min • Level: 3

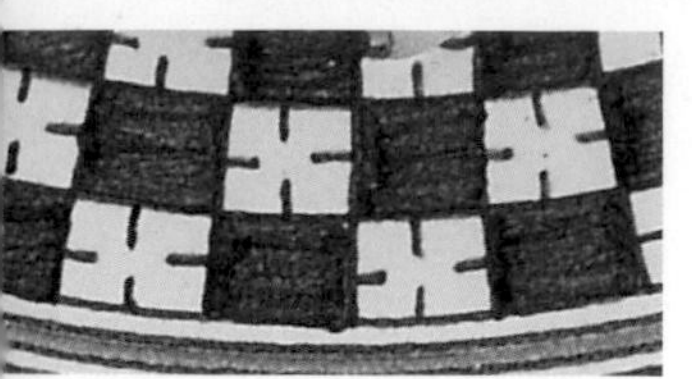

Pumpkin tortelli

Tortelli di zucca mantovani

- 1 quantity plain pasta dough (see page 156)

Filling

- 4 lb (2 kg) firm pumpkin flesh
- 12 oz (350 g) *mostarda di frutta* or spicy fruit chutney
- $1\frac{1}{2}$ cups (200 g) very finely crushed amaretti cookies
- $\frac{1}{2}$ teaspoon freshly grated nutmeg
- freshly grated zest of $\frac{1}{2}$ lemon,
- 1 tablespoon freshly squeezed lemon juice
- $\frac{1}{2}$ cup (60 g) freshly grated Parmesan cheese + extra as required
- salt and freshly ground black pepper

Sauce

- $\frac{3}{4}$ cup (180 g) butter, melted
- 1 cup (125 g) freshly grated Parmesan cheese
- zest of $\frac{1}{2}$ lemon, cut into julienne strips

Mostarda di frutta *is a savory fruit preserve which is available in Italian delicatessens. In the original Mantuan version of this recipe the mostarda traditionally used was made using only apples or pears.Substitute with a spicy fruit chutney.*

Prepare the pasta dough. • Preheat the oven to 350°F (180°C/gas 4). Remove and discard the seeds from the pumpkin but leave the skin intact. Cut into chunks and arrange on an oiled baking sheet. Bake until the pumpkin is tender, 25–30 minutes. Let cool slightly. • Scrape the cooked pumpkin flesh away from the skin and chop in a food processor until smooth. Place the purée in a large bowl. • Add the *mostarda di frutta*, amaretti, nutmeg, lemon zest, lemon juice, and Parmesan. Season with salt and pepper. The mixture should be quite stiff; if it is too moist add 2–3 tablespoons of extra Parmesan and mix well. • Cover and let rest in the refrigerator overnight. • Roll out the pasta dough into a very thin, almost transparent sheet. • Use a fluted pastry cutter to cut the pasta into 4-inch (10-cm) squares. Place heaped teaspoons of the filling in the center of each square. Moisten the edges of the dough and fold over into triangles to seal. • Cook the pasta in small batches in a large pot of salted boiling water for 2–3 minutes per batch. Transfer the cooked tortelli to a heated serving dish using a slotted spoon. Arrange in layers, drizzling each layer with a little of the melted butter and sprinkling with a little of the Parmesan. • When all the tortelli are cooked, drizzle with the remaining butter and sprinkle with the remaining Parmesan. Garnish with shreds of lemon zest and serve hot.

Serves: 4–6 • Prep: 1 hr + time to make pasta + 12 hr to rest filling • Cooking: 50 min • Level: 3

Tortellini with cream

Tortellini alla panna

- 1 quantity plain pasta dough (see page 156)

Filling

- 2 oz (60 g) boneless lean pork, coarsely chopped
- 2 oz (60 g) chicken breast, coarsely chopped
- $\frac{1}{4}$ cup (60 g) butter
- 2 oz (60 g) prosciutto (Parma) ham
- 4 oz (125 g) mortadella, finely chopped
- 2 eggs
- 6 tablespoons freshly grated Parmesan cheese
- $\frac{1}{4}$ teaspoon freshly grated nutmeg
- salt and freshly ground black pepper

Sauce

- $\frac{1}{3}$ cup (90 g) butter
- 1 cup (250 g) heavy (double) cream
- 1 truffle, white or black
- $\frac{1}{2}$ cup (60 g) freshly grated Parmesan cheese

Prepare the pasta dough. • Sauté the pork and chicken in the butter in a large frying pan over medium heat for about 5 minutes, or until cooked through. • Remove from the pan and chop finely in a food processor. • Sauté the prosciutto and mortadella in the same pan over medium heat for 2–3 minutes. • Mix the pork, chicken, prosciutto, and mortadella in a large bowl. Add the eggs, Parmesan, and nutmeg. Season with salt and pepper. Set aside. • Roll out the pasta dough to a thin, almost transparent sheet. • Cut the pasta into long sheets about 4-inches (10-cm) wide. Place heaped teaspoons of the filling down the center of the sheets of pasta at intervals of about 2 inches (5 cm). Moisten the edges of the dough and fold over to seal, pressing down gently between the mounds of filling. Use a fluted pastry cutter to cut between the mounds. • Cook the pasta in batches in a large pot of salted, boiling water for 4–5 minutes. • Melt the butter in a large saucepan over low heat. Stir in the cream and simmer for 3 minutes. • Use a slotted spoon to transfer the pasta to the pan with the cream. Add the Parmesan and shavings of truffle. Toss gently over medium-low heat for 2–3 minutes. • Serve hot.

Serves: 4–6 • Prep: 25 min + time to make pasta
Cooking: 25 min • Level: 3

RICE & RISOTTO

Most of the rice in Italy is grown in the north, especially in the Po River Valley which runs through Piedmont and Lombardy. Not surprisingly, rice is far more common in the cooking styles of the northern regions, and it is here that risotto first came to light. All Italian rices are short-grain, and the many different varieties are divided into four major categories, largely depending on how long they take to cook: *comune* or *originario* (mainly used in light soups and sweet dishes such as fritters and cakes); *semifino* (mainly used in heavier soups like minestrone, and for timballi); *fino* (mainly used for stuffings and baked dishes), and *superfino* (mainly used for risottos). The two most common risotto rices are Arborio and Carnaroli. For the inexperienced risotto cook, the most difficult thing is getting the timing right. The grains of rice should be just tender but never mushy or overcooked.

Leek and rosemary risotto (see page 198)

Risotto with lemon and marjoram

RISOTTO WITH ZUCCHINI FLOWERS

Risotto ai fiori di zucca

- 2 tablespoons extra-virgin olive oil
- 2 shallots, finely chopped
- 4 small zucchini (courgettes), cut into small cubes
- 10–12 zucchini (courgette) flowers, coarsely chopped + 1–2 extra whole, to garnish
- 2 cups (400 g) Italian risotto rice
- 1/3 cup (90 ml) dry white wine
- 4 cups (1 liter) boiling vegetable stock, homemade (see page 112), or bouillon cube
- leaves from 3 sprigs basil, torn
- 1/2 cup (60 g) freshly grated Parmesan cheese
- 1/4 cup (60 g) butter
- salt and freshly ground black pepper

Heat the oil in a large saucepan over medium heat. Add the shallots and sauté until transparent, about 3 minutes. • Add the zucchini and one-third of the chopped zucchini flowers. Sauté until the flowers begin to soften. • Add the rice and sauté for 2 minutes. • Pour in the wine and cook until it evaporates. • Begin adding the stock, 1/2 cup (125 ml) at a time, cooking and stirring until each addition has been absorbed and the rice is tender, 15–18 minutes. • Add the remaining chopped zucchini flowers and the basil. Mix well and remove from the heat. • Stir in the Parmesan and butter. Season with salt and pepper. Cover and let rest for 2 minutes. • Garnish with the whole zucchini flowers and serve hot.

Serves: 4 • Prep: 15 min • Cooking: 30 min • Level: 2

RISOTTO WITH BELL PEPPERS

Risotto ai peperoni

- 3 large bell peppers (capsicums), mixed colors
- 1/3 cup (90 g) butter
- 1 onion, finely chopped
- 2 cups (400 g) Italian risotto rice
- 1 tablespoon finely chopped thyme
- 4 cups (1 liter) boiling vegetable stock, homemade (see page 112) or bouillon cube
- salt and freshly ground black pepper
- 1/2 cup (60 g) freshly grated Parmesan cheese
- 1 tablespoon finely chopped parsley

Cut the bell peppers in half and set aside four halves. Chop the rest into small pieces. • Heat 2 tablespoons of butter in a large frying pan and sauté the onion until softened, 3–4 minutes. • Add the rice and cook for 2 minutes, stirring constantly. Add the thyme and diced bell peppers. • Begin adding the stock, 1/2 cup (125 ml) at a time, cooking and stirring until each addition has been absorbed and the rice is tender, 15–18 minutes. • Season with salt and pepper and stir in the Parmesan, parsley, and remaining butter. • Spoon the risotto into the reserved bell pepper halves and serve.

Serves: 4 • Prep: 20 min • Cooking: 25 min • Level: 1

FISH STOCK

Brodo di pesce

- 8 cups (2 liters) water
- 1 lb (500 g) fish trimmings (heads, skin, shells)
- 1 onion, chopped
- 1 carrot, chopped
- 1 stalk celery
- 1 medium tomato
- 1 bunch parsley
- 1 bay leaf
- 1 large slice lemon
- 1/2 cup (125 ml) dry white wine
- 2 teaspoons coarse sea salt
- 6 black peppercorns

Put the water in a large pot and add the fish trimmings, onion, carrot, celery, tomato, parsley, bay leaf, lemon slice, wine, salt, and peppercorns. • Bring to a boil over high heat, then reduce the heat to low and simmer for 20 minutes, skimming the foam at regular intervals with a slotted spoon. • Strain the stock, discarding the fish and vegetables.

Makes: about 4 cups (1 liter) • Prep: 15 min • Cooking: 50 min • Level: 1

RISOTTO WITH LEMON AND MARJORAM

Risotto al limone e maggiorana

- 2 tablespoons extra-virgin olive oil
- 1/3 cup (90 g) butter
- 1 onion, finely chopped
- 2 cloves garlic, finely chopped
- 2 cups (400 g) Italian risotto rice
- 4 cups (1 liter) boiling vegetable stock, homemade (see page 112) or bouillon cube
- salt and freshly ground white pepper
- 1 tablespoon finely grated lemon zest
- 1 cup (125 g) freshly grated Parmesan cheese
- fresh marjoram leaves, to garnish

Heat the oil and half the butter in a large frying pan and sauté the onion and garlic until softened, 3–4 minutes. • Add the rice and cook for 2 minutes, stirring constantly. • Begin adding the stock, 1/2 cup (125 ml) at a time, cooking and stirring until each addition has been absorbed and the rice is tender, 15–18 minutes. • Remove from the heat and season with salt and white pepper. Sprinkle with the lemon zest, Parmesan, and marjoram. Dot with the remaining butter, letting it melt into the rice. Serve hot.

Serves: 4 • Prep: 20 min • Cooking: 25 min • Level: 1

Spring vegetable risotto

Porcini mushroom risotto

Risotto ai funghi porcini

- 1 oz (30 g) dried porcini mushrooms
- 1 cup (250 ml) warm water
- ¼ cup (60 ml) extra-virgin olive oil
- 1 small onion, finely chopped
- ½ cup (125 ml) dry white wine
- 2 cups (400 g) Italian risotto rice
- 4 cups (1 liter) boiling vegetable stock homemade (see page 112) or bouillon cube
- salt and freshly ground black pepper
- 2 tablespoons finely chopped parsley

Soak the mushrooms in the water for 20 minutes. Drain, reserving the water, and chop coarsely. • Heat the oil in a large, heavy saucepan over medium heat. Add the onion and sauté until soft. • Add the mushrooms and sauté for 2–3 minutes. Add the rice and cook for 2 minutes, stirring constantly. • Pour in the wine, and when it has been absorbed, stir in the mushroom water. • Begin adding the stock, ½ cup (125 ml) at a time, cooking and stirring until each addition has been absorbed and the rice is tender, 15–18 minutes. • Season with salt and pepper. Add the parsley, mix well, and serve hot.

Serves: 4 • Prep: 30 min • Cooking: 25 min • Level: 1

Risotto with beans

Panissa

- 8 oz (250 g) fresh cranberry or red kidney beans, shelled
- 4 cups (1 liter) boiling vegetable stock homemade (see page 112), or bouillon cube
- ⅓ cup (90 g) finely chopped lard
- ⅓ cup (90 g) finely chopped pancetta
- 1 small onion, finely chopped
- 2 cups (400 g) Italian risotto rice
- 1 cup (250 ml) full-bodied red wine
- salt and freshly ground white or black pepper

This hearty winter dish comes from Piedmont. If fresh beans are unavailable, use dry beans. Soak them in cold water for 10–12 hours, then simmer until tender, about 1 hour 30 minutes.

Cook the beans in the stock in a covered pot over low heat until tender, about 40 minutes. • Place the lard and pancetta in a heavy saucepan over low heat. When the fat has melted, add the onion and sauté for 5 minutes. • Pour in the rice and stir for 2 minutes. • Add the wine, ½ cup (125 ml) at a time. When it has been absorbed, begin adding, ½ cup (125 ml) at a time, the hot beans and their stock. • Stir constantly until each addition is absorbed, until the rice is cooked, about 15–18 minutes. • Season with salt and pepper and serve hot.

Serves: 4 • Prep: 30 min • Cooking: 1 hr 10 min • Level: 2

Spring vegetable risotto

Risotto di primavera

- 2 artichokes
- juice of 1 lemon
- 3 large ripe tomatoes
- 2 tablespoons extra virgin olive oil
- ⅓ cup (90 g) butter
- 1 medium onion, finely chopped
- 1 stalk celery, finely chopped
- 4 tablespoons finely chopped parsley
- 1 large carrot, cut in small cubes
- 2 medium potatoes, peeled and cut in small cubes
- salt
- 4 cups (1 liter) boiling beef stock homemade (see page 104), or bouillon cube
- 2 cups (300 g) frozen peas
- 4 oz (125 g) green beans, coarsely chopped
- 5 oz (150 g) fresh spinach, coarsely chopped
- 8 oz (250 g) asparagus tips, coarsely chopped
- 2 cups (400 g) Italian risotto rice
- ¼ cup (30 g) freshly grated Parmesan cheese
- freshly ground black pepper

Clean the artichokes by pulling the tough outer leaves down and snapping them off. Cut off the top third of the leaves and trim the stalk. Cut in half and use a sharp knife to remove any fuzzy choke. Slice thinly and drizzle with the lemon juice. • Blanch the tomatoes in boiling water for 2 minutes. Drain and peel them. Chop the peeled tomatoes, discarding the seeds. • Heat the oil and half the butter in a large frying pan over medium heat. Add the onion, celery, and parsley and sauté until tender, about 5 minutes. • Add the carrot, potatoes, artichokes, and tomatoes to the pan and season with salt. Sauté for 2–3 minutes and then add a ½ cup (125 ml) of stock. Simmer over low heat until the potatoes and the carrots begin to soften, about 10 minutes. • Add the peas, green beans, spinach, and asparagus. Add the rice and stir for 2 minutes. • Begin adding the stock, ½ cup (125 ml) at a time, cooking and stirring until each addition has been absorbed and the rice is tender, 15–18 minutes. • Remove from the heat and add the Parmesan and the remaining butter. Season with pepper and serve hot.

Serves: 4–6 • Prep: 20 min • Cooking: 40 min • Level: 1

Shrimp risotto

Sicilian rice

Riso siciliano

- 2 cups (400 g) short-grain rice
- salt
- 1 small onion, thinly sliced
- $\frac{1}{4}$ cup (60 ml) extra-virgin olive oil
- 2 salt-cured anchovy fillets
- $\frac{1}{2}$ cup (125 ml) dry white wine
- 1 tablespoon Italian red or white wine vinegar
- 4–5 fresh or canned tomatoes, peeled and coarsely chopped
- juice of 2 lemons
- 1 dried chile pepper, crumbled
- 1 teaspoon finely chopped marjoram
- 3–4 leaves fresh basil
- 8 large, fleshy black olives, pitted and cut into quarters

Bring plenty of salted water to a boil in a large saucepan. Add the rice and cook for until just tender, about 15 minutes. • While the rice is cooking, sauté the onion in the oil over medium heat until softened, 3–4 minutes. • Add the anchovies, crushing them with a fork, until they dissolve into the oil. • Add the wine and vinegar and simmer, uncovered, until the liquid has evaporated. • Add the tomatoes, lemon juice, chile pepper, marjoram, basil, and olives, and simmer over medium heat for 7–8 minutes, stirring now and then. • Drain the rice and transfer to a heated serving dish. Pour the sauce over the top. Serve at once.

Serves: 4 • Prep: 15 min • Cooking: 25 min • Level: 1

Shrimp risotto

Risotto con gamberi

- 8 cups (2 liters) water
- 2 medium onions
- 1 stalk celery, coarsely chopped
- 1 large carrot, coarsely chopped
- 1 bay leaf
- salt
- 1 lb (500 g) fresh shrimp (prawn) tails
- $\frac{1}{4}$ cup (60 ml) extra virgin olive oil
- $\frac{1}{3}$ cup (90 g) butter
- 1 clove garlic, finely chopped
- 2 cups (400 g) Italian risotto rice
- $\frac{1}{3}$ cup (90 ml) dry white wine
- freshly ground black pepper

Bring the water to a boil in a large saucepan over medium heat. Cut one of the onions in half and add to the saucepan. Add the celery, carrot, and bay leaf. Season with salt. Cover and simmer over low heat until the vegetables are very tender, about 30 minutes. • Add the shrimp and cook until tender, 3–5 minutes. Remove from the heat. Transfer the shrimps to a plate using a slotted spoon. • Filter the stock, discarding the vegetables. Return the filtered stock to the saucepan and keep it warm over very low heat. • Shell the shrimps and devein them. • Chop the remaining onion finely. Heat the oil and 2 tablespoons of butter in a large saucepan over medium heat. Add the chopped onion and garlic. Sauté until softened, 3–4 minutes. • Add the shrimps and rice. Sauté for 2 minutes. • Add the wine and let it evaporate. • Add $\frac{1}{2}$ cup (125 ml) of the stock and stir until it has been absorbed. Keep adding the stock, $\frac{1}{2}$ cup (125 ml) at a time, cooking and stirring until each addition has been absorbed and the rice is tender, 15–18 minutes. • Remove from the heat and add the remaining butter. Season generously with pepper and serve hot.

Serves: 4 • Prep: 15 • Cooking: 55 min • Level: 2

Leek and rosemary risotto

Risotto con porri e rosmarino

- $\frac{1}{3}$ cup (90 g) butter
- 2 leeks, thinly sliced
- $\frac{1}{3}$ cup (90 ml) water
- salt
- 2 tablespoons extra-virgin olive oil
- 1 shallot, finely chopped
- 2 cups (400 g) Italian risotto rice
- $\frac{1}{3}$ cup (90 ml) dry white wine
- 3 cups (750 ml) boiling vegetable stock, homemade (se page 112) or bouillon cube
- finely grated zest of 1 lemon
- 2 tablespoons finely chopped rosemary + extra, to garnish
- freshly ground black pepper
- $\frac{2}{3}$ cup (100 g) freshly grated Parmesan cheese

Melt $\frac{1}{4}$ cup (60 g) of the butter in a large frying pan over low heat. Add the leeks and sauté until they begin to soften, 2–3 minutes. • Add the water and season with salt. Cook until the leeks begin to break down, about 20 minutes. • Heat the oil in another large frying pan over medium heat. Add the shallot and sauté until transparent, 3–4 minutes. • Add the rice and sauté for 2 minutes. • Pour in the wine and cook until it evaporates, 2–3 minutes. • Add the leeks and their cooking juices, and mix well. • Add $\frac{1}{2}$ cup (125 ml) of the stock and cook until it is absorbed. Stir in the lemon zest and rosemary and season with salt and pepper. Keep adding the stock, $\frac{1}{2}$ cup (125 ml) at a time, cooking and stirring until each addition has been absorbed and the rice is tender, 15–18 minutes. • Stir in the remaining butter and the Parmesan. • Garnish with the rosemary and serve hot.

Serves: 4 • Prep: 15 • Cooking: 55 min • Level: 1

Neapolitan baked rice

Sartu

Sauce
- 3 tablespoons extra virgin olive oil
- 1/4 cup (60 g) butter
- 1 small onion, finely chopped
- 1 clove garlic, finely chopped
- 2 tablespoons finely chopped basil
- 2 lb (1 kg) ripe tomatoes, peeled and chopped
- salt and freshly ground black pepper

Meatballs
- 1/2 cup (60 g) fine dry bread crumbs + a little extra, as required
- 1/4 cup (60 ml) vegetable stock, homemade (see page 112) or bouillon cube
- 8 oz (250 g) lean ground (minced) beef
- 2 tablespoons freshly grated Parmesan cheese
- 1 egg, lightly beaten
- salt and freshly ground black pepper
- 1/3 cup (50 g) all-purpose (plain) flour
- 1 cup (250 ml) olive oil, for frying

This is quite a complicated dish and will take an entire afternoon to make but it is well worth the effort.

Sauce: Heat the oil and butter in a large frying pan over medium heat. Add the onion, garlic, and basil and sauté until the onion is softened, 3–4 minutes. • Add the tomatoes and season with salt and pepper. Partially cover the pan and simmer over low heat for 1 hour. • Press the sauce through a fine mesh strainer and transfer to a bowl. • Meatballs: Moisten the bread crumbs with the stock in a large bowl. Add the meat, Parmesan, and egg. Season with salt and pepper. Mix well. The mixture should be stiff enough to hold its shape. If it is too moist, add some more bread crumbs and mix well. • Shape into meatballs the size of marbles. • Roll the meatballs in the flour, ensuring that they are evenly coated. • Heat the oil in a large frying pan over medium heat. Fry the meatballs until cooked through and lightly browned, about 5 minutes. Drain on paper towels. • Béchamel Sauce: Melt the butter in a large saucepan over medium heat. Add the flour and mix well. Remove from the heat and add a little of the milk. Mix well. Add the remaining milk and mix well to prevent lumps forming. • Simmer over medium heat until the sauce thickens, about 5 minutes. • Remove from the heat and let cool slightly. Add the Parmesan and egg yolk. Season with salt and pepper. • Filling: Melt 2 tablespoons of the butter in a large frying pan over low heat. Add the pancetta and sauté until lightly browned, 3–4 minutes. • Add the peas and sauté for 2 minutes. Add 1/4 cup (60 ml) of the stock, cover, and simmer until the peas begin to break down, about 20 minutes. Remove from the heat. • Place half the tomato sauce in a large saucepan over medium heat. Add the rice and a ladle or two of the stock and mix well. Simmer for 5 minutes, stirring constantly, until the rice has absorbed all the liquid. Add a little more stock and simmer, stirring constantly, until the rice has absorbed all the liquid. Repeat until you have used all the stock and the rice is just tender, about 15 minutes. • Remove from the heat. Add 2 tablespoons of the parmesan, the egg, and egg yolk. Season with salt and pepper. Mix well and transfer to a bowl. Let cool. • Place the sausage in a small saucepan with 1/2 cup (125 ml) of water. Simmer over medium heat for 5 minutes. Drain and slice thinly. • Melt 1/3 cup (90 g) of the butter in a saucepan over medium heat. Add the mushrooms and simmer until tender, about 10 minutes. • Add the chicken liver, season with salt and pepper, and simmer until the liver is cooked through, about 5 minutes. Remove from the heat. • Put the remaining tomato sauce into a large saucepan over very low heat. Add the liver mixture, sausage, and meatballs. Warm over medium heat, 2–3 minutes. • Preheat the oven to 350°F (180°C/gas 4). • Oil a deep-sided baking pan with a capacity of about 8 cups (2 liters). • Put two-thirds of the rice mixture into the prepared pan. Press the mixture into the pan so that it coats the base and sides evenly. Use the back of a spoon to smooth the surface of the rice. • Spoon the meat mixture into the rice case. Cover with a layer of the peas followed by the mozzarella. Sprinkle with the remaining Parmesan. Dot with 1/4 cup (60 g) of the remaining butter. Add the Béchamel. • Cover with the remaining rice, smoothing the surface with the back of a spoon. • Melt the remaining butter in a small saucepan over low heat. • Sprinkle the Sartù with the bread crumbs and drizzle with the butter. • Bake until the top is crisp and lightly browned, about 40 minutes. • Let rest for 10 minutes before turning out onto a serving dish. Serve hot.

Serves: 6–8 • Prep: 1 hr 20 min + 20 min to rest • Cooking: 3 hr 30 min • Level: 3

Béchamel Sauce
- 2 tablespoons butter
- 1/4 cup (30 g) all-purpose (plain) flour
- 1 1/4 cups (300 ml) milk
- 1 tablespoon freshly grated Parmesan cheese
- 1 egg yolk
- salt and freshly ground black pepper

Filling
- 3/4 cup (200 g) butter
- 1/2 cup (60 g) pancetta, chopped
- 2 cups (300 g) frozen peas
- 2 1/2 cups (600 ml) vegetable stock, homemade (see page 112) or bouillon cube
- 2 cups (400 g) short-grain rice
- 1/4 cup (30 g) freshly grated Parmesan cheese
- 1 egg + 1 egg yolk
- salt and freshly ground black pepper
- 2 large Italian sausages
- 1 oz (30 g) dried mushrooms, soaked in warm water for 15 minutes, drained, and chopped
- 4 chicken livers, sliced
- 8 oz (250 g) fresh mozzarella cheese, drained and sliced
- 2 tablespoons fine dry bread crumbs

GNOCCHI & POLENTA

Gnocchi are small pieces of pasta, usually made with potatoes and flour, but also with semolina, polenta, spinach and ricotta, and other ingredients. They are cooked in boiling water and served with melted butter and fresh herbs, or cheese, tomato, and meat sauces. Semolina gnocchi, also known as *gnocchi alla romana*, are baked in the oven; many of the other types of gnocchi can also be served gratin-style. Polenta as we know it today is made from coarsely ground corn flour. However, polenta recipes are present in Italian cook books long before corn was introduced to Italy from the Americas. Before then, it was made with crushed fava (broad) beans and was a cheap and nutritious food for the poor. From the 18th century onward, corn flour polenta became a staple food of poor people all over northern Italy. During the 20th century polenta was shunned at first, but became popular again as people realized just how good—and healthy—this traditional dish can be.

Potato gnocchi and leek gratin (see page 209)

Potato gnocchi with butter and sage

Potato gnocchi with butter and sage

Gnocchi con burro e salvia

Potato Gnocchi
- 2 lb (1 kg) starchy potatoes
- 2 large egg yolks
- salt
- 2 cups (300 g) all-purpose (plain) flour

Sauce
- 1/2 cup (125 g) butter, melted
- 2–3 sprigs fresh sage
- 1 cup (150 g) freshly grated Parmesan cheese

Gnocchi: Cook the potatoes in a large pot of salted boiling water until tender, 20–25 minutes. Drain and slip off their skins. Mash until smooth. • Gradually stir in the egg yolks, salt, and enough of the flour to obtain a smooth dough that is just a little sticky. • Take a piece of dough and roll it on a lightly floured work surface into a rope about 1/2 inch (1 cm) in diameter. Cut into pieces about 1 inch (2.5 cm) long. Repeat with all the dough. • To give the gnocchi their special grooves, twist around the tines of a fork. • Set a large pot of salted water to boil. Cook the gnocchi in batches. Lower the first batch (20–24 gnocchi) gently into the boiling water. After a few minutes they will rise to the surface. Simmer for 1–2 minutes, then scoop out with a slotted spoon. Place on a heated serving dish. Repeat until all the gnocchi are cooked. • Melt the butter with the sage and drizzle over the gnocchi. Sprinkle with the Parmesan and serve hot.

Serves: 4–6 • Prep: 30 min + 1 hr to rest • Cooking: 45 min • Level: 2

Potato gnocchi and leek gratin

Gnocchi gratinati con porri

Prepare the gnocchi following the instructions in the recipe on this page. • Sauce: Preheat the oven to 400°F (200°C/gas 6). • Grease one large or 4–6 individual ovenproof dishes. • Beat the cream and cornstarch in a small bowl. • Melt the butter in a large frying pan over medium heat. Add the leeks and sauté until they begin to soften, 3–4 minutes. • Add 3 tablespoons of water and cook until the leeks are tender, about 5 minutes. • Add the cognac and cook over high heat until it evaporates, 2–3 minutes. • Lower the heat and sprinkle with the cornstarch. Stir in the cream and simmer, stirring often, until thickened, 5 minutes. Add the nutmeg and season with salt and pepper. • Place the cooked gnocchi in the prepared baking dish(es). Spoon the leek sauce over the top. Sprinkle with Parmesan. • Bake until lightly browned, 5–10 minutes. • Garnish with basil and serve hot.

Serves 4–6 • Prep: 30 min + time to make the gnocchi • Cooking: 40 min • Level: 2

- 1 quantity potato gnocchi (see recipe left)

Sauce
- 2 tablespoons butter
- 5 small leeks, thinly sliced
- 2 tablespoons cognac
- 1 tablespoon cornstarch (cornflour)
- 1 1/4 cups (300 ml) heavy (double) cream
- 1/4 teaspoon freshly grated nutmeg
- salt and freshly ground black pepper
- 3/4 cup (90 g) freshly grated Parmesan cheese
- sprigs of basil, to garnish

Gnocchi with broccoli and pancetta

Gnocchi con broccoli e pancetta

- 1 quantity potato gnocchi (see recipe above)
- 14 oz (450 g) broccoli, broken up into small florets
- 1/2 cup (125 ml) extra-virgin olive oil
- 4 cloves garlic, finely chopped
- 1 red chile pepper, finely chopped
- 5 oz (150 g) diced pancetta
- salt and freshly ground black pepper
- 1/2 cup (60 g) freshly grated pecorino cheese

Prepare the gnocchi following the instructions in the recipe on this page. • Sauce: Cook the broccoli in a large pan of salted boiling water until just tender, 6–8 minutes. Remove with a slotted spoon, reserving the cooking water. • Heat the oil in a frying pan over medium heat and sauté the garlic, chile, and pancetta for 5 minutes. • Add the broccoli. Season with salt and pepper. Simmer for 10 minutes. • Bring the reserved cooking water to a boil. Cook the gnocchi in small batches following the instructions above. • Add to the pan with the sauce. • Sprinkle with pecorino and serve hot.

Serves: 4–6 • Prep: 25 min + time to make the gnocchi • Cooking: 25 min • Level: 1

Gnocchi with four-cheese sauce

Gnocchi ai quattro formaggi

Prepare the gnocchi following the instructions in the recipe on this page. • Prepare the Béchamel sauce. • When the Béchamel is ready, add the four cheeses and stir over low heat until they have melted and the sauce is smooth and creamy. Season with salt and pepper. • Cook the gnocchi in a large pot of salted boiling water following the instructions above. • Place the gnocchi in a heated serving dish and pour the cheese sauce over the top. Toss gently and serve hot.

Serves: 4–6 • Prep: 20 min + time to make the gnocchi • Cooking: 30 min • Level: 2

- 1 quantity potato gnocchi (see recipe above)
- 1/2 quantity Béchamel sauce (see page 151)
- 8 oz (250 g) Fontina cheese, freshly grated
- 4 oz (125 g) Gorgonzola cheese, coarsely chopped
- 4 oz (125 g) mascarpone cheese
- 1 cup (120 g) freshly grated Parmesan cheese
- salt and freshly ground black pepper

Brown gnocchi with cheese fondue sauce

Saffron gnocchi in meat sauce

Gnocchetti allo zafferano

Gnocchi

- 2⅔ cups (400 g) semolina flour
- ½ teaspoon salt
- ¼ teaspoon saffron strands, crumbled and dissolved in ¾ cup (180 ml) lukewarm water + more as needed

Meat Sauce

- ¼ cup (60 ml) extra-virgin olive oil
- 1 onion, finely chopped
- 3 oz (90 g) pancetta, bacon, or lard, finely chopped
- 12 oz (350 g) lean ground (minced) pork
- ½ cup (125 ml) dry red wine
- 2 (14-oz/400-g) cans tomatoes, with juice
- 4 leaves fresh basil, torn
- salt and freshly ground black pepper
- 1 cup (125 g) freshly grated aged pecorino cheese

Gnocchi: Sift the flour and salt into a bowl. Mix in enough saffron water to make a smooth dough. • Knead until smooth and elastic, 3–5 minutes. Shape into a ball, wrap in plastic wrap (cling film), and let rest for 30 minutes. • Heat the oil in a heavy saucepan over low heat and add the onion and pancetta. Cover and simmer for 10 minutes. • Add the pork and sauté over high heat until well browned, 5–7 minutes. • Pour in the wine and let it evaporate, 5 minutes. • Stir in the tomatoes and basil and season with salt and pepper. Simmer over low heat, partially covered, for at least 2 hours, adding stock or hot water if the sauce begins to stick to the pan. • Form the dough into logs ¼-inch (5 mm) in diameter and cut into ½-inch (1-cm) lengths. • Lay on a dry cloth dusted with semolina. • Cook the gnocchi in small batches in a large pot of salted boiling water until they rise to the surface, 2–3 minutes. • Drain and serve in the sauce, sprinkled with pecorino.

Serves: 6 • Prep: 1 hr + 30 min to rest the dough • Cooking: 40 min • Level: 2

Pumpkin gnocchi with sausage sauce

Gnocchi di zucca con sugo di salsicce

Gnocchi

- 2½ lb (1.25 kg) pumpkin or winter squash, cut into large pieces, unpeeled but seeded
- 2 large eggs
- ¼ cup (50 g) amaretti cookies, crumbled
- 4 tablespoons fresh bread crumbs
- ¼ cup (30 g) freshly grated Parmesan cheese
- ¼ teaspoon ground nutmeg
- salt and freshly ground white pepper

Sauce

- 1 onion, finely chopped
- ¼ cup (60 g) butter
- 8 oz (250 g) Italian sausage, crumbled
- 1 clove garlic, finely chopped
- 1 tablespoon tomato paste (concentrate) mixed in 1 tablespoon water
- salt
- ¼ cup (30 g) all-purpose (plain) flour

Gnocchi: Preheat the oven to 400°F (200°C/ gas 6). • Bake the pieces of pumpkin on a large baking sheet until tender, 40–45 minutes. • Let cool a little then use a tablespoon to remove the flesh. Chop in a food processor. • Transfer the pumpkin to a large bowl and mix in the eggs, amaretti, bread crumbs, and Parmesan. Season with nutmeg, salt, and pepper. • Sauce: Sauté the onion in the butter in a small saucepan over medium heat until softened, 3–4 minutes. Add the crumbled sausage and garlic and simmer over low heat for 10 minutes. • Add the tomato paste mixture. Season with salt and remove from the heat. • Form tablespoons of the gnocchi mixture into balls the size of walnuts, pressing them into an oval shape. • Dip in the flour until well coated. • Cook the gnocchi in small batches in a large pot of salted boiling water until they rise to the surface, 2–3 minutes. • Use a slotted spoon to transfer to heated serving dishes and serve hot with the sauce.

Serves: 4 • Prep: 45 min • Cooking: 1 hr 15 min • Level: 2

Brown gnocchi with cheese fondue sauce

Gnocchi integrale con fonduta

- 14 oz (400 g) Fontina or other mild cheese suitable for melting, sliced
- ⅔ cup (150 ml) milk
- 2 lb (1 kg) starchy potatoes, peeled
- ⅔ cup (100 g) all-purpose (plain) flour
- ⅔ cup (100 g) buckwheat flour
- salt and freshly ground black pepper
- 1 tablespoon butter
- 2 large egg yolks, lightly beaten

Place the cheese in a bowl and cover with the milk. Leave to soak. • Cook the potatoes in a large pot of salted boiling water until tender, 20–25 minutes. Drain and mash until smooth. • Place in a large bowl. Gradually stir in both flours. Season with salt and pepper. Mix well to make a smooth dough. • Knead the dough on a lightly floured work surface until smooth, 3–4 minutes. • Roll the dough into ropes about ¾-inch (2 cm) in diameter. Cut into pieces about 1 inch (2.5 cm) long. • Lay on a lightly floured clean cloth to dry. • Place the cheese and 3 tablespoons of the milk in a double boiler over barely simmering water. Add the butter and stir until the cheese has melted, about 5 minutes. • Stir in the egg yolks one at a time. • Cook, stirring constantly, until the sauce is thick, about 5 minutes. Season with salt and pepper • Cook the gnocchi in small batches in a large pot of salted boiling water until they rise to the surface. Scoop out with a slotted spoon and place in a large heated serving bowl. Pour the cheese fondue sauce over the top. Mix gently and serve hot.

Serves: 4 • Prep: 30 min • Cooking: 45 min • Level: 2

BAKED POLENTA IN CHEESE SAUCE

Polenta al forno con la Ricotta

- 1 quantity polenta (see page 220)
- 3 tablespoons butter
- 1 tablespoon all-purpose (plain) flour
- 1 cup (250) ml milk
- $1/2$ teaspoon freshly ground nutmeg
- 12 oz (350 g) Gorgonzola cheese, chopped
- 12 oz (350 g) Emmental (or Gruyère) cheese, thinly sliced
- $3/4$ cup (90 g) freshly grated Parmesan cheese

Prepare the polenta following the instructions on page 220. Set aside to cool for at least 3 hours. • Preheat the oven to 400°F (200°C/gas 6). • Melt 2 tablespoons of the butter in a saucepan. Add the flour and cook over low heat for 1–2 minutes, stirring continuously. • Begin adding the milk, a little at a time, stirring continuously until the sauce is smooth. Season with the nutmeg. • Turn up the heat and add the Gorgonzola, Emmental, and Parmesan, a handful at a time, stirring constantly until smooth. • Butter an ovenproof baking dish large enough to hold the polenta and sauce in a layer about 2 inches (5 cm) thick. • Cut the polenta into $3/4$-inch (2-cm) cubes. • Cover the bottom of the dish with half the polenta and pour half the sauce over the top. Put the remaining polenta on top and cover with the remaining sauce. • Bake until golden brown, 25–30 minutes.

Serves: 6–8 • Prep: 20 min + 4 hr to make and cool the polenta • Cooking: 30 min • Level: 2

POTATO POLENTA WITH SPARERIBS

Polenta di patate con rosticciana

This hearty dish is a meal in itself. Serve with a tossed green salad and a glass of full-bodied red wine.

- 2 lb (1 kg) potatoes, peeled
- $1/2$ cup (75 g) polenta (coarse-grain cornmeal)
- $1/2$ cup (75 g) buckwheat flour
- 2–3 cups (500–750 ml) boiling water
- 3 tablespoons butter
- 3 tablespoons extra-virgin olive oil
- 2 onions, thinly sliced
- salt and freshly ground black pepper
- 6 oz (180 g) fresh Asiago (or Fontina) cheese, in slivers
- 2 lb (1 kg) pork spareribs

Cook the potatoes in a large pot of salted boiling water until tender, 25 minutes. Mash until smooth. Place in the pot where the polenta is to be cooked. • Add the cornmeal and buckwheat flour, mix well, and continue to mix while adding the water. • Cook over medium-low heat, stirring energetically. • Melt the butter and oil over medium heat in a small saucepan. Add the onion and sauté until soft. • Add the onion to the polenta. Stir continuously. • After 20 minutes, add a little salt, a generous pinch of pepper, and the cheese. Stir for 10–15 more minutes. • Meanwhile, season the spareribs generously with salt and pepper and place them under a hot broiler. Broil until deep golden brown. • When the polenta is ready, turn it out onto a heated serving platter and top with the spareribs. Serve immediately.

Serves: 4–6 • Prep: 30 min • Cooking: 50 min • Level: 1

POLENTA BAKED WITH RICOTTA AND TOMATOES

Polenta al forno con ricotta e pomodoro

- 1 quantity polenta (see page 220)
- 8 oz (250 g) fresh ricotta cheese, drained
- 3 tablespoons extra-virgin olive oil
- 3 tablespoons lard
- 1 medium onion, finely chopped
- 3 tablespoons finely chopped parsley
- 1 (14-oz/400 g) can tomatoes, with juice
- freshly ground black pepper
- $1/2$ cup (60 g) freshly grated pecorino or Parmesan cheese

Prepare the polenta following the instructions on page 220. Place the cooked polenta in an oiled baking dish and let cool. • Preheat the oven to 350°F (180°C/gas 4). • Press the ricotta through a fine mesh strainer. • Heat the oil and lard in a large frying pan over medium heat. Add the onion and sauté until softened, about 5 minutes. • Add the parsley and tomatoes. Mix well. Season with salt and pepper. Simmer over low for 15 minutes. • Turn the polenta out onto a cutting board and let cool. • Slice the polenta and arrange a layer in an oiled baking dish. Add half the ricotta and spoon one-third of the sauce over the top. Sprinkle with pecorino. Add another layer of polenta, the remaining ricotta, and half of the remaining sauce. Sprinkle with pecorino and then cover with the remaining polenta. Cover with the remaining sauce and sprinkle with the remaining pecorino. • Bake until the top is golden brown, 20–25 minutes. • Let stand for 5–10 minutes before serving.

Serves: 6–8 • Prep: 20 min • Cooking: 1 hr 15 min • Level: 2

EGGS

Most egg dishes are easy, quick, and nourishing. Served with a salad, they make ideal light lunches and rapid dinners for busy cooks. The frittata—or Italian omelet—is a great way to prepare eggs Italian style. We have included a host of frittata recipes, from simple herb and vegetable frittatas that can be made in a frying pan or baked in the oven, to more elaborate dishes such as Crabmeat frittata (see page 237) or Baked stuffed egg rolls (see page 237). Crêpes, also known as *crespelle* in Italian, are another popular egg-based dish. Despite French claims on them, crêpes were actually invented in Renaissance Florence and introduced to France by Catherine de' Medici's retinue of cooks who accompanied her to Paris following her marriage to the French king, Henry II, in the 16th century. The mouthwatering dish shown here (left) is one of the best savory crêpe recipes we know. Try it!

Ricotta and zucchini crepes (see page 237)

Scrambled eggs with tomatoes

Eggs with olive sauce

Uova brusche

- 8 basil leaves, finely chopped
- 3 tablespoons finely chopped parsley
- 2 tablespoons capers, finely chopped
- 5 oz (150 g) green olives, pitted and finely chopped
- 1 cup (125 g) freshly grated Parmesan cheese
- 1 cup (100 g) fine dry bread crumbs
- 1/2 cup (125 ml) dry white wine
- freshly ground black pepper to taste
- 1/4 cup (60 ml) extra-virgin olive oil
- 12 hard-boiled eggs, sliced in half lengthwise

Mix the basil, parsley, capers, and olives together in a bowl. Stir in the Parmesan and bread crumbs. Gradually stir in the wine. • Add the pepper and gradually stir in the oil. The mixture should be thick but still fluid. • Place the eggs on a platter with the yolks facing up. Pour the mixture over the eggs and serve.

Serves: 6 • Prep: 10 min • Level: 1

Tomato and egg bake

Uova con pomodorini ripieni al forno

- 12–16 cherry tomatoes
- 1/2 cup (75 g) fine dry bread crumbs
- 3 large eggs and 1 large egg yolk
- 1/2 cup (125 ml) heavy (double) cream
- 1/2 cup (125 ml) milk
- 2 tablespoons freshly grated Emmental cheese
- 2 tablespoons freshly grated Parmesan cheese
- salt and freshly ground black pepper
- 1 quantity pesto (see page 130)

Slice the tops off the tomatoes. Scoop out the seeds and sprinkle the shells with salt. Drain upside-down on a chopping board or in a colander for 15 minutes. • Toast the bread crumbs in a nonstick frying pan over medium heat until browned, 2–3 minutes. Let cool. • Preheat the oven to 350°F (180°C/gas 4). • Oil a baking dish. • Beat the eggs and egg yolk, cream, milk, Emmental, and Parmesan in a medium bowl until frothy. Season with salt and pepper. • Mix the toasted crumbs with the pesto and spoon the mixture inside the tomatoes. • Arrange the tomatoes in the prepared baking dish, not too close together. Put the tops back on and drizzle with the remaining oil. • Pour the egg mixture into the dish around the tomatoes. Bake until set, about 30 minutes. Serve hot.

Serves: 4 · Prep: 20 min · Cooking: 50 min · Level: 1

Baked eggs with fontina

Uova al forno con Fontina

- 6 thin slices whole-wheat (wholemeal) bread
- 1/4 cup (60 ml) milk
- 8 oz (250 g) Fontina cheese, thinly sliced
- 2 tablespoons butter, cut into flakes
- 6 large eggs

Preheat the oven to 350°F (180°C/gas 4). • Butter a medium baking dish. • Dip the bread in the milk and arrange in the prepared baking dish. Top with half the Fontina and butter. • Bake until the bread is golden and the cheese is bubbling, about 10 minutes. • Break the eggs into the dish and cover each one with the remaining slices of Fontina. • Bake until the egg white is cooked and the cheese has melted, 10–15 minutes. • Serve hot.

Serves: 4 • Prep: 15 min • Cooking: 20–25 min • Level: 1

Scrambled eggs with tomatoes

Uova strapazzate col pomodoro

- 2 tablespoons butter
- 4–6 tomatoes, peeled and coarsely chopped
- 2 tablespoons finely chopped basil
- 8 large eggs, lightly beaten
- salt and freshly ground black pepper

Melt the butter in a large saucepan over medium heat. • Add the tomatoes and basil. and simmer until the liquid from the tomatoes has reduced, about 10 minutes. • Add the eggs and season with salt and pepper. Simmer, stirring from time to time, until the eggs are cooked through and the mixture is thick and creamy, 7–10 minutes. • Serve hot.

Serves: 4 • Prep: 5 min • Cooking: 20 min • Level: 1

Eggs

Leek frittata

Leek frittata

Frittata con porri

- 12 large eggs, lightly beaten
- salt and freshly ground black pepper
- 4 large leeks, very thinly sliced
- 2 tablespoons extra-virgin olive oil
- 1 tablespoon butter

Beat the eggs in a large bowl with a pinch of salt and pepper. Add the leeks and mix well. • Heat the oil and butter in a large frying pan over medium heat. Add the egg mixture and cook until the bottom is firm and cooked, about 5 minutes. • Slide the frittata onto a plate, flip it onto another plate and then slide it back into the pan. Cook until firm and lightly browned and the egg is cooked through, 3–5 minutes. • Serve hot.

Serves: 6 • Prep: 5 min • Cooking: 10 min • Level: 1

Zucchini frittata

Tortino di zucchini

- 3 large zucchini (courgettes)
- 1/2 cup (75 g) all-purpose (plain) flour
- 1/2 cup (125 ml) extra-virgin olive oil
- 6 large eggs
- salt and freshly ground black pepper

Slice the zucchini into thin wheels and coat with flour, shaking off any excess. • Heat all but 2 tablespoons of the oil in a large frying pan over high heat. • Sauté the zucchini until tender and lightly browned, about 8 minutes. Drain on paper towels. • Discard the oil and replace with the remaining oil. Arrange the zucchini in a single layer in the pan and return to medium-high heat. • Beat the eggs lightly with the salt and pepper, then pour over the zucchini. Cook until the bottom is firm and cooked, about 5 minutes. • Slide the frittata onto a plate, flip it onto another plate and then slide it back into the pan. Cook until firm and lightly browned and the egg is cooked through, 3–5 minutes. • Serve hot.

Serves: 4 • Prep: 10 min • Cooking: 15–20 min • Level: 1

Frittata with mint

Frittata alla menta

- 6 large eggs
- 2 tablespoons fine dry bread crumbs
- 1 small bunch parsley, finely chopped
- 25 leaves fresh mint, torn
- salt and freshly ground black pepper
- 1–2 tablespoons extra-virgin olive oil

Break the eggs into a bowl and beat until frothy. Stir in the bread crumbs, parsley, and mint. Season with salt and pepper. • Heat the oil in a large frying pan. Pour in the egg mixture and cook until set on top, 4–5 minutes. • To turn the frittata, place a large plate over the pan, turn it upside down and then slide the egg mixture back into the pan, browned side up. Cook for 4 minutes more. It should be firm and lightly browned on both sides. Serve hot.

Serves: 4 • Prep: 10 min • Cooking: 10 min • Level: 1

Tomato and bell pepper frittata

Frittata di pomodori e peperoni

- 1 small yellow bell pepper (capsicum), seeded and coarsely chopped
- 1 small red bell pepper (capsicum), seeded and coarsely chopped
- 1 onion, thinly sliced
- 2 tablespoons extra-virgin olive oil
- 12 oz (350 g) cherry tomatoes, coarsely chopped
- 4 leaves fresh basil, torn
- salt
- 6 large eggs

Sauté the bell peppers and onion in the oil in a large frying pan over medium heat for until the bell peppers and onions are tender, about 10 minutes. • Stir in the tomatoes and basil. Season with salt. • Beat the eggs in a medium bowl until frothy. Season with salt. • Pour the eggs into the frying pan. Stir well and cook until the eggs have set. • Turn on the broiler (grill) and broil the frittata for until the top is golden, 3–4 minutes. Serve hot.

Serves: 4 • Prep: 20 min • Cooking: 25 min • Level: 1

Baked stuffed egg rolls

Frittatine ripiene

- 6 oz (180 g) frozen spinach
- 1/3 cup (90 g) butter
- 1 clove garlic, finely chopped
- salt and freshly ground black pepper
- 4 large eggs, lightly beaten
- 2 tablespoons extra-virgin olive oil
- 1/2 quantity meat sauce (see page 132)
- 2 tablespoons freshly grated Parmesan cheese

Try this dish with a variety of different fillings: boiled artichoke hearts drizzled with butter and sprinkled with Parmesan; cooked asparagus with butter; mushrooms sautéed with garlic, butter, and fresh thyme; or slices of mozzarella and ham.

Preheat the oven to 400°F (200°C/gas 6). • Cook the spinach in a little salted boiling water until tender, about 5 minutes. Drain well and chop finely. • Heat 1/4 cup (60 g) of butter in a frying pan over medium heat and sauté the garlic until pale gold, 3–4 minutes. Add the spinach and sauté for 5 minutes. • Cook half the beaten eggs in a large frying pan with half the oil until set, about 3 minutes. • Transfer the cooked egg to a large baking sheet and repeat with the remaining egg. • Spread with the filling and roll up. Cut each roll into 3 or 4 sections (to fit your baking dish). Place in the oiled baking dish and drizzle with the remaining butter (melted). Season with salt and pepper. • Cover with the sauce and sprinkle with Parmesan. • Bake for 10 minutes. • Serve hot.

Serves: 2–4 • Prep: 20 min • Cooking: 20 min • Level: 2

Ricotta and zucchini crêpes

Crespelle alla con zucchine e ricotta

Crêpes
- 1 2/3 cups (250 g) all-purpose (plain) flour
- 2 cups (500 ml) milk
- 4 large eggs
- 1 tablespoon finely chopped thyme
- 1 tablespoon finely chopped parsley
- 1/4 teaspoon salt
- 1 tablespoon butter

Ricotta Filling
- 3 medium zucchini (courgettes), sliced
- 2 tablespoons butter
- 24 zucchini (courgette) flowers, carefully washed
- 14 oz (400 g) fresh ricotta cheese, drained
- 1/2 cup (60 g) pine nuts, toasted
- 1/4 teaspoon freshly ground nutmeg
- 1 1/4 cups (300 ml) heavy (double) cream
- 4 tablespoons freshly grated Parmesan cheese

Crêpes: Mix the flour and milk in a large bowl. Add the eggs, thyme, and parsley and beat well. Season with salt. • Melt the butter in a small frying pan over medium heat. • Pour in just enough batter to cover the pan, tilting it so that it thinly covers the bottom. • Cook until the crêpe is pale gold on the underside. Use a large spatula to flip and cook the other side. Repeat until all the batter is cooked. Stack the cooked crêpes one on top of another in a warm oven. • Preheat the oven to 400°F (200°C/gas 6). • Butter a large baking dish. • Ricotta Filling: Sauté the zucchini in the butter in a large frying pan over medium heat until softened, 10 minutes. • Add the zucchini flowers, ricotta, pine nuts, and nutmeg. Simmer for 3 minutes. • Place 2–3 tablespoons of filling in the center of each crêpe. Fold the crêpes in half and then in half again to form triangles. • Arrange the filled crêpes in the baking dish. • Pour the cream over the top and sprinkle with Parmesan. • Cover with aluminum foil and bake for 10 minutes. Remove the foil and bake until the crêpes are golden brown, 8–10 minutes.

Serves: 4–6 · Prep: 45 min · Cooking: 35 min · Level: 2

Crabmeat omelet

Frittata al granchio

- 1/2 cup (75 g) all-purpose (plain) flour
- 14 oz (400 g) crabmeat, diced
- 1/4 cup (60 ml) extra-virgin olive oil
- 8 large eggs
- salt and freshly ground black pepper

Lightly flour the crab meat. Heat half the oil in a medium frying pan and sauté the crabmeat for 4–5 minutes. • Beat the eggs with the salt and pepper in a bowl then add the crabmeat and mix well. • Heat the remaining oil in the same frying pan and pour in the egg mixture. Cook for 4–5 minutes. • Turn the omelet carefully and cook for 4 minutes more. It should be firm and lightly browned on both sides. • Serve hot.

Serves: 4 • Prep: 10 min • Cooking: 15 min • Level: 1

Onion and pecorino frittata

Frittata di cipolle e Pecorino

- 8 small onions, thinly sliced
- 3 tablespoons extra-virgin olive oil
- 8 large eggs
- 5 oz (150 g) mature pecorino cheese, cut into flakes
- 1 tablespoon torn basil
- salt to taste
- 1 tablespoon finely chopped parsley

Sauté the onions with the oil in a large frying pan over medium heat for 5 minutes. • Beat the eggs in a medium bowl until frothy. Stir in the pecorino, basil, and salt. • Pour the egg mixture into the pan and cook until set on top, about 5 minutes. • Turn the frittata carefully and cook for 4 minutes more. It should be firm and lightly browned on both sides. • Sprinkle with the parsley and serve hot.

Serves: 4–6 • Prep: 15 min • Cooking: 15 min • Level: 1

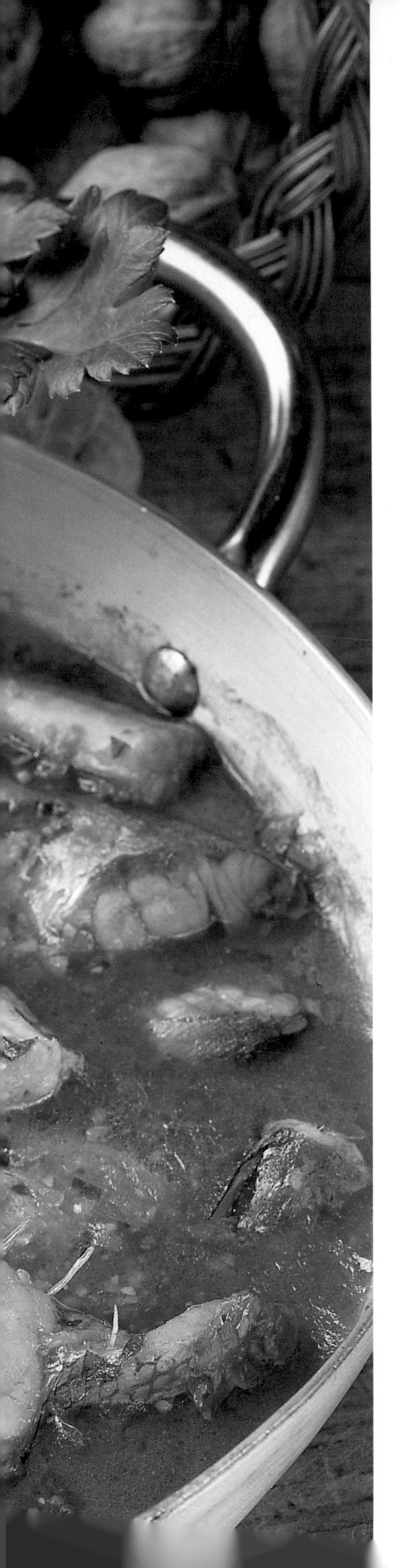

SEAFOOD

The long thin Italian peninsula stretches down into the Mediterranean and is surrounded on every side by the sea. This proximity means that fish and seafood have always played an important role in Italian cooking styles. Large and vibrant fish markets are held every morning in many Italian sea towns (try to visit the one under the Rialto Bridge in Venice, or the seafood section in the huge Vucciria market in Palermo) where local housewives mingle with restaurant owners in search of perfect seafood. Much of the success of your seafood dish will depend on the quality of the fish you buy. Absolute freshness is the most essential quality; really fresh fish has very little odor, so hold it to your nose and smell it before you buy it!

Ligurian fish stew (see page 260)

Crusty baked cod with carrots

Fresh tuna with oregano

Tonno all'origano

- 1 (14-oz/400-g) can tomatoes, with juice
- 1 clove garlic, finely chopped
- 1 tablespoon salt-cured capers, rinsed
- 1 teaspoon dried oregano
- salt and freshly ground black pepper
- 4 slices of very fresh tuna, about 6 oz (180 g) each, preferably taken from the belly of the fish
- 1/3 cup (90 ml) extra-virgin olive oil

Preheat the oven to 350°F (180°C/gas 4). • Place the tomatoes in a mixing bowl with the garlic, capers, oregano, a little salt, and a generous sprinkling of pepper. • Rinse the tuna and dry with paper towels. • Pour just over half the oil into a large ovenproof dish and arrange the tuna slices in a single layer. • Cover with the tomato mixture and drizzle with the remaining oil. • Bake until tender, about 30 minutes. • Serve hot.

Serves: 4 • Prep: 10 min • Cooking: 30 min • Level: 1

Crusty baked cod with carrots

Merluzzo agli aromi e senape con carote

Preheat the oven to 400°F (200°C/gas 6). • Blanch the carrots in a large pot of boiling water for 3 minutes. Drain and arrange in an oiled baking dish. Drizzle with 2 tablespoons of the oil. • Place the bread, parsley, garlic, and mustard in the bowl of a food processor. Blend until finely chopped. • Add 1/4 cup (60 ml) of the remaining oil and mix well. Season with salt and pepper. • Brush the cod with oil and dip it in the bread mixture, ensuring that each piece is evenly coated. • Arrange the coated cod on the bed of carrots. Drizzle with the remaining oil and bake until the fish is cooked through and the coating is lightly browned, 10–15 minutes. • Garnish with parsley and serve hot.

Serves: 4 • Prep: 15 min • Cooking: 15 min • Level: 1

- 6 large carrots, sliced
- 1/2 cup (125 ml) extra-virgin olive oil
- 2 large slices day-old bread, crumbled
- 2 tablespoons finely chopped parsley
- 1 clove garlic, finely chopped
- 1 teaspoon wholegrain mustard
- salt and freshly ground black pepper
- 2 lb (1 kg) cod fillets

Grouper with pesto

Cernia con il pesto

- 2 quantities pesto (see page 130)
- 4 large grouper steaks, about 8 oz (250 g) each
- 4 salt-cured anchovy fillets
- 3 tablespoons extra-virgin olive oil
- 2 large tomatoes, peeled and chopped
- salt and freshly ground black pepper

Prepare the pesto. • Rinse the grouper steaks under cold running water and dry with paper towels. • Heat a broiler (grill) to very hot and broil the grouper until tender, about 5 minutes each side. Place in a warm oven. • Crush the anchovies with the back of a fork. • Heat the oil in a heavy-bottomed saucepan and add the tomatoes and anchovies. Simmer over medium heat for 10 minutes. • Add the basil sauce to the pan and heat, without letting it boil. • Pour the sauce over the grouper steaks and serve at once.

Serves: 4 • Prep: 10 min • Cooking: 20 min • Level: 1

Broiled swordfish with lemon sauce

Pesce spada al limone

Pour about half the oil into a small blender and gradually add the hot water and lemon juice, processing continuously as you do so. (Alternatively, place the oil in a small, heatproof bowl and gradually beat in the water and juice with a balloon whisk, adding a little at a time). • Stir in the parsley, garlic, oregano, salt, and pepper. • Place the bowl over a pan of boiling water to heat for 3–4 minutes before serving. • Coat the swordfish steaks with the remaining oil and broil (grill) or barbecue them until tender, 4–5 minutes each side. • Serve hot with the sauce.

Serves: 4 • Prep: 10 min • Cooking: 8–10 min • Level: 1

- 2/3 cup (150 ml) extra-virgin olive oil
- 1/4 cup (60 ml) hot water
- 1/3 cup (90 ml) freshly squeezed lemon juice
- 1 tablespoon finely chopped parsley
- 1 clove garlic, finely chopped
- 1 tablespoon finely chopped oregano
- salt and freshly ground black pepper
- 4 steaks or slices swordfish, about 6 oz (180 g) each, preferably taken from the belly of the fish

Gilthead sea bream with spinach

Gilthead sea bream Puglia-style

Orata alla pugliese

- 2 lb (1 kg) gilthead sea bream fillets
- 1/2 cup (125 ml) extra-virgin olive oil
- juice of 1 large lemon
- 1 tablespoon each finely chopped parsley, thyme, sage, bay leaves
- 4 cloves garlic, finely chopped
- salt and freshly ground white pepper
- 4 slices firm-textured bread, toasted

Gilthead sea bream is a delicately-flavored fish found in the Mediterranean and the temperate areas of the Atlantic Ocean. If not available, replace with another mild, sweet fish with firm texture.

Place the fillets in a deep-sided dish and pour in the oil and lemon juice. Sprinkle with the parsley, thyme, sage, bay leaves, garlic, salt, and pepper. Marinate for 1 hour. • Broil (grill) the fillets on both sides until tender, 4–5 minutes each side, basting frequently with the marinade. • Arrange the toast on a heated serving platter and cover with the fillets. Spoon a little of the marinade over the top and serve hot.

Serves: 4 • Prep: 10 min + 1 hr to marinate • Cooking: 10 min • Level: 1

Rustic gilthead sea bream

Orate alla buona massaia

- 1 tablespoon extra virgin olive oil
- 1/4 cup (60 g) butter
- 2 salt-cured anchovies, rinsed and chopped
- 1 large onion, finely chopped
- 4 tablespoons finely chopped parsley
- 2 sage leaves, finely chopped
- 12 oz (350 g) white mushrooms, chopped
- 1/2 cup (125 ml) dry white wine
- salt and freshly ground black pepper
- 2 tablespoons all-purpose (plain) flour
- 2 large gilthead sea bream, gutted
- 1 clove garlic, crushed
- juice of 1 lemon

Heat the oil and half the butter in a large saucepan over medium heat. Add the anchovies and onion. Sauté, mashing the anchovies with a fork, until they have broken down and the onion is transparent, 3–4 minutes. • Add the parsley, sage, and mushrooms. Sauté for 2 minutes. • Add the white wine and season with salt and pepper. • Put the flour on a plate. Dredge the fish in the flour, ensuring that it is evenly coated. Shake gently to remove any excess flour. • Add the fish to the pan and simmer until cooked through and the sauce is reduced, 5–7 minutes each side. • Place the fish in a heated serving dish. • Add the garlic, remaining butter, and lemon juice to the pan and mix well. Bring to a boil. • Spoon over the fish. Garnish with parsley and serve hot.

Serves: 4 • Prep: 10 min • Cooking: 25 min • Level: 2

Salt-baked gilthead sea bream

Orata al sale

- 2 large gilthead sea bream, gutted
- 5 lb (2.5 kg) coarse sea salt

Many different kinds of fish can be cooked in this way. Try striped bass, red snapper, rockfish, tilefish, and grouper.

Preheat the oven to 400°F (200°C/gas 6). • Rinse the gutted fish without removing the scales, gills, or fins. Dry with paper towels. • Put half the salt into the bottom of a (preferably earthenware) roasting pan into which the fish will fit snugly. Put the fish on top and cover with the remaining salt. The fish should be completely covered—adjust the quantity of salt as required. • Bake for 30 minutes. • Serve the fish directly from the roasting pan, breaking the crust at the table. Peel off the skin, spoon the fish off the bone, and serve hot.

Serves: 6 • Prep: 10 min • Cooking: 30 min • Level: 1

Gilthead sea bream with spinach

Orata agli spinaci

- 2 gilthead sea bream, 1 1/2 lb (750 g) each
- 1 onion, chopped
- 2 cloves garlic, sliced
- 2 tablespoons finely chopped parsley
- 1/4 teaspoon freshly grated nutmeg
- salt and freshly ground black pepper
- 1/2 cup (125 ml) dry white wine
- 1/2 cup (125 ml) extra-virgin olive oil
- 4 tablespoons golden raisins (sultanas)
- 1 1/2 lb (750 g) spinach
- 1/4 cup (60 g) butter
- 2 tablespoons pine nuts
- 4 salt-cured anchovy fillets

Place the gutted fish in a large saucepan. • Cover with the onion, garlic, parsley, nutmeg, salt, and pepper. Pour in the wine and half the oil. Turn the fish in the marinade a few times. Marinate for 2 hours. • Place the golden raisins in a small bowl and cover with warm water. Soak for 15 minutes. • Cook the spinach in a little salted water until tender, about 5 minutes. Drain and chop finely. • Place the pan with the fish and marinade over medium heat. Bring to a boil and simmer until tender, about 20 minutes. Turn once, half way through the cooking time. • Drain the liquid from the fish. Cover with half the butter and place in a warm oven. • Strain the cooking liquid. Return to the pan with the anchovies and simmer until the anchovies have dissolved. Add the spinach and drained golden raisins. Serve hot with the fish .

Serves: 4 • Prep: 15 min • Cooking: 30 min • Level: 1

Sea bass with vegetable sauce

Sea bass with vegetable sauce

Branzino alla salsa

- 2 lb (1 kg) potatoes, peeled
- 1 sea bass, weighing about 2 lb (1 kg), gutted
- 1 large onion, sliced
- 2 large ripe tomatoes, sliced
- 1/2 teaspoon dried oregano
- salt and freshly ground black pepper
- 1 bay leaf
- 4 tablespoons freshly chopped parsley
- 4 basil leaves, torn
- 2 cloves garlic, lightly crushed but whole
- 1/2 oz (15 g) dried mushrooms, soaked in warm water for 15 minutes, drained, and chopped
- 1/2 cup (125 m)l dry white wine
- 1/3 cup (90 ml) water
- 2 tablespoons all-purpose (plain) flour
- 2/3 cup (150 ml) heavy (double) cream
- 2 tablespoons butter

Boil the potatoes in a large pot of salted water until tender, about 25 minutes. • Cut the fish into 1-inch (3-cm) sections. • Preheat the oven to 375°F (190°C/gas 5). • Place the onion and tomatoes in a large oval baking dish. Top with the fish, including the head and tail. Sprinkle with oregano and season with salt and pepper. Add the bay leaf, parsley, basil, garlic, mushrooms, wine, and water. • Bake until the fish is cooked through, about 20 minutes. • Spoon the vegetables onto a heated serving dish. Place the fish on top, arranging it carefully so that it keeps its fish shape on the dish. • Beat the flour and cream in a small bowl. • Filter the cooking juices through a fine mesh strainer into a small saucepan. You should have about 1 cup (250 ml) of filtered liquid. • Add the cream mixture to the saucepan with the filtered cooking juices. Mix well and simmer over low heat, stirring constantly, until the sauce thickens, 3–4 minutes. Remove from the heat and add the butter. Mix well and check the seasoning. • Drizzle the sauce over the fish. Serve with hot with the potatoes.

Serves: 4 • Prep: 20 min • Cooking: 30 min • Level: 2

Roasted sea bass

Branzino al cartoccio

Preheat the oven to 400°C (200°F/gas 6). • Rinse the fish carefully under cold running water and pat dry with paper towels. • Mix the rosemary, parsley, and garlic in a small bowl. Season with salt and pepper. • Stuff the fish with the herb mixture. • Arrange the lemon slices along the opening in the fish. Season with salt and pepper. • Place the fish in a sheet of aluminum foil and transfer to a baking dish. Drizzle with the olive oil and fold the foil over the fish. • Bake until the fish is tender, 15–20 minutes. • Serve hot.

Serves: 4 • Prep: 15 min • Cooking: 25 min • Level: 1

- 1 sea bass, about 2 lb (1 kg), cleaned and gutted
- 1 tablespoon finely chopped rosemary
- 1 tablespoon finely chopped parsley
- 2 cloves garlic, lightly crushed
- 1/2 lemon, thinly sliced
- salt and freshly ground black pepper
- 1/4 cup (60 ml) extra-virgin olive oil

Sole meunière

Sogliola alla mugnaia

Lightly flour the sole fillets. • Heat the butter with the oil in a large frying pan (you may need two pans to cook them all at once) and fry the fillets for 3 minutes each side, turning carefully with a broad spatula as they can break easily. • Season lightly with salt and pepper. • Add the lemon juice and wine and cook for 3 more minutes. • Turn the sole in the cooking juices, sprinkle with parsley, and transfer to a heated serving platter. • Pour the cooking juices over the top and serve hot.

Serves: 6 • Prep: 25 min • Cooking: 10 min • Level: 2

- 1 cup (150 g) all-purpose (plain) flour
- 6 sole fillets, about 8 oz (250 g) each
- 2 tablespoons butter
- 1/4 cup (60 ml) extra-virgin olive oil
- salt and freshly ground black pepper
- juice of 2 lemons
- 1/2 cup (125 ml) dry white wine
- 2 tablespoons finely chopped parsley

Stuffed sardine rolls

Stuffed sardine rolls

Sardi a beccaficu

- $1\frac{1}{2}$ lb (750 g) fresh large sardines
- $\frac{1}{2}$ cup (125 ml) extra-virgin olive oil
- $1\frac{3}{4}$ cups (100 g) fresh bread crumbs
- 8–10 salt-cured anchovy fillets
- 3 tablespoons golden raisins (sultanas), soaked and drained
- 3 tablespoons pine nuts
- 1 tablespoon capers
- 6 large black olives, pitted and chopped
- 1 tablespoon finely chopped parsley
- 1 tablespoon freshly squeezed lemon juice
- grated zest of $\frac{1}{2}$ lemon
- 1 teaspoon sugar
- salt and freshly ground black pepper
- bay leaves

Preheat the oven to 400°F (200°C/gas 6). • Scale the sardines and remove the heads and viscera. Use kitchen scissors to slit them along their bellies, remove the bones, and open them out flat. Rinse and dry with paper towels. • Heat $\frac{1}{4}$ cup (60 ml) of the oil in a large frying pan over medium heat and add two-thirds of the bread crumbs. Stir for 1–2 minutes, then set aside in a bowl. • Pour 1 tablespoon of fresh oil into the pan and add the anchovies, crushing them with a fork over low heat so that they turn into a paste. • Stir into the bread crumbs, followed by the raisins, pine nuts, capers, olives, parsley, lemon juice and zest, sugar, a little salt, and a generous sprinkling of pepper. Mix well. • Lay the sardines out flat, skin side downward, and spread some of the mixture on each one. • Roll the sardines up, starting at the head end, and place in an oiled baking dish. Pack them closely together, tail downward, and wedge a bay leaf between each one. • Sprinkle with the remaining bread crumbs and drizzle with the remaining oil. • Bake for 20–25 minutes. • Serve hot or at room temperature.

Serves: 4 • Prep: 30 min • Cooking: 25 min • Level: 1

Sardines in sweet and sour marinade

Sardelle in Saor

- 2 lb (1 kg) very fresh sardines
- $\frac{2}{3}$ cup (100 g) all-purpose (plain) flour
- 1 cup (250 ml) olive oil, for frying
- salt
- $1\frac{1}{2}$ lb (750 g) white onions, thinly sliced
- $\frac{1}{2}$ cup (125 ml) extra-virgin olive oil
- $1\frac{1}{4}$ cups (310 ml) white wine vinegar

Carefully remove the scales from the sardines, take off their heads, then cut down the middle of their bellies and eviscerate (gut) them. Dust lightly with flour. • Heat the frying oil in a large frying pan until very hot. Fry the fish in small batches until golden brown. • Drain well on paper towels and season with salt. • Remove the pan from the heat, let cool slightly, and then carefully pour off the oil into a heatproof receptacle. • Sauté the onions in the extra-virgin olive oil in the same pan until pale golden brown, 5 minutes. • Pour in the vinegar and let it reduce by half. • Arrange the sardines and onions in layers in a baking dish, finishing with a layer of onions. Pour the liquid over the top. • Refrigerate for 24 hours before serving.

Serves: 6 • Prep: 20 min + 24 hr to marinate • Cooking: 20 min • Level: 1

Leghorn mullet

Triglie alla Livornese

- 8 mullet, about $1\frac{1}{2}$ lb (750 g), cleaned and gutted
- salt and freshly ground black pepper
- $\frac{1}{2}$ cup (75 g) all-purpose (plain) flour
- $\frac{1}{4}$ cup (60 ml) extra-virgin olive oil
- 2 cloves garlic, finely chopped
- 1 stalk celery, finely chopped
- 2 tablespoons finely chopped parsley
- 1 (14-oz/400-g) can tomatoes, with juice

Sprinkle the fish with salt and pepper and dredge in the flour. • Heat half the oil in a large, heavy-bottomed saucepan and cook the fish for 5 minutes on each side. Remove from the pan and set aside in a warm oven. • Clean the pan and heat the remaining oil in it. Sauté the garlic, celery, and half the parsley for 4–5 minutes, then add the tomatoes. Simmer over medium heat for 15 minutes. • Place the mullet on a heated serving dish and spoon the tomato sauce over the top. Sprinkle with the remaining parsley and serve hot.

Serves: 4 • Prep: 15 min • Cooking: 35 min • Level: 1

Mixed deep-fried fish

Mini seafood kebabs

Spiedini alla marinara

- 8 small squid, cleaned
- 1 swordfish steak, about 8 oz (250 g)
- 8 jumbo shrimp (king prawns)
- 2 cloves garlic, finely sliced
- 1/4 cup (60 ml) dry white wine
- 1/4 cup (60 ml) extra-virgin olive oil
- salt and freshly ground black pepper
- 4 oz (125 g) mixed salad greens
- 1 tablespoon finely chopped parsley

Remove the tentacles from the squid, reserving them. • Skin the swordfish and remove the bone. Cut into 8 bite-size pieces. • Shell the shrimp and wash them carefully. • Thread the seafood onto the skewers alternating 2 pieces of swordfish, 2 shrimp, 2 pieces of squid tentacle, and 2 squid on each skewer. • Arrange the kebabs in a dish and sprinkle with the garlic. • Drizzle with the wine and 1 tablespoon of the oil. Season with salt and pepper. • Let the kebabs marinade for 30 minutes in the fridge. • Preheat the broiler (grill) on a medium setting. Drizzle the kebabs with the remaining oil and broil for 5 minutes. • Turn them over and broil for another 5 minutes. Arrange the salad on serving dishes. • Transfer the kebabs to the serving dishes and sprinkle with the parsley. • Serve hot.

Serves: 2–4 • Prep: 35 min + 30 min to marinate • Cooking: 10 min • Level: 2

Mixed grilled seafood

Grigliata mista di pesce

Grill the seafood outdoors on your barbecue. Be sure to buy only the freshest fish; the best way to tell if it is fresh is by smelling it. Very fresh fish and seafood has almost no odor.

- 4 fillets fresh sole, about 5 oz (150 g) each
- 8 large fresh shrimp (prawn) tails
- 4 fillets monkfish
- 8 medium squid, cleaned
- 1/4 cup (60 ml) extra-virgin olive oil
- 1/4 cup fine dry bread crumbs
- 2 tablespoons finely chopped parsley
- salt and freshly ground black pepper
- 1 lemon, cut in wedges

Rinse the seafood carefully in cold running water and dry with paper towels. • Place the sole, shrimp, monkfish, and squid on a large tray and drizzle with half the oil. Sprinkle with the bread crumbs. • Grill over the glowing embers of a barbecue for 10 minutes, basting often with a basting brush dipped in the remaining oil. Turn the seafood and cook the other sides, basting frequently. • When the fish is tender and well cooked, place on a large heated serving platter. Sprinkle with the parsley, season with salt and pepper, and arrange the lemon wedges around the edges.

Serves: 4 • Prep: 20 min • Cooking: 20 min • Level: 2

Mixed deep-fried seafood

Fritto misto

- 14 oz (450 g) calamari, cleaned
- 14 oz (450 g) shrimp
- 12 oz (350 g) baby cuttlefish
- 2 cups (300 g) all-purpose (plain) flour
- 4 cups (1 liter) olive oil, for frying
- salt
- 1 lemon, cut into wedges

Cut the calamari bodies into rings and leave the tentacles whole. • Do not shell the shrimp. • Sprinkle the flour in a large dish and dredge all the seafood in it, shaking off the excess. Place the floured fish on a large sheet of aluminum foil laid on a work surface or in a tray or platter. • Heat the oil in a deep fryer to very hot. Deep-fry the fish in batches until golden brown all over. Drain well and pat dry with paper towels. • Season with salt lightly and transfer to a serving plate. Decorate with the wedges of lemon. • Serve hot.

Serves: 4 • Prep: 20 min • Cooking: 20–25 min • Level: 2

Stuffed squid with tomato

Seppie ripiene al pomodoro

- 3 lb (1.5 kg) starchy potatoes, peeled
- 2 large eggs, lightly beaten
- 1 cup (125 g) fine dry bread crumbs
- 1 cup (125 g) freshly grated pecorino or Parmesan cheese
- 3 cloves garlic, finely chopped
- 3 tablespoons finely chopped parsley
- salt and freshly ground black pepper
- 6 medium squid, cleaned
- 1/4 cup (60 ml) extra-virgin olive oil
- 1 (14-oz/400-g) cam tomatoes, with juice

Cook the potatoes in a large pot of salted boiling water until tender, 20–25 minutes. Drain well and mash until smooth. • Place the potato purée in a large bowl. Add the eggs, bread crumbs, cheese, 1 clove of garlic, and the parsley. Season with salt and pepper. Mix well. • Spoon the stuffing into the squid. Secure each one using a cocktail stick. • Heat the oil in a large frying pan over medium heat. Add the garlic and sauté until pale golden brown, 2–3 minutes. • Add the tomatoes and season with salt and pepper. Mix well and then add the stuffed squid. Simmer, turning the squid from time to time, until tender, about 35 minutes. Prick with a toothpick to see if they are ready—it should penetrate easily. • Place in a heated serving dish. • Spoon the sauce over the squid. Serve hot.

Serves: 4–6 • Prep: 20 min • Cooking: 1 hr • Level: 2

Liguria stuffed squid

Totani ripieni alla Ligure

- 2 lb (1 kg) medium-sized squid, cleaned
- 1/4 cup (60 ml) extra-virgin olive oil
- 1/4 cup (60 g) butter
- 2 cloves garlic, chopped
- 2 tablespoons finely chopped parsley
- 1 large onion, finely chopped
- 1 large carrot, finely chopped
- 2 stalks celery, finely chopped
- 4 oz (125 g) prosciutto (Parma ham), cut into small cubes
- leaves from 3 sprigs basil, chopped
- 1 tablespoon Marsala wine
- 1 tablespoon cognac or brandy
- 2 large eggs
- generous 3/4 cup(100 g) freshly grated parmesan cheese
- 2 tablespoons milk
- 2 cups (120 g) fresh bread crumbs
- salt and freshly ground black pepper
- 1/2 cup (125 ml) dry white wine
- boiled rice, to serve

Clean the squid. Remove and discard the eyes, hard part, and the ink sac. Wash well. Chop the tentacles. • Heat half the oil and half the butter in a large Dutch oven or earthenware dish over medium heat. Add the garlic, parsley, half the onion, half the carrot, half the celery, the prosciutto, and basil. Sauté until the vegetables are very tender and have begun to break down, 15 minutes. • Add the Marsala and cognac and simmer for 3 minutes. • Remove from the heat and purée in a blender. Do not wash the pan. • Beat the eggs and Parmesan in a bowl. • Drizzle the milk over the bread crumbs to moisten. Mix the purée, bread crumbs, chopped tentacles, and eggs in a large bowl. Season with salt and pepper. • Fill the squid with this mixture and close the opening with a needle and thread. • Heat the remaining oil and butter in the pan you used before over a medium heat. Sauté the remaining onion, carrot, and celery until softened, 5 minutes. • Preheat the oven to 350°F (180°C/gas 4). • Arrange the stuffed squid in the casserole and cook over medium heat for 2–3 minutes. Add the wine and simmer for 20 minutes. • Place in the oven and bake for 40 minutes. • Serve hot with boiled rice.

Serves: 6 • Prep: 45 min • Cooking: 80 min • Level: 3

Stuffed mussels

MUSSEL WITH TOMATOES

Cozze al pomodoro

- 3 lb (1.5 kg) mussels, in shell
- 4 medium tomatoes, peeled and chopped
- 3 tablespoons finely chopped parsley
- 3 cloves garlic, finely chopped
- 1/4 cup (60 ml) extra-virgin olive oil
- salt and freshly ground black pepper
- 4 large, thick slices bread, toasted and, if liked, rubbed with garlic

Soak the mussels in cold water for 1 hour. • Scrub the mussels thoroughly, removing any beards and discarding broken shells. Rinse well. • Sauté the tomatoes, 2 tablespoons of parsley, and 2 cloves of garlic in the oil in a large frying pan over medium heat for 2–3 minutes. Add the mussels and cook until they open up. Discard any that do not open. • Sprinkle with the remaining parsley and garlic. Season with salt and pepper and cook for 4–5 minutes more. • Arrange the toasted bread in individual serving dishes and spoon the mussels and the cooking juices over the top. • Serve hot.

Serves: 4 • Prep: 10 min + 1 hr to soak • Cooking: 10 min Level: 1

STUFFED MUSSELS

Cozze alla Metapontina

- 2 lb (1 kg) mussels, in shell
- 3 large ripe tomatoes
- 1/2 cup (125 ml) extra virgin olive oil
- 2 cups (120 g) fresh bread crumbs
- 2 cloves garlic, finely chopped
- 3 tablespoons finely chopped parsley
- 1/2 cup (60 g) freshly grated pecorino or Parmesan cheese
- salt and freshly ground black pepper
- sprigs of parsley, to garnish

Soak the mussels in cold water for 1 hour. • Preheat the oven to 425°F (220°C/gas 7). Scrub the mussels and shuck with a sharp knife. Remove and discard the empty half of each shell. • Arrange the mussels on an oiled baking sheet. • Blanch the tomatoes in boiling water for 2 minutes. Drain and peel. Chop the peeled tomatoes. • Heat half the oil in a large frying pan over medium heat. Add the tomatoes and sauté until they begin to break down, about 10 minutes. • Add the bread crumbs, garlic, parsley, and pecorino. Season with salt and pepper and mix well. • Spoon a little of the filling into each of the mussel shells. Drizzle with the remaining oil and bake until cooked through and browned, 12–15 minutes. • Garnish with parsley and serve hot or at room temperature.

Serves: 4 • Prep: 20 min • Cooking: 20 min • Level: 1

SPICY MUSSEL STEW

Pepata di cozze

- 2 lb (1 kg) mussels, in shell
- 1/4 cup (60 ml) extra-virgin olive oil
- 2 cloves garlic
- 1/2 cup (125 ml) dry white wine
- salt
- 2 teaspoons freshly ground black pepper
- juice of 1 lemon

Soak the mussels in cold water for 1 hour. • Scrub the mussels thoroughly, removing any beards and discarding broken shells. Rinse well. • Heat the oil in a large frying pan and sauté the garlic for 1 minute. Add the mussels and increase the heat. • Season with the salt and pepper and moisten with the wine. • Cover and cook until all the mussels have opened, 7–10 minutes. Discard any that have not opened. • Turn off the heat, pour away some of the liquid, if it is excessive, and drizzle with the lemon juice. • Mix well and serve immediately.

Serves: 4 • Prep: 30 min • Cooking: 10 min • Level: 1

CLAMS WITH WHITE WINE

Vongole al vino bianco

- 4 lb (2 kg) fresh clams, in shell
- 3/4 cup (200 ml) extra-virgin olive oil
- 2 medium onions, finely chopped
- 1 cup (250 ml) dry while wine
- 1/4 cup (60 ml) boiling water
- salt and freshly ground black pepper
- 2 tablespoons finely chopped parsley
- 1 clove garlic, finely chopped (optional)

Soak the clams in cold water for 1 hour. Rinse thoroughly in cold running water. • Heat the oil in a large frying pan and sauté the onions until light gold. • Add the clams, followed by the wine and then the water. Season with salt and pepper. Cover tightly and simmer over low heat for 10 minutes. • By this time the clams should have opened. Discard any that have not opened. • Sprinkle with parsley and garlic, if using, and serve hot.

Serves: 6 • Prep: 20 min + 1 hr to soak • Cooking: 15 min Level: 1

Octopus with potatoes and green beans

Tuscan fish stew

Cacciucco

- 4 lb (2 kg) mixed fish, such as smooth hound, stargazer, eel, scorpion fish, and gurnard
- ½ onion, finely chopped
- 1 carrot, finely chopped
- 1 stalk celery, finely chopped
- 1 sprig parsley, finely chopped
- 4 cloves garlic
- 1 red chile pepper, thinly sliced
- ⅔ cup (150 ml) extra-virgin olive oil
- salt and freshly ground black pepper to taste
- 1 lb (500 g) octopus and squid, cleaned and coarsely chopped
- ½ cup (125 ml) dry white wine
- 2 lb (1 kg) ripe tomatoes, peeled and chopped
- 12 jumbo shrimp (king prawn) tails, shelled
- 6 slices firm-textured bread, toasted

Clean the large fish and remove the heads. Set them aside for later. Leave the smaller fish whole but clean inside. • Sauté the onion, carrot, celery, parsley, 3 cloves of garlic, and chile pepper in the oil in a large saucepan over medium heat until the garlic is lightly golden. Season with salt and pepper. • Add the octopus and squid and cook over high heat until any liquid has evaporated. • Pour in the wine and let it evaporate. • Stir in the tomatoes. Cover and cook for 10 minutes. • Remove the octopus and squid and set aside. Add the reserved fish heads and the smaller whole fish. Cook for 25 minutes, adding a little hot water if the sauce starts to dry out and stick to the bottom of the pan. • Remove the fish and set aside. • Transfer the sauce to a food processor and process until purèed. Return the sauce to the pan and add all the fish, cut into pieces. Simmer over low heat for 15 minutes, add a little water if necessary. • Put the octopus and squid back in the pan and add the shrimp. Bring to a boil and simmer for about 30 minutes. • Serve the soup in bowls, with hot *bruschette* (toasted bread rubbed with garlic).

Serves: 6 • Prep: 50 min • Cooking: 1 hr 30 min • Level: 3

Ligurian fish stew

Buridda

- 1 tablespoon dried mushrooms, soaked in warm water for 15 minutes and drained
- 2 salt-cured anchovy fillets, rinsed and chopped
- 6 walnuts, chopped
- ⅓ cup (90 ml) dry white wine
- 2 tablespoons extra-virgin olive oil
- 1 clove garlic, lightly crushed but whole
- 1 large onion, finely chopped
- 2 tablespoons finely chopped parsley
- 1 ripe tomato, peeled, deseeded, and chopped
- 2 lb (1 kg) mixed fish, such as monk fish and halibut, cleaned, skinned, and cut into pieces
- salt
- freshly baked bread, to serve

Crush the mushrooms, anchovy, and walnuts with a mortar and pestle to make a smooth paste. • Add the wine and mix well. • Heat the oil in a large saucepan over a medium heat. Add the garlic and sauté until softened, 3 minutes. • Discard the garlic. Add the onion and parsley to the pan and sauté until the onion is softened but not browned, 3 minutes. • Add the tomatoes and mushroom mixture. Mix well before adding the fish. • Add the fish beginning with the one with the firmest flesh which will require slightly longer to cook. • Simmer until the fish is cooked through, about 15 minutes. Season with salt and transfer to serving dishes. • Serve hot with freshly baked bread.

Serves: 4 • Prep: 10 min • Cooking: 25 min • Level: 1

Octopus with potatoes and green beans

Polpo con patate e fagiolini

- 3 lb (1.5 g) octopus, cleaned
- 1 onion
- 1 carrot
- 1 piece root ginger
- 1 sprig parsley
- 2 lb (1 kg) boiling potatoes, peeled and cut into bite size pieces
- 1 lb (500 g) green beans
- ⅓ cup (90 ml) extra-virgin olive oil
- 1 tablespoon finely chopped parsley
- 1 clove garlic, finely chopped
- salt and freshly ground black pepper

Place the octopus, onion, carrot, ginger, and sprig of parsley in a large pan and cover with water. Bring to a boil then simmer over medium-low heat until tender, about 1 hour. • Let the octopus cool in the cooking water for at least 3 hours; this will make it tender. • Cook the potatoes in a large pot of salted boiling water until tender, 25 minutes. Drain and set aside. • Cook the green beans in a large pot of salted boiling water until tender, about 8 minutes. • Drain well and set aside. • Heat the oil in a large frying pan or saucepan over medium heat. • Add the chopped parsley and garlic. Sautè until the garlic is pale gold and slightly softened, 2–3 minutes. Season with salt and pepper. • Add the green beans, potatoes, and octopus and toss well. • Transfer to a serving dish and serve hot or at room temperature.

Serves: 6 • Prep: 5 min • Cooking: 30 min • Level: 1

POULTRY

Chicken is a favorite meat in Italy. It is a common takeaway food, with rosticcerias and supermarkets offering whole grilled and spit roasted chickens ready to go at accessible prices. This is a much healthier option than the fried chicken fast food sold by international chains in many other parts of the world but mercifully still absent from most parts of Italy. In this chapter we have included more than a dozen recipes for preparing chicken at home, from the classic Hunter's chicken (see page 274), to Tuscan fried chicken (photograph left, see page 266 for recipe), and the wonderfully succulent Spring chicken roasted in sea salt (see page 265). In traditional Italian cooking, chicken was just one, often interchangeable, meat source from among the *animali da cortile* (small farmyard animals, such as chickens, rabbits, ducks, turkeys, geese, and guinea fowl). We have completed the chapter with a selection of recipes for these other meats.

Tuscan fried chicken (see page 266)

Lemon and herb roast chicken

Barbecued chicken

Pollo alla diavola

- 2 spring chickens, about 1½ lb (750 g) each, cleaned
- salt and freshly ground black pepper
- ½ cup (125 ml) extra-virgin olive oil

The Italian name for this dish, alla diavola, *means "the devil's way" and is a reference to how the chicken is barbecued over hot embers, just as some people believe sinners will be "barbecued" when they get to hell.*

Rinse the chickens under cold running water and dry with paper towels. • Place the chickens on their backs and, using a sharp knife, cut down the middle so that they can be opened out like a book but are still in one piece. • Sprinkle the chickens generously with salt and pepper. Heat 2 tablespoons of the oil in a large frying and brown the chickens on both sides over high heat. This will take 8–10 minutes. • Place the chickens on the barbecue (or under the broiler) and drizzle with a little more of the oil. Cook until tender, about 30 minutes, turning often and basting with oil as required. Sprinkle with more salt and pepper, if liked. • Serve hot.

Serves: 4–6 • Prep: 10 min • Cooking: 40 min • Level: 1

Lemon and herb roast chicken

Pollo arrosto al limone e alle erbe

- 1 chicken, about 3 lb (1.5 kg)
- salt and freshly ground black pepper
- 2–3 sprigs fresh thyme
- 5 slices prosciutto (Parma ham)
- 3 bay leaves
- ½ lemon + 12 lemon slices
- 1 tablespoon extra-virgin olive oil
- 3 sprigs tarragon
- 8 cloves garlic
- 1 tablespoon brandy

Preheat the oven to 400°F (200°C/gas 6). • Season the cavity of the chicken with salt and pepper. Place the thyme inside. Wrap the outside with the prosciutto and bay leaves and tie the legs against the body with kitchen string. • Season with salt and pepper and rub with half the lemon. Brush with the oil and cover the breast with a sheet of aluminum oil. • Place the chicken in a baking dish (it should fit snugly). • Bake for 20 minutes. • Discard the foil. Place the lemon slices, tarragon, and garlic on the chicken, tucking some under the slices of prosciutto. • Roast until the juices run clean, about 45 minutes, turning once or twice and basting with the cooking juices. • Remove the kitchen string and place in a warm oven. • Add the brandy to the cooking juices in the pan and simmer over low heat until it evaporates. • Serve the chicken hot with the sauce.

Serves: 4 • Prep: 30 min • Cooking: 1 hr 15 min • Level: 2

Chicken with fennel seeds

Pollo ai semi di finocchio

- 1 chicken, about 3 lb (1.5 kg)
- 3 oz (90 g) pancetta, finely chopped
- 2 cloves garlic, finely chopped
- 1 heaped teaspoon each, finely chopped fresh sage and rosemary
- 1 tablespoon finely chopped parsley
- 1 teaspoon fennel seeds
- ⅓ cup (90 ml) extra-virgin olive oil
- salt and freshly ground black pepper

Preheat the oven to 350°F (180°C/gas 4). • Rinse the chicken inside and out and dry with paper towels. • Mix the pancetta, garlic, sage, rosemary, parsley, fennel seeds, salt, and pepper in a small bowl and place in the cavity. Use a trussing needle and thread to sew up the opening. • Pour half the olive oil into a roasting pan, place the chicken in it and drizzle with the remaining oil. Season with salt and pepper. • Roast until the chicken is very tender, about 1 hour. • Serve hot.

Serves: 4 • Prep: 20 min • Cooking: 1 hr • Level: 1

Spring chicken roasted in sea salt

Pollo novello al sale

- 8 lb (4 kg) coarse sea salt
- 3 sprigs fresh sage
- 3 sprigs fresh rosemary
- 1 chicken, about 3 lb (1.5 kg)
- 1 clove garlic, whole

Preheat the oven to 375°F (190°C/gas 5.) • Spread 3 lb (1.5 kg) of coarse salt on the bottom of an attractive high-sided baking dish. • Tie the herbs together and insert, with the garlic, into the abdominal cavity of the chicken. • Place the chicken in the baking dish and cover with the remaining salt. No parts of the chicken should be visible. • Bake until the chicken is very tender, about 1 hour 30 minutes. • Bring to the table as is. Open the salt encrusted chicken just before serving.

Serves: 4 • Prep: 10 min • Cooking: 1 hr 30 min • Level: 1

Tuscan fried chicken

Pollo fritto alla toscana

- 3 lb (1.5 kg) chicken thighs
- 3 tablespoons finely chopped parsley
- juice of 1 large lemon
- 5 tablespoons extra-virgin olive oil
- salt and freshly ground black pepper
- 2 large eggs
- ½ cup (75 g) all-purpose (plain) flour
- 2 cups (500 ml) sunflower oil, for frying

If liked, dip the chicken into a bowl of fine dry bread crumbs after the egg. This is not strictly traditional but delicious all the same. You can also spice up the marinade by adding 1 tablespoon of French mustard or cognac or a few drops of either Worcestershire or Tabasco sauce.

Place the chicken in a large bowl and sprinkle with the parsley. Add the lemon juice and olive oil. Season with salt and pepper. Cover and let marinate for 2 hours. • Beat the eggs until frothy in a medium bowl. • Place the flour in a bowl. • Heat the sunflower oil to very hot in a deep frying pan or deep fryer over medium heat. • Drain the chicken from the marinade. • Dredge in the flour, ensuring that it is evenly coated. Shake to remove any excess flour. Dip each piece of chicken in the beaten egg. • Fry in two batches in the hot oil until cooked through and golden brown, about 15 minutes each batch. • Drain on paper towels • Serve hot.

Serves: 4–6 • Prep: 15 min + 2 hr to marinate the meat
Cooking: 30 min • Level: 1

Boiled chicken with anchovy sauce

Pollo lesso in salsa di acciughe

- 1 carrot, cut in 4
- 1 leek, cut in 4
- 1 stalk celery, chopped
- zest of 1 lemon
- 1 chicken, about (3 lb/1.5 kg)
- 3 sprigs rosemary
- 1 sprig thyme
- 1 sprig parsley
- 1 bay leaf
- ½ cup (125 ml) extra-virgin olive oil
- 2 cloves garlic, lightly crushed but whole
- 8 salt-cured anchovy fillets
- 1 tablespoon salt-cured capers, rinsed
- sprigs of parsley, to garnish
- 1 lemon, cut into wedges, to garnish

Bring 3 quarts (3 liters) of water to a boil in a large saucepan over medium heat. Add the carrot, leek, celery, and lemon zest. Add the chicken. • Tie a sprig of rosemary, the thyme, a sprig of parsley, and the bay leaf together with a piece of thread and add to the saucepan. • Cover and simmer until the chicken is tender, about 1 hour 30 minutes. • Heat the oil in a small frying pan over medium heat. Add the garlic and remaining rosemary and sauté until the garlic turns pale gold, 3–4 minutes. • Discard the garlic and rosemary. Add the anchovies and simmer for 5 minutes, mashing with a fork until they dissolve into the oil. • Add the capers and simmer for 5 minutes. • Drain the chicken, reserving the stock for another recipe. Discard the skin from the chicken and place the flesh on a serving dish. Drizzle with the sauce. Garnish with the remaining parsley and wedges of lemon. • Serve hot.

Serves: 4 • Prep: 20 min • Cooking: 1 hr 30 min • Level: 1

Roast chicken with orange

Pollo all'arancia

- 2 tablespoons orange marmalade
- 2 small chickens, about 3 lb (1.5 kg) in total combined weight
- salt and freshly ground black pepper
- ¼ cup (60 ml) extra virgin olive oil
- freshly grated zest of 3 oranges
- freshly squeezed juice of 6 large oranges
- zest of 1 orange, cut into julienne strips, to garnish

Spread 1 tablespoon of the marmalade in the cavity of each chicken. Sprinkle each chicken with salt and pepper. • Heat the oil in a Dutch oven or heavy saucepan over medium-high heat. Add the orange zest. Add the chickens and sauté, turning so that they are sealed all over, about 10 minutes. • Add half the orange juice. Cover and simmer over very low heat until the meat is tender, about 2 hours. • Add the remaining orange juice gradually during the cooking time to keep the dish moist. • Transfer to a serving dish and drizzle with the cooking juices. Garnish with orange zest and serve hot.

Serves: 4–6 • Prep: 10 min • Cooking: 2 hr 10 min • Level: 2

Chicken scaloppine with lemon and cognac

Scaloppine di pollo al limone

- $1/2$ cup (75 g) all-purpose (plain) flour
- 2 skinless, boneless chicken breasts, thinly sliced
- $1/3$ cup (90 g) butter
- 2 oz (60 g) prosciutto (Parma ham), sliced into ribbons
- $1/3$ cup (90 ml) dry white wine
- 2 tablespoons cognac
- 4 tablespoons finely chopped parsley
- juice of 1 lemon
- pinch cayenne pepper
- salt

Place the flour on a plate. Dip the chicken in the flour, ensuring that each piece is evenly coated. Shake gently to remove any excess flour. • Melt half the butter in a large frying pan over medium-high heat. Add the prosciutto and sauté until crisp, about 2 minutes. • Add the chicken in a single layer (make sure the pieces don't overlap). Sauté until browned on both sides, about 5 minutes. • Add the wine and cognac and cook until evaporated, 4–5 minutes. • Add the parsley and lemon juice. Dust with cayenne pepper and season with salt. Simmer until the meat is cooked through, about 2 minutes. Transfer to a heated serving dish. • Remove the pan from the heat and add the remaining butter. Let the butter melt and mix well. Drizzle the sauce over the chicken and serve hot.

Serves: 4 • Prep: 10 min • Cooking: 15 min • Level: 2

Fricasséd chicken with parsley and lemon

Pollo in fricassea

- 2 tablespoons butter
- 3 tablespoons extra-virgin olive oil
- 2 tablespoons all-purpose flour
- $1\frac{1}{2}$ cups (375 ml) chicken stock, homemade (see page 104) or bouillon cube
- 1 carrot, cut in half lengthwise
- 1 stalk celery, cut in half lengthwise
- 4 sprigs parsley
- 1 onion, cut in quarters
- 1 chicken, about 3 lb (1.5 kg), cut into 6–8 pieces
- salt and freshly ground black pepper
- 3 egg yolks, lightly beaten
- juice of 1 lemon
- 2 tablespoons finely chopped parsley

Heat the butter and oil in a large, heavy-bottomed pan. Add the flour and simmer over low heat, stirring often, until it turns reddish-brown. • Add $2/3$ cup (180 ml) of the stock and, stirring constantly, bring the mixture to a boil. • Tie the pieces of carrot, celery, and the sprigs of parsley together and add to the pan with the onion. Simmer for 5 minutes, then add the chicken pieces. • Season with salt and pepper, then cover and simmer until the chicken is tender, about 30 minutes. Add more stock during cooking if the pan becomes dry. • When the chicken is tender, remove and discard the pieces of onion and the bunch of carrot, celery, and parsley. • Add the egg yolks, lemon juice, and parsley. Stir rapidly until the egg is cooked. Serve immediately.

Serves: 4 • Prep: 20 min • Cooking: 50 min • Level: 2

Chicken breast with cheese sauce

Filetti di pollo al formaggio

- $1/4$ cup (60 ml) extra-virgin olive oil
- 2 boneless skinless chicken breast, thinly sliced
- salt and freshly ground black pepper
- 6 oz (180 g) Fontina cheese, sliced
- 2 oz (60 g) ham, finely chopped
- $3/4$ cup (180 ml) milk

Heat the oil in a large frying pan over medium heat. Add the chicken and sauté until golden brown on both sides, about 5 minutes. Season with salt and pepper. • Cover each slice of chicken with slices of cheese and a sprinkling of ham. Carefully pour the milk over the top. • Simmer until the cheese has melted and the milk has reduced to a creamy sauce. • Serve hot.

Serves: 4 • Prep: 10 min • Cooking: 25 min • Level: 1

Grilled turkey breasts

Petti di tacchino grigliati

- 2 lb (1 kg) boneless skinless turkey breasts, cut in 12 slices
- $2/3$ cup (150 ml) extra-virgin olive oil
- $1/2$ cup (125 ml) white wine vinegar
- 4 cloves, crushed
- 2 cloves garlic, finely chopped
- 2 tablespoons finely chopped marjoram
- salt and freshly ground black pepper

Place the turkey in a bowl. Mix the oil, vinegar, cloves, garlic, marjoram, salt, and pepper together and pour over the turkey. Marinate in the refrigerator for at least 3 hours. • Cook the breasts under a broiler (grill) or over the hot embers of a barbecue. Baste with the marinade as they cook to stop them from drying out. Serve hot.

Serves: 6 • Prep: 10 min + 3 hr to marinate • Cooking: 15–20 min • Level: 1

Chicken with red wine

Pollo al vino

- 1 clove
- 1 clove garlic
- 1 stalk celery
- sprig of parsley
- sprig of basil
- 1 bay leaf
- 14 oz (400 g) pickling onions, peeled
- 3 tablespoons extra virgin olive oil
- 3 oz (90 g) pancetta
- 1 chicken, about 3 lb (1.5 kg), cut into 6–8 pieces
- 1/2 cup (75 g) all-purpose(plain) flour
- 1/4 cup (60 ml) cognac
- 2 cups (500 ml) Barolo or other full bodied red wine
- 1 teaspoon black peppercorns
- salt
- 1/4 cup (60) g butter

Replace the chicken with the same amount of duck for a slightly different but equally delicious dish.

Push the clove into the garlic. Tie the garlic, celery, parsley, basil, and bay leaf together using kitchen string. • Blanch the onions in boiling water for 3 minutes. Drain and cool under cold running water. Drain well. • Heat the oil in a large Dutch oven or earthenware casserole over medium heat. Add the pancetta and sauté until browned, about 5 minutes. • Dredge the chicken in half the flour, ensuring that it is evenly coated. Shake to remove any excess flour. • Add the onions and chicken to the pan. Sauté until the chicken is lightly browned all over, 5–7 minutes. • Add the cognac and light it using a match. When the flames have gone out add the wine, peppercorns, and the bunch of herbs. Season with salt and cook over high heat for 6–7 minutes. • Lower the heat and simmer until the chicken is cooked through, about 30 minutes. Turn the chicken from time to time while it is cooking. • Beat together the butter and 1 tablespoon of flour in a small bowl. • Remove the pan from the heat and transfer the chicken and onions to a heated serving dish using a slotted spoon. Remove and discard the bunch of herbs. • Add the butter mixture to the pan and stir until well mixed. Place over low heat, stirring constantly, until the sauce thickens, 3–4 minutes. • Drizzle the sauce over the chicken and serve hot.

Serves: 4 • Prep: 20 min • Cooking: 50 min • Level: 2

Chicken galantine

Galantina di pollo

This is a fairly complicated dish, but if you have the time it really is worth the effort. In Italy, this dish is served around Christmas time when it provides a welcome light change after all the hearty festive food and again at the peak of summer when other meat dishes seem too heavy to face in the heat.

- 1 lb (500 g) lean ground (minced) beef
- 6 oz (180 g) lean ground (minced) pork
- 6 oz (180 g) ground (minced) turkey breast
- 6 oz (180 g) ground (minced) suckling veal
- 4 oz (125 g) ground (minced) mortadella
- 1/2 cup (60 g) shelled pistachios
- 1 egg
- 1 oz (30 g) black truffle, finely sliced (optional)
- salt and freshly ground black pepper
- 1 chicken, boned, weighing about 4 lb (2 kg)
- 1 onion, cut in half
- 1 carrot, cut in 3
- 1 stalk celery, cut in 3
- 2 sprigs parsley
- 7–8 peppercorns
- 1 chicken stock cube
- 2 gelatin cubes
- juice of 1/2 lemon

Combine the beef, pork, turkey, veal, and mortadella in a large bowl. Mix well and add the pistachios, egg, and truffle, if using. Sprinkle with salt and pepper and mix thoroughly. • Stuff the boned chicken with the mixture and sew up the neck and stomach cavities with a trussing needle and string. • Use your hands to give it a rectangular shape. Wrap in a piece of cheesecloth (muslin) and tie with kitchen string. • Place a large saucepan of salted water over medium heat. Add the onion, carrot, celery, parsley, peppercorns, and stock cube. • When the water is boiling, carefully add the stuffed chicken and simmer over low heat for1 hour 30 minutes. • Remove from the heat and drain the stock. • Remove the cheesecloth and place the chicken between two trays, with a weight on top. • When cool, transfer to the refrigerator, with the weight still on top, and leave for at least 12 hours. • In the meantime prepare the gelatin, following the directions on the packet. Be sure to add the lemon juice while the gelatin is still liquid. • Serve the galantine thinly sliced on a serving dish, topped with the diced gelatin.

Serves: 6–8 • Prep: 40 min + 12 hr to chill • Cooking: 1 hr 30 min • Level: 3

Duck baked in a bread crust

Duck baked in a bread crust

Anatra in crosta

- 1 quantity basic dough (see page 60)
- 2 whole eggs + 1 egg yolk
- 1/2 cup (125 g) butter, softened
- 1/3 cup (90 ml) milk
- 1 tablespoon sugar
- 1/3 cup (50 g) all-purpose (plain) flour + more as needed
- salt and freshly ground black pepper
- 3 tablespoons extra-virgin olive oil
- 1 large onion, finely chopped
- 1 clove garlic, finely chopped
- 3 tablespoons finely chopped fresh herbs, such as parsley, rosemary, and basil
- 8 oz (250 g) ground (minced) lean beef
- 2 Italian pork sausages, skinned and crumbled
- 2 tablespoons chopped walnuts
- 1 tablespoon chopped pistachios
- 1 small black truffle, thinly sliced (optional)
- 1 duck, about 4 lb (2 kg)

Prepare the basic dough without letting it rise. Place the dough on a lightly floured surface and knead, gradually incorporating 2 eggs, the butter, milk, and sugar. Reserve 1 tablespoon of the milk. Add enough flour to prevent the dough from becoming too sticky. Season with salt and pepper and knead until smooth and elastic, 15 minutes. • Transfer to an oiled bowl, cover, and let rise for 3 hours. • Preheat the oven to 350°F (180°C/gas 4). • Heat the oil in a small saucepan over a medium heat. Sauté the onion, garlic, and herbs until the onion begins to soften, 2–3 minutes. Remove from the heat. • Mix the beef, sausage meat, onion mixture, walnuts, pistachios, and truffle, if using, in a large bowl. Season with salt and pepper. • Spoon the mixture into the cavity of the duck. • Transfer the duck to an oiled roasting pan. Roast until the duck is cooked and the juices run clear when stuck with a skewer, about 1 hour 30 minutes. • Remove from the oven. • Roll out the dough on a lightly floured work surface into a rectangle large enough to wrap around the duck. • Beat the remaining egg yolk with the reserved milk. • Wrap the duck in the bread dough, pinching the dough together to seal the closed. Transfer to a large roasting pan and brush all over with the egg mixture. • Bake until the bread is cooked through, about 1 hour. • Remove from the oven and serve hot.

Serves: 4–6 • Prep: 45 min + 3 hr to rise • Cooking: 3 hr • Level: 3

Roast duck with fresh figs

Anatra arrosto con fichi

This dish comes from Sicily, where it is made in late summer when fresh figs are at their succulent best.

- 1 duck, about 4 lb (2 kg)
- salt and freshly ground black pepper
- 2 onions, finely chopped
- 1 clove garlic, finely chopped
- 2 bay leaves
- 1 sprig thyme
- 1 cup (250 ml) dry sherry
- 1 cup (150 g) all-purpose (plain) flour
- 1/3 cup (90 ml) chicken stock, homemade (see page 104) or bouillon cube
- 1 lb (500 g) fresh figs, cut in half
- 1/4 cup (60 g) butter

Preheat the oven to 250°F (130°C/gas 1/2). • Season the duck with salt and pepper. Pierce the skin all over to encourage the slow release of fat during roasting. • Place the duck in a large baking dish. Roast for 3 hours. • Add the onions, garlic, bay leaves, and thyme and roast until the onions have softened, 15 minutes. • Increase the oven temperature to 350°F (180°C/gas 4). • Pour the sherry over the duck and cook until the meat is very tender, about 45 minutes. • Remove the duck from the pan. Cut into halves or quarters. Set aside. • Drain the cooking juices in the pan into a saucepan. Stir in 3 tablespoons of the flour and stir over low heat until thickened. • Stir in the stock and simmer for 5 minutes. • Return the duck to the baking dish. Spoon the sauce over the top. • Peel the figs and roll in the remaining flour until well coated. • Sauté the figs in the butter in a large frying pan over medium heat for 5 minutes. • Add the figs to the duck and cook over low heat for 5 minutes. • Serve hot.

Serves: 4–6 • Prep: 40 min • Cooking:4 hr • Level: 2

Glutton's pheasant

Faraona alla ghiotta

- 1 large pheasant, cleaned but with its liver reserved
- 1 small onion, finely chopped
- 2 cloves garlic, finely chopped
- 1 tablespoon capers preserved in salt, rinsed and drained
- 2 sage leaves, torn
- 1 carrot, chopped
- 1 stalk celery, chopped
- 6 salt-cured anchovy fillets, chopped
- 1 tablespoon finely chopped wild fennel
- 1 tablespoon butter
- 1 cup (125 g) fine dry bread crumbs
- ½ cup (125 ml) dry white wine
- grated zest of 1 lemon
- salt and freshly ground black pepper
- 4 oz (125 g) sliced prosciutto (Parma ham)

Preheat the oven to 350°F (180°C/gas 4). • Chop the pheasant liver. Mix in a bowl with the onion, garlic, capers, sage, carrot, celery, anchovies, and fennel. Add the butter, bread crumbs, wine, and lemon zest. Season with salt and pepper and mix well. Spoon the mixture into the cavity of the pheasant. • Transfer the pheasant to an oiled roasting pan and cover with slices of prosciutto. • Roast until the pheasant is cooked through and its juices run clear when stuck with a skewer, about 1 hour 15–30 minutes. • Serve hot.

Serves: 2–4 • Prep: 10 min • Cooking: 1 hr 20 min • Level: 2

Turkey with prosciutto

Tacchino al prosciutto

- 1 tender young turkey, about 4 lb (2 kg), boneless
- 4 oz (125 g) prosciutto (Parma ham), chopped
- 4 cloves, crushed
- 1 tablespoon finely chopped rosemary
- 1 tablespoon finely chopped sage
- salt and freshly ground black pepper
- ¼ cup (60 ml) water
- 2 tablespoons butter
- 1 cup (250 ml) heavy (double) cream

Preheat the oven to 375°F (190°C/gas 5). • Rinse the turkey under cold running water and dry with paper towels. • Sprinkle with the prosciutto, cloves, rosemary, sage, salt, and pepper, and rub the turkey all over. Wrap in ovenproof parchment paper and drizzle with the water. • Bake until tender, about 3 hours. • Unwrap the turkey and carve. • Heat the butter in a frying pan and add the turkey. Pour in the cream, season with salt and pepper, and simmer over medium heat for 10 minutes, or until most of the cream is absorbed. • Serve hot.

Serves: 6 • Prep: 25 min • Cooking: 3 hr 15 min • Level: 2

Christmas roast turkey

Tacchino natalizio

This is a recipe from Lombardy, the region around Milan. Traditionally served at Christmas, it makes a wonderful main course throughout the year.

Ask your butcher to remove the bones from the turkey through an incision in the neck. • Finely chop the turkey liver and place in a bowl with the beef, sausages, egg, apples, chestnuts, prunes, salt, pepper, nutmeg, and brandy. Mix well. • Stuff the turkey with the mixture and close the incision with a trussing needle and kitchen thread. • Butter a Dutch oven or cast-iron pot that will hold the turkey snugly. Cover the bottom of the pot with the strips of lard, add the turkey, and place the rosemary and sage on top. • Brown over medium heat for 30 minutes, turning often so that the turkey colors evenly. • Preheat the oven to 400°F (200°C/gas 6). • Drain the fat from the turkey and discard. Pour in the wine and cook until it evaporates. • Add a ladleful of stock, cover and roast for 3 hours. Baste the turkey with the cooking juices (and a little extra stock, if the pan dries out) during cooking. • The turkey should be very tender and with a crisp, golden skin.

Serves: 8 • Prep: 45 min • Cooking: 3 hr 30 min • Level: 2

- 1 small turkey, boneless, about 8 lb (4 kg), with liver
- 4 oz (125 g) ground (minced) beef
- 6 oz (180 g) Italian sausages, skinned and crumbled
- 1 egg
- 2 apples (such as Golden Delicious), peeled, cored, and diced
- 12 chestnuts, boiled in chicken stock until soft, peeled and cut in half
- 12 prunes, soaked in warm water for 5 minutes, then pitted and chopped
- salt and freshly ground black pepper
- pinch of nutmeg
- ½ cup (125 ml) brandy
- 2 tablespoons butter
- 8 strips lard
- 6 twigs fresh rosemary
- 12 leaves fresh sage
- ½ cup (125 ml) dry white wine
- ½ cup (125 ml) beef stock, homemade (see recipe, page 104) or bouillon cube

VEAL & BEEF

Veal and beef are the two most popular meats in every region of Italy. They can be prepared in dozens of different ways and are braised, stewed, fried, boiled, and roasted into an infinite array of dishes. Among Italian veal dishes, *scaloppine* are especially well liked. However, getting well-cut *scaloppine* outside Italy can sometimes be a challenge. Ask your butcher to cut the *scaloppine* across the grain of the meat from a solid piece of veal topside (top round). Before you cook them, the *scaloppine* should be gently flattened using a meat pounder. Besides a number of *scaloppine* recipes, we have included some old favorites, such as Veal with tuna sauce (see page 282), Florentine steak (see page 288), Sautéed veal chops, Milanese-style (see page 291), Meatballs in tomato sauce (see page 291), and Ossobuco (see page 299).

Roast veal roulade (see page 299)

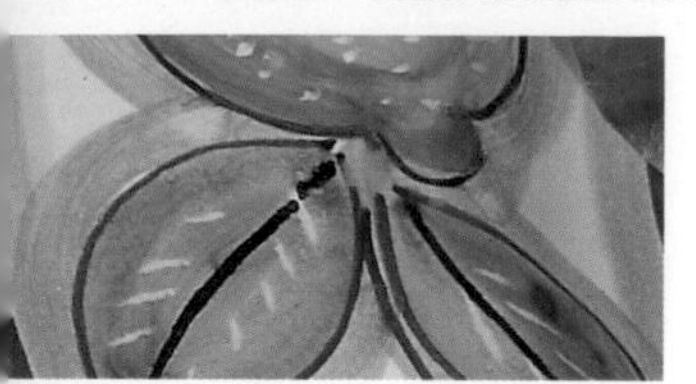

Veal with tuna sauce

Genoese stuffed veal

Cima alla genovese

- 2 lb (1 kg) boned veal roast
- 8 oz (250 g) ground (minced) veal or beef
- 6 oz (180 g) ground (minced) pork
- 4 oz (125 g) lard, very finely chopped
- 8 oz (250 g) day-old bread, without crust, soaked in milk, and squeezed
- 3 tablespoons freshly grated Parmesan cheese
- 8 oz (250 g) boiled Swiss chard (silver beet), squeezed and finely chopped
- 2 tablespoons finely chopped marjoram
- 4 tablespoons pistachios
- 4 large eggs, beaten
- 1/8 teaspoon freshly grated nutmeg
- salt and freshly ground white pepper
- 3 quarts (3 liters) vegetable stock, homemade (see page 112) or bouillon cube

Cut a pocket into the piece of veal or beef. • Mix the ground veal, pork, lard, bread, Parmesan, Swiss chard, marjoram, pistachios, eggs, nutmeg, salt, and pepper in a bowl. Stuff the veal with this mixture. Use a trussing needle and thread to stitch up the pocket. • Place in a heavy saucepan and cover with hot stock. Place over high heat and bring the stock to a boil. • Lower the heat and simmer gently until the meat is very tender, about 2 hours. • Cool the veal in the stock. • Serve at room temperature, sliced, with pickled vegetables and mayonnaise.

Serves: 6 • Prep: 25 min • Cooking: 2 hr • Level: 2

Veal with tuna sauce

Vitello tonnato

Serve this delicacy from Lombardy during the heat of summer. The tuna sauce can be chilled before serving.

- 1 bottle very dry white wine
- carrot, finely chopped
- 3 cloves
- 2 bay leaves
- salt and freshly ground black pepper
- 2 lb (1 kg) boned veal roast
- 1/2 cup (125 g) mayonnaise
- 8 oz (250 g) canned tuna, drained and crumbled
- 2 tablespoons lemon juice
- 1 tablespoon white wine vinegar
- 1 tablespoon salt-cured capers, rinsed
- 1–2 cups (250–500 ml) beef stock, homemade (see page 104) or bouillon cube

Pour the wine into a large bowl, reserving 1/2 cup (125 ml). • Add the carrot, onion, cloves, and bay leaves. Season with salt and pepper and add the meat. Cover and let marinate for 1 day. • Place the mayonnaise, tuna, lemon juice, vinegar, capers, and reserved wine in a food processor and chop until smooth. • Place in a bowl, cover, and set aside. • Remove the meat from the marinade and wrap it in a piece of muslin (cheesecloth). Secure the muslin, tying the ends with kitchen string. • Place in a large saucepan over medium heat. Add the marinade and simmer until tender, about 2 hours. If the cooking liquid reduces too much during cooking, add a little stock. • Remove the meat from the pan and transfer to a cutting board. Remove the muslin and slice the meat thinly. Let cool. • Arrange on a serving dish. Spoon the tuna sauce over the meat and serve.

Serves: 6 • Prep: 25 min + 24 hr to marinate the meat
Cooking: 2 hr • Level: 2

Beef with tomato sauce

Stracotto

- 2 cloves garlic, lightly crushed but whole
- 8 leaves fresh sage
- 1/4 cup (60 ml) extra-virgin olive oil
- salt and freshly ground black pepper
- 2 lb (1 kg) boned veal roast
- 2/3 cup (150 ml) dry red wine
- 1 large onion, finely chopped
- 2 bay leaves
- 1 (14-oz/400-g) can tomatoes, with juice

Sauté the garlic and sage in the oil in a large Dutch oven (casserole) for 5 minutes. Season with salt and pepper. • Add the beef and sauté until browned all over, 7–10 minutes. • Pour in the wine and let it evaporate. • Add the onion, bay leaves, and tomatoes. Cover and simmer over low heat until the meat is tender, 2–3 hours. Stir occasionally to make sure the sauce does not stick to the pan. • Slice and serve hot.

Serves: 6 • Prep: 15 min • Cooking: 2–3 hr • Level: 1

Veal roast with polenta

Arrosto di vitello con polenta

- 2 lb (1 kg) boned veal roast
- 8 oz (250 g) thinly sliced pancetta
- 6 leaves fresh sage
- 1 tablespoon rosemary leaves
- 1 clove garlic, finely sliced
- salt and freshly ground black pepper
- 1/4 cup (60 ml) extra-virgin olive oil
- 1 quantity polenta (see page 220)

Preheat the oven to 425°F (220°C/gas 7). • Wrap the veal in the slices of pancetta. Sprinkle with sage, rosemary, and garlic. Season with salt and pepper. Tie firmly with kitchen string. • Transfer the veal to a large roasting pan and drizzle with the oil. • Roast for 20 minutes. • Lower the oven temperature to 300°F (150°C/gas 1) and roast until tender, about 1 hour. • Turn off the oven but leave the veal in the oven for 20 minutes more. • Slice thinly and serve hot with freshly made polenta.

Serves: 4–6 • Prep: 25 min • Cooking: 1 hr 40 min • Level: 2

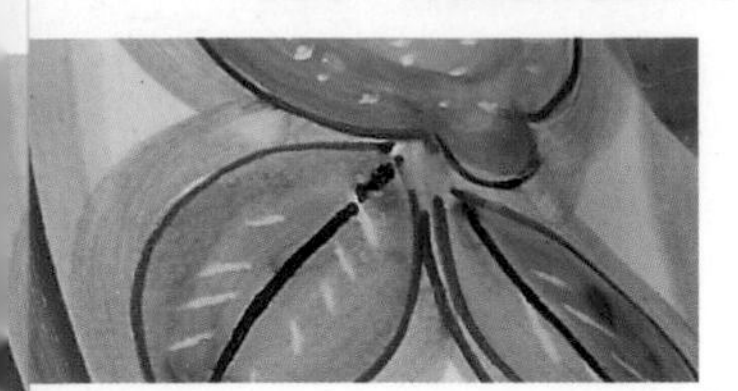

Veal scaloppine with Marsala

Veal scaloppine with Marsala

Scaloppine di vitello al marsala

- 1 lb (500 g) veal scaloppine (escalopes)
- 1/4 cup (30 g) all-purpose (plain) flour
- 1/3 cup (90 g) butter
- 1/3 cup (90 ml) dry Marsala wine
- salt and freshly ground black pepper

Remove any small pieces of fat from the scaloppine. • Pound the meat lightly, dredge in the flour, and shake thoroughly. • Melt half the butter in a large frying pan over medium heat. Add the veal in a single layer, making sure that the pieces do not overlap. Cook until lightly browned, about 2 minutes on each side. • Add the Marsala and simmer for 3 minutes. Season with salt and pepper. • Place the meat on a heated serving dish. Remove the pan from the heat and add the remaining butter. Let the butter melt and mix well. Drizzle over the meat and serve hot.

Serves: 4 • Prep: 10 min • Cooking: 10 min • Level: 1

Veal scaloppine with capers and oregano

Scaloppine alla pizzaiola

Blanch the tomatoes in boiling water for 1 minute. Slip off the skins, gently squeeze out as many seeds as possible, and chop coarsely. • Sauté the garlic in 2 tablespoons of oil in a large frying pan until pale gold. Discard the garlic. • Stir in the tomatoes and season with salt and pepper. Cook over high heat for 10 minutes, stirring often. • Melt the butter with the remaining oil in a large frying pan. Add the veal and cook until lightly browned, about 2 minutes on each side. • Add the tomato sauce and capers and simmer for 2 minutes. • Transfer to a serving plate, sprinkle with the oregano, and serve hot.

Serves: 4–6 • Prep: 10 min • Cooking: 20 min • Level: 1

- 6 large tomatoes
- 1 clove garlic, lightly crushed but whole
- 1/4 cup (60 ml) extra-virgin olive oil
- salt and freshly ground black pepper
- 1 tablespoon butter
- 1½ lb (750 g) veal scaloppine (escalopes)
- 2 tablespoons salt-cured capers, rinsed
- 1/4 teaspoon dried oregano

Veal scaloppine with prosciutto

Saltimbocca alla romana

- 1 lb (500 g) veal scaloppine (escalopes)
- 4 oz (125 g) prosciutto (Parma ham)
- 8 leaves sage
- 4 tablespoons all-purpose (plain) flour
- 2 tablespoons butter
- 3 tablespoons extra-virgin olive oil
- salt and freshly ground black pepper
- 1/2 cup (125 ml) dry white wine

This quick and easy recipe is a classic of Roman cuisine. Its success depends very much on the quality of the veal.

Pound the meat lightly, dredge in the flour, and shake thoroughly. • Place half a slice of prosciutto on each slice of veal and top with a sage leaf. • Use a cocktail stick to fix the ham and sage to the slice of veal. • Melt the butter and oil in a large frying pan. Add the veal slices with the ham facing downward. Brown over high heat, then turn and brown the other side. Season with salt and pepper. • Pour in the wine and cook for 5–6 minutes more. • Serve hot.

Serves: 4 • Prep: 15 min • Cooking: 10 min • Level: 1

Bari-style veal rolls

Involtini alla barese

Lay the slices of veal out flat. Sprinkle with the garlic, parsley, and cheese. • Roll the veal up and secure with cocktail sticks. • Sauté the onion and bay leaves in the oil in a large frying pan until softened, about 5 minutes. • Add the veal rolls and simmer over medium heat for 5 minutes. Season with salt and pepper. • Pour in the tomatoes, partially cover the pan, and simmer until the tomatoes reduce and the meat is tender, 15–20 minutes. • Remove the bay leaves and serve hot.

Serves: 4–6 • Prep: 15 min • Cooking: 25–30 min • Level: 1

- 1½ lb (750 g) veal scaloppine (escalopes)
- 3 cloves garlic, finely chopped
- 2 tablespoons finely chopped parsley
- 8 oz (250 g) pecorino cheese, cut in cubes
- 1 medium onion, finely chopped
- 2 bay leaves
- 2 tablespoons extra-virgin olive oil
- salt and freshly ground black pepper
- 1 (14-oz/400-g) can tomatoes, with juice

18%vol

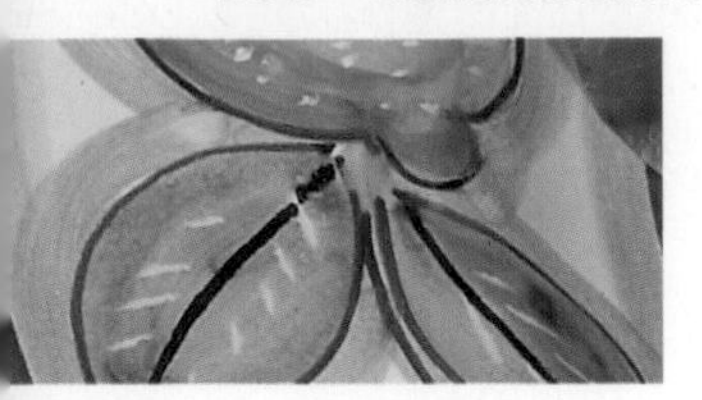

Tenderloin steak with mushrooms

Filetto di manzo ai funghi

- $\frac{1}{3}$ cup (90 ml) extra-virgin olive oil
- 1 lb (500 g) beef tenderloin
- salt and freshly ground black pepper
- 12 oz (350 g) mixed wild mushrooms
- 2 cloves garlic, finely chopped
- 2 tablespoons finely chopped parsley
- $\frac{1}{2}$ cup (125 ml) dry white wine

Vary the cooking time of the steak according to how you like it done.

Heat 3 tablespoons of oil in a large frying pan over high heat. Season the meat with salt and pepper and sauté for 10–15 minutes. The outside should be nicely browned, but it should still be pink in the center. Remove from the heat and set aside in a warm oven. • Sauté the mushrooms, garlic, and parsley in the remaining oil in the same pan until tender, 8–10 minutes (timing will depend on the type of mushrooms you are using). • Pour in the wine and cook until it has evaporated. Season with salt and pepper. • Slice the beef and spoon the mushroom sauce over the top. Serve hot.

Serves: 4 • Prep: 20 min • Cooking: 20–25 min • Level: 1

Sliced steak with cherry tomatoes

Tagliata con pomodorini

There are many slight variations on this dish which has become a modern classic in restaurants all over Italy. Vary the cooking time of the steak so that it is cooked rare, medium, or well done to your liking.

Season the steak generously with salt and pepper. • Heat 2 tablespoons of the oil in a large grill pan and add the steak. Cook until done to your liking, 8–15 minutes. • Place the salad greens on a large serving plate. • Slice the beef and arrange over the salad. Top with the tomatoes and drizzle with the remaining oil and the vinegar. Season with salt and pepper and serve hot.

Serves: 4 • Prep: 15 min • Cooking: 8–15 min • Level: 1

- 2 lb (1 kg) thick boned sirloin steak
- salt and freshly ground black pepper
- $\frac{1}{3}$ cup (90 ml) extra-virgin olive oil
- 1 bunch fresh arugula (rocket) or other tender salad greens
- 16–20 cherry tomatoes, whole or cut in half
- $\frac{1}{4}$ cup (60 ml) balsamic vinegar

Florentine beef steak

Bistecca alla fiorentina

- 2 lb (1 kg) T-bone steak at least $1\frac{1}{2}$ inches (4 cm) thick
- salt and freshly ground black pepper

This dish is the ultimate treat for steak-lovers. In Italy, the steak is cut from Tuscan-bred Chianina beef and hung for at least 6 days. It is cooked over the embers of a charcoal or wood-burning grill and eaten so rare that the meat nearest the bone is only just warm.

Season the steak with pepper. • Place on a grill about 4 inches (10 cm) above the glowing embers. • After 4–5 minutes the steak will come away easily from the grill. Sprinkle the seared surface with a little salt, turn and cook the other side, sprinkling with more salt and pepper. • It should be well-browned on the outside, juicy inside. • Serve at once.

Serves: 2 • Prep: 1 min • Cooking: 10 min • Level: 1

Tenderloin steak with balsamic vinegar

Filetto all'aceto balsamico

Melt the butter in a heavy-bottomed pan over high heat. When it is foaming, add the shallot and then the meat. Cook until lightly browned, about 4 minutes each side. • Pour in the balsamic vinegar and season with salt and pepper. Simmer for 1–2 minutes more. • Set the meat aside in a warm oven on a heated serving dish. • Return the cooking juices to the heat and simmer until they foam. Add the cornstarch and stir until thickened. • Pour the sauce over the meat and serve hot.

Serves: 4 • Prep: 10 min • Cooking: 10 min • Level: 1

- 2 tablespoons butter
- 1 shallot, finely chopped
- $1\frac{1}{2}$ lb (750 g) tenderloin steak, cut in 4 slices
- $\frac{1}{2}$ cup (125 ml) balsamic vinegar
- salt and freshly ground black pepper
- 1 tablespoon cornstarch (cornflour)

Sautéed veal chops, Milanese-style

Sautéed veal chops, Milanese-style

Cotolette alla milanese

- 4 large single-rib veal chops
- 2 large eggs
- 1½ cups (150 g) fine dry bread crumbs
- ½ cup (125 g) butter
- 1 tablespoon extra virgin olive oil
- salt
- wedges of lemon, to garnish
- mixed salad greens, to serve

This classic Milanese dish is very similar to what we know as an Austrian dish called Wiener schnitzel.

Lightly pound the meat to flatten. • Beat the eggs in a bowl. • Place the bread crumbs on a large plate. • Dip the veal first in the egg and then in the bread crumbs, shaking off any excess. • Melt two-thirds of the butter in a large frying pan over medium heat. Add the oil. • Place the veal chops in the pan and fry until the meat is tender and lightly browned, 3–4 minutes each side. Do not turn more than once, as the veal will absorb too much fat and become dry. • Place on a heated serving dish. • Garnish with wedges of lemon. Serve hot with the salad.

Serves: 4 • Prep: 10 min • Cooking: 10 min • Level: 2

Meatballs in tomato sauce

Polpette al pomodoro

Heat the oil in a large heavy saucepan over medium heat and sauté until softened, about 5 minutes. • Add the tomatoes, basil, salt, and pepper. Simmer over medium heat for 10 minutes. • Place the bread crumbs in a large bowl with the milk. Stir in the meat, pecorino, eggs, parsley, and garlic. Season with salt and pepper and mix well. • Shape into meatballs and add to the tomato sauce. Simmer until cooked through, 15–20 minutes, turning carefully once or twice. • Serve hot.

Serves: 4 • Prep: 15 min • Cooking: 30 min • Level: 1

- ¼ cup (60 ml) extra-virgin olive oil
- 1 small onion, finely chopped
- 1 (14-oz/400-g) can tomatoes, with juice
- 6 fresh basil leaves
- salt and freshly ground black pepper
- 1 cup (100 g) fine dry bread crumbs
- ¼ cup (60 ml) milk
- 14 oz (400 g) ground (minced) beef or veal
- 1 cup (200 g) freshly grated pecorino cheese
- 2 eggs, beaten
- 2 tablespoons finely chopped parsley
- 2 cloves garlic, finely chopped

Bolognese cutlets

Cotolette alla bolognese

- 4–8 veal cutlets, about 1 lb (500 g) total
- 1 egg
- salt
- 1 cup (100 g) fine dry bread crumbs
- ½ cup (125 g) butter
- 6 thin slices prosciutto (Parma ham)
- 4 oz (125 g) Parmesan cheese, in small shavings
- 1 cup (250 g) sieved tomatoes (passata)
- ½ cup (125 ml) beef stock, homemade (see page 104) or bouillon cube

For an extra special dish, sprinkle shavings of raw white truffle on top of the melted cheese just before serving.

Beat the veal lightly with a meat pounder. • Beat the egg in a shallow dish with the salt. • Dip the cutlets into the egg and then coat with the bread crumbs, pressing so they stick. • Fry the cutlets in the butter until golden brown, 2–3 minutes each side. • Arrange the veal in a single layer in a very wide frying pan. Place a slice of prosciutto on each and cover with Parmesan shavings. • Mix the sieved tomatoes with the meat stock and pour into the pan. Cover and simmer until the cheese has melted, about 15 minutes. • Serve hot.

Serves: 4 • Prep: 15 min • Cooking: 15 min • Level: 1

Fried cutlets with tomato and basil

Cotolette al pomodoro e basilico

Blanch the tomatoes in boiling water for 30 seconds. • Slip off the skins, remove the seeds, and coarsely chop. Place them in a colander and sprinkle with salt. Add the basil and let drain for 15 minutes. • Make a few cuts around the edges of the cutlets. Dip the cutlets in the eggs and then in the bread crumbs. Press down well so that the bread crumbs stick all over. • Melt the butter in a large frying pan. Add the cutlets and cook until cooked through and golden, 3–4 minutes each side. • Drain well on paper towels and season with salt and pepper. Top with the tomato. Drizzle with the oil and serve hot.

Serves: 4 • Prep: 30 min • Cooking: 10 min • Level: 2

- 2 tomatoes
- salt and freshly ground black pepper
- 1 bunch basil
- 4 veal cutlets with bone about ½ inch (1 cm) thick
- 2 eggs, lightly beaten
- 1 cup (125 g) fine dry bread crumbs
- 7 tablespoons butter
- 1 tablespoon extra-virgin olive oil

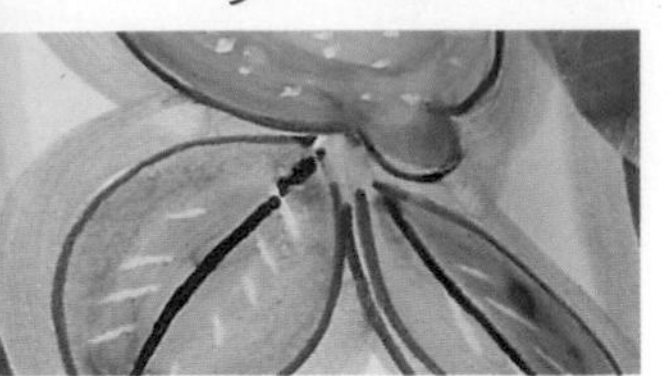

Meatballs with salad

MEATBALLS WITH SALAD

Polpette con insalata

- 2 large zucchini (courgettes)
- 1 large yellow bell pepper (capsicum), seeded and very thinly sliced
- 6 oz (180 g) mixed salad greens
- 1/4 cup (60 ml) extra-virgin olive oil
- 1 tablespoon balsamic vinegar
- salt and freshly ground black pepper
- 14 oz (400 g) ground (minced) beef
- 2 oz (60 g) mortadella, finely chopped
- 1 clove garlic, finely chopped
- 1 large egg, beaten
- 1 tablespoon freshly grated Parmesan cheese
- 1 tablespoon finely chopped parsley
- 2 teaspoons finely chopped mint
- grated zest of 1/2 lemon
- 1/2 cup (60 g) fine dry bread crumbs
- 1 cup (250 ml) sunflower oil, for frying

Trim the zucchini and slice very thinly lengthwise. Blanch in a pot of boiling water for 1 minute. • Use a slotted spoon to transfer to a bowl of ice water. Drain well and place on a clean cloth to dry. • Arrange the zucchini, bell pepper, and salad greens on individual serving plates. • Beat the olive oil and balsamic vinegar to make a dressing. Season with salt and pepper. • Mix the beef, mortadella, and garlic in a large bowl. Add the egg, Parmesan, parsley, mint, and lemon zest. Season with salt and pepper and mix well. • Shape the mixture into meatballs the size of walnuts. Roll the meatballs in the bread crumbs. • Heat the sunflower oil in a large frying pan over medium heat. Fry the meatballs in two batches until browned and cooked through, 5–7 minutes per batch. • Drain well on paper towels. • Drizzle the dressing over the salad and add the meatballs to the serving plates. • Serve hot.

Serves: 4 • Prep: 20 min • Cooking: 15 min • Level: 1

SICILIAN STUFFED BEEF ROLL

Farsumaru

Mix the ground beef and sausage meat in a large bowl. • Add the raw egg, pecorino, parsley, onion, garlic, salt, and pepper, and combine well. • Place the slice of beef flat between 2 sheets of parchment paper and beat gently until it is about 1/4 inch (5 mm) thick. • Lay the meat flat and cover with the prosciutto and pancetta. Spread the ground meat mixture over the top, leaving a border around the edge. • Slice the pointed ends off the eggs and place them "nose to tail" down the center of the beef. • Lay the Provolone on either side of the eggs. • Carefully roll up. Tie with kitchen string at regular intervals. • Heat the oil in a large heavy saucepan, and brown the meat roll all over. • Pour in the wine and cook, uncovered, until it has reduced. • Add the tomato paste. Cover and simmer over very low heat for about 1 hour, turning several times. • Just before serving, remove the string and transfer to a heated serving plate. • Carve into thick slices and spoon the cooking liquid over the top. Serve hot.

Serves: 6 • Prep: 30 min • Cooking: 1 hr 15 min • Level: 2

- 4 oz (125 g) ground (minced) beef
- 8 oz (250 g) Italian sausage meat
- 1 large egg
- 1/2 cup (60 g) freshly grated pecorino cheese
- 1 tablespoon finely chopped parsley
- 2 tablespoons finely chopped onion
- 2 cloves garlic, finely chopped
- salt and freshly ground black pepper
- a single, thick slice of lean beef, weighing about 1 1/2 lb (750 g)
- 7 oz (200 g) prosciutto or ham, sliced
- 4 slices pancetta, chopped
- 3 hard-boiled eggs
- 4 oz (125 g) mature Provolone cheese, cut into narrow strips
- 1/4 cup (60 ml) extra-virgin olive oil
- 1/2 cup (125 ml) dry red wine
- 1 tablespoon tomato paste, diluted in 1 cup (250 ml) hot water

MEAT LOAF WITH MUSHROOMS

Polpettone con i funghi

- 6 oz (180 g) white bread
- 2 cups (500 ml) milk
- 1 1/4 lb (600 g) lean ground (minced) veal
- 2 eggs
- 1/2 cup (60 g) freshly grated pecorino cheese
- 1/2 cup (60 g) finely chopped prosciutto
- salt and freshly ground black pepper
- 2 tablespoons fine dry bread crumbs

Preheat the oven to 350°F (180°C/gas 4). • Remove the crusts from the bread and soak it in the milk for 5 minutes. Squeeze well and place the bread in a mixing bowl. Add the veal, eggs, pecorino, prosciutto, salt, and pepper. • Shape the mixture into a meat loaf and roll carefully first in the bread crumbs then in the flour. • Heat the oil in an ovenproof Dutch oven or casserole over medium heat and brown the loaf on all sides, 7–10 minutes. • Pour in the wine and simmer until it has evaporated, about 5 minutes. • Add the tomatoes, mushrooms, garlic, and parsley. Stir well. • Bake until golden brown and cooked through, about 45 minutes. • Serve hot or at room temperature.

Serves: 6 • Prep: 20 min • Cooking: 1 hr • Level: 1

- 2 tablespoons all-purpose (plain) flour
- 1/4 cup (60 ml) extra-virgin oil
- 1/2 cup (125 ml) dry white wine
- 4 large ripe tomatoes, peeled and chopped
- 8 oz (250 g) white mushrooms, chopped
- 1 clove garlic, chopped
- 2 tablespoons finely chopped parsley

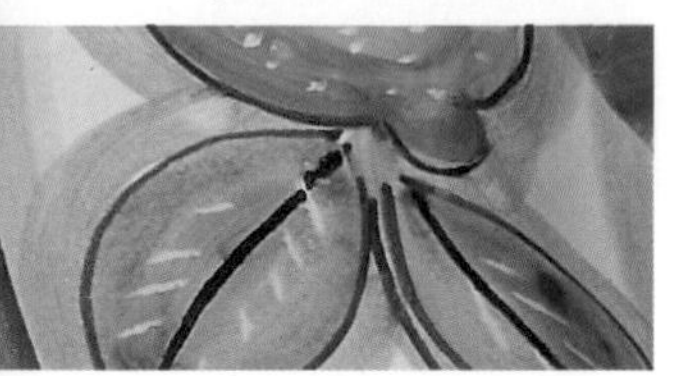

Venetian-style liver

Veal & Beef

Veal & Beef

BREADED LIVER WITH TANGY DRESSING

Fegato in agrodolce

- juice of 1 lemon
- 1/2 teaspoon sugar
- 1 large egg, lightly beaten
- 1/2 cup (75 g) all-purpose (plain) flour
- 1 cup (120 g) fine dry bread crumbs
- 1 1/4 lb (600 g) calf's liver, sliced
- 1/3 cup (100 g) butter
- salt

Beat the lemon juice and sugar in a small bowl. • Beat the egg in another bowl. • Place the flour and bread crumbs on separate plates. • Dip each piece of liver in the flour and then in the egg. Finally coat each piece with bread crumbs, shaking off any excess. • Melt the butter in a large frying pan over medium heat. Fry the liver until golden brown and cooked through, about 5 minutes on each side. • Season with salt. Drizzle with the lemon juice mixture and serve hot.

Serves: 4 • Prep: 15 min • Cooking: 10 min • Level: 1

FLORENTINE-STYLE TRIPE

Trippa alla fiorentina

Rinse the tripe thoroughly under cold running water, drain, dry with a clean cloth and cut into thin strips with kitchen scissors or a very sharp knife. • Sauté the onion, carrot, and celery in the oil in a heavy-bottomed casserole for 5 minutes. • Add the tripe and season with salt and pepper. Continue cooking for 3–4 minutes, stirring often. • Add the wine and cook over high heat, uncovered, for 5–6 minutes to reduce. • Mix in the tomatoes, check the seasoning, cover and simmer for 30 minutes, stirring occasionally. If necessary, reduce the amount of liquid by cooking uncovered over a higher heat for a few minutes. • Sprinkle with the cheese and serve hot.

Serves: 4 • Prep: 20 min • Cooking: 45 min • Level: 1

- 2 lb (1 kg) ready-to-cook calf's honeycomb tripe
- 1 large onion, finely chopped
- 1 large carrot, finely chopped
- 1 stick celery, finely chopped
- 1/4 cup (60 ml) extra-virgin olive oil
- salt and freshly ground black pepper
- 1/2 cup (125 ml) dry white wine
- 1 (14-oz/400-g) can tomatoes, with juice
- 1 cup (120 g) freshly grated Parmesan cheese

VENETIAN-STYLE LIVER

Fegato alla veneziana

- 1 1/2 lb (750 g) white onions, thinly sliced
- 1/4 cup (60 g) butter
- 2 tablespoons extra-virgin olive oil
- 1 1/2 lb (750 g) calf's liver, cut into thin strips
- salt and freshly ground black pepper
- 2 tablespoons finely chopped parsley
- freshly cooked mashed potatoes, to serve

This is a classic recipe from Venice. The slight sweetness of the onion balances the liver's hint of bitterness, combining to make a superb dish. Serve hot with freshly cooked mashed potatoes.

Place the onions, butter, and oil in a very large frying over low heat. Let them sweat gently for 15 minutes, then add the liver. • Cook over a high heat, stirring and turning constantly for 5 minutes at most. Sprinkle with salt just before removing from the heat (or the liver will become tough). • Season with pepper, sprinkle with the parsley, and serve hot.

Serves: 6 • Prep: 15 min • Cooking: 20 min • Level: 1

TRUFFLED KIDNEYS

Rognoni trifolati alla salvia

Slice the kidneys in half and remove the fatty parts and sinews. Cut into thin slices and set aside in a bowl with the cold water and vinegar for about 1 hour. • Heat the oil and butter in a heavy-bottomed pan over medium-high heat. Add the garlic, parsley, and sage and sauté for 2–3 minutes. • Add the drained kidneys. Season with salt and pepper and pour in the wine. • Sauté for 5 minutes only, or the kidneys will become tough. • Serve hot with the cooking juices.

Serves: 4 • Prep: 15 min + 1 hr to marinate • Cooking: 8 min Level: 1

- 1 lb (500 g) calf's kidneys
- 2 cups (500 ml) cold water
- 1 cup (250 g) vinegar
- 1/4 cup (60 ml) extra-virgin olive oil
- 1 tablespoon butter
- 2 cloves garlic, finely chopped
- 1 tablespoon finely chopped parsley
- 5 sage leaves
- salt and freshly ground black pepper
- 1/2 cup (125 ml) red wine

LAMB

Lamb is a popular meat all over Italy. Pan roasting or roasting in the oven are the most common ways of preparing it and roast lamb is a classic dish—especially at Easter—but also throughout the rest of the year (see our recipes on pages 304, 306, and 312). Grilled and fried lamb chops are also favorite dishes and they are often listed on menus as *scottadito* or "finger burners," which refers to the fact that they are best eaten by hand. See our recipe for Grilled lamb chops (page 312). In Lazio, the region around Rome, very young lamb is a traditional dish and is known as *abbacchio*. In the strictest sense, *abbacchio* is the meat of a lamb that is fed only on its mother's milk, before it begins to eat grass. Kid, or goat meat (sometimes called chevron in North America), is very similar to lamb, and interchangeable with lamb for most of the recipes in this chapter. Kid is still a fairly common meat in Italy, although more difficult to find in the United States.

Roast lamb with capers, olives, and anchovies (see page 304)

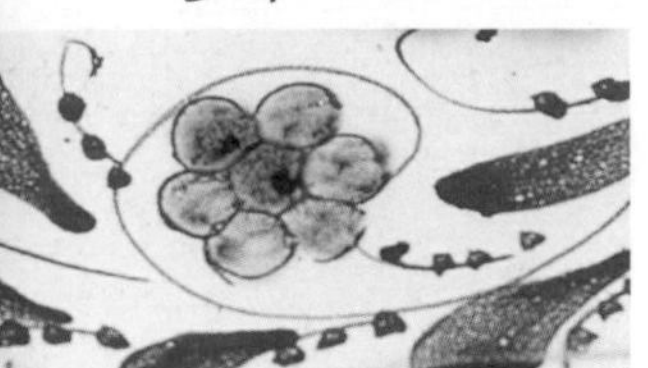

Roast lamb with capers, olives, and anchovies

Agnello al forno con capperi, olive e acciughe

- 3 lb (1.5 kg) leg or shoulder of lamb
- salt and freshly ground black pepper
- 1 tablespoon finely chopped rosemary
- 1 tablespoon finely chopped thyme
- 2 onions, thinly sliced
- 2 cloves garlic, finely chopped
- 1 bay leaf, finely chopped
- 2 tablespoons extra-virgin olive oil
- 3 salt-cured anchovies, finely chopped
- 2 tablespoons salt-cured capers, chopped
- 16 black olives, pitted
- juice of 1/2 lemon mixed with 2/3 cup (150 ml) dry white wine

Preheat the oven to 425°F (220°C/gas 7). • Oil a baking dish. • Season the lamb with salt and pepper and sprinkle with the rosemary and thyme. • Place the onions, garlic, and bay leaf in the prepared dish. Place the lamb on top and drizzle with the oil. • Roast for 10 minutes. • Lower the oven temperature to 350°F (180°C/gas 4) and roast for 30 minutes. • Remove from the oven and add the anchovies, capers, olives, and wine mixture. • Roast until the lamb is tender, about 45 minutes. Baste the lamb occasionally with the cooking juices. • Remove the lamb and place on a heated serving dish. • Spoon the cooking juices and onions around the lamb and serve hot.

Serves: 4–6 • Prep: 20 min • Cooking: 1 hr 30 min • Level: 1

Roast lamb with potatoes, onions, and tomatoes

Agnello al forno con patate, cipolle, e pomodorini

- 1/4 cup (60 ml) extra-virgin olive oil
- 3 lb (1.5 kg) leg or shoulder of lamb, cut into 6–8 pieces
- 4 large onions, coarsely chopped
- 10 cherry tomatoes
- 1 1/4 lb (600 g) starchy potatoes, peeled and sliced about 1/4-inch (5-mm) thick
- salt and freshly ground black pepper
- 1/2 teaspoon dried oregano

Preheat the oven to 350°F (180°C/gas 4). • Heat the oil in a large roasting pan. Add the lamb, onions, tomatoes, and potatoes. Baste with the hot oil, spooning it over the vegetables and meat several times. Sprinkle with salt, pepper, and oregano. • Roast until the lamb is tender and the potatoes are crisp, about 1 hour 30 minutes. Baste the lamb and vegetables from time to time during cooking. • Transfer to a heated serving dish. Serve hot.

Serves: 4–6 • Prep: 10 min. • Cooking: 1 hr 30 min – 2 hr Level: 1

Lamb in butter, oil, and white wine

Agnello all'agro

- 3 lb (1.5 kg) leg or shoulder of lamb, cut into 6–8 pieces
- 2 tablespoons butter
- 2 tablespoons extra-virgin olive oil
- salt and freshly ground black pepper
- 1/2 cup (125 ml) dry white wine
- juice of 2 lemons

Brown the lamb in the butter and oil over high heat in a Dutch oven or heavy saucepan, about 5 minutes. • Season with salt and pepper, mix well, and pour in half the wine and lemon juice. • Reduce the heat to medium-low, partially cover the pan and simmer until the meat is very tender, about 1 hour 30 minutes. Gradually stir in the remaining wine and lemon juice as the sauce reduces. • Serve hot.

Serves: 4–6 • Prep: 10 min. • Cooking: 1 hr 45 min • Level: 1

Roast suckling lamb with pancetta

Agnello o capretto pillottato al forno

- 2 1/2 lb (1.2 kg) suckling lamb on the bone
- 4–6 small sprigs rosemary
- 2 cloves garlic, coarsely chopped
- 1/2 cup (60 g) coarsely chopped pancetta
- salt and freshly ground black pepper

Preheat the oven to 350°F (180°C/gas 4). • Make several small incisions in the lamb using a sharp knife. Insert the pieces of rosemary, garlic, and pancetta into the incisions. • Place in an oiled roasting pan. Sprinkle with salt and pepper. • Roast until the meat is tender and cooked through, about 1 hour 30 minutes. Baste the lamb from time to time during cooking. • Serve hot.

Serves: 4–6 • Prep: 10 min. • Cooking: 1 hr 30 min • Level: 1

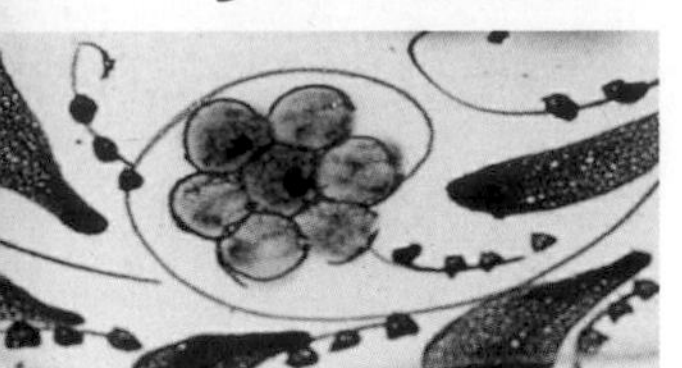

Lamb fricassee

Agnello in fricassea

- 3 tablespoons butter
- 2 tablespoons extra-virgin olive oil
- 1 large onion, finely chopped
- $2\frac{1}{2}$ lb (1.25 kg) lamb shoulder, boned and cut into bite-size pieces
- $\frac{1}{2}$ cup (125 ml) dry white wine
- $1\frac{1}{2}$ cups (375 ml) boiling vegetable stock, homemade (see page 112) or bouillon cube
- 3 tomatoes, peeled and chopped
- 4 large potatoes, peeled and cut into bite size pieces (optional)
- 3 artichoke hearts, cut into bite-size segments (optional)
- 2 large eggs
- salt and freshly ground black pepper
- 2 tablespoons pine nuts
- juice of 1 lemon
- 1 tablespoon finely chopped parsley

Heat the butter and oil in a Dutch oven or heavy saucepan over medium heat. Add the onion and sauté until it begins to soften, 2–3 minutes. • Add the lamb and brown all over, 5–7 minutes. • Add the wine and let evaporate, 3–5 minutes. • Add the stock and tomatoes. Lower the heat, cover, and simmer for 1 hour. • Add the potatoes and artichokes, if using. Cover and simmer until tender, about 30 minutes. • Beat the eggs, salt, pepper, pine nuts, lemon juice, and parsley in a bowl. • Add the egg mixture to the pan and stir until the sauce thickens slightly. • Serve hot.

Serves: 4–6 • Prep: 15 min • Cooking: 1 hr 40 min • Level: 2

Easter lamb

Agnello di Pasqua

Lamb is a traditional dish to serve at Easter in Italy. Normally the lamb is killed very young for this dish so that the meat is very pale and has a delicate flavor. In this particular version, the peas are a symbol of spring.

Preheat the oven to 375°F (190°C/gas 5). • Heat the oil in a large roasting pan over medium heat. Add the onions and sauté until pale golden brown, about 5 minutes. • Add the lamb and pancetta and sauté until lightly browned all over, about 5 minutes. • Add the wine and let it evaporate. • Roast in the oven for 45 minutes. • Add the peas. Season with salt and pepper. Add a little more wine if the meat is beginning to dry out. • Return to the oven and roast until the meat is cooked through, about 45 minutes. • Beat the eggs, pecorino, and parsley in a bowl. • Pour this mixture over the cooked meat and bake until set, 3–5 minutes. • Serve hot.

Serves: 4–6 • Prep: 25 min • Cooking: 1 hr 45 min • Level: 2

- $\frac{1}{4}$ cup (60 ml) extra-virgin olive oil
- 2 medium onions, coarsely chopped
- $2\frac{1}{2}$ lb (1.2 kg) suckling lamb on the bone, cut into 6–8 pieces
- $\frac{1}{2}$ cup (60 g) chopped pancetta, (optional)
- $\frac{1}{2}$ cup (125 ml) dry white wine
- 3 cups (450 g) frozen peas
- salt and freshly ground black pepper
- 3 large eggs, lightly beaten
- $\frac{3}{4}$ cup (90 g) freshly grated pecorino cheese
- 3 tablespoons finely chopped parsley

Sweet and sour lamb

Agnello in agrodolce

- $\frac{1}{4}$ cup (60 ml) extra-virgin olive oil
- 1 large onion, finely chopped
- 2 lb (1 kg) boned lamb shoulder, cut into cubes
- 4 large tomatoes, peeled and chopped
- $\frac{1}{2}$ cup (125 ml) milk
- salt and freshly ground black pepper to taste
- $\frac{1}{4}$ cup (50 g) sugar
- $\frac{1}{2}$ cup (125 ml) white wine vinegar

Heat the oil in a heavy-bottomed saucepan over medium-high heat and sauté the onion until softened, 3–4 minutes. • Add the lamb and sauté until browned, 5–7 minutes. • Add the tomatoes and milk. Season with salt and pepper. Reduce heat to low and simmer until the lamb is very tender, about 1 hour. • When the lamb is almost done, add the sugar and vinegar. Simmer for 10 more minutes, then serve hot.

Serves: 4–6 • Prep: 10 min • Cooking: 1 hr 15 min • Level: 1

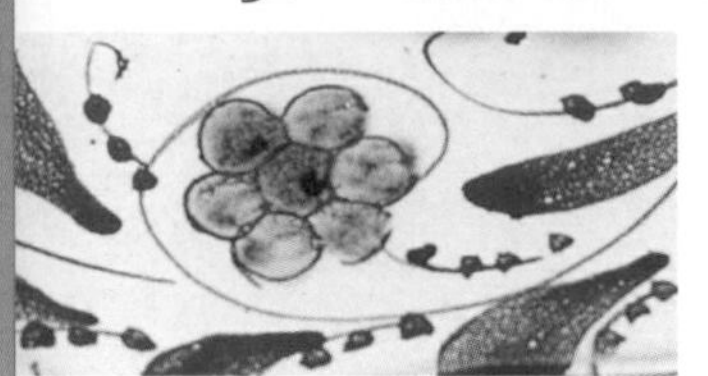

Breaded lamb chops

Costolette d'agnello fritte

- 2 lb (1 kg) thin, single-rib lamb chops
- salt
- 1/2 cup (75 g) all-purpose (plain) flour
- 1 egg
- 1 cup (125 g) fine dry bread crumbs
- 1–2 cups (250–500 ml) olive oil, for frying

Pound the chops lightly to spread the meat as much as possible. • Sprinkle with salt and dredge in the flour, shaking to remove excess. • Dip in the egg and coat well with the bread crumbs. • Heat the oil in a heavy-bottomed pan and fry the chops, turning often, until golden brown on both sides, about 10 minutes. • Drain on paper towels and serve very hot.

Serves: 4 • Prep: 10 min • Cooking: 10 min • Level: 1

Lamb chops with tomatoes and peppers

Costolette d'agnello al pomodoro

Heat half the oil in a large frying pan over medium heat. Add the lamb chops and sauté until browned all over, 5–7 minutes. Remove from the heat. • Heat the remaining oil in the same pan over medium heat. Add the onions, bell peppers, olives, and parsley. Sauté until the vegetables are softened, about 5 minutes. Season with salt and pepper. • Add the lamb chops and their cooking juices. Mix well and then add the tomatoes. Bring to a boil, cover, then simmer until the sauce is thick and the meat is tender, 30–40 minutes. • Serve hot.

Serves: 4–6 • Prep: 5 min • Cooking: 50 min • Level: 2

- 1/3 cup (90 ml) extra-virgin olive oil
- 2 1/2 lb (1.2 kg) thick lamb loin chops
- 2 medium onions, finely chopped
- 2 red bell peppers (capsicums), seeded and cut in short strips
- 1 1/2 cups (150 g) pitted green olives, halved
- 2 tablespoons freshly chopped parsley
- salt and freshly ground black pepper
- 2 (14-oz/400-g) cans tomatoes, with juice

Grilled lamb chops

Costolette a scottadito

- 2 lb (1 kg) thin, single-rib lamb chops
- 2 tablespoons extra-virgin olive oil
- salt and freshly ground black pepper

Place the chops on a large plate and drizzle with the oil, if using. Sprinkle with salt and a generous grinding of pepper. • Arrange the chops under in a grill pan and place over high heat. Turn frequently until well-cooked. If you don't have a grill pan, arrange the chops on a broiler rack and place under the broiler. Turn frequently until they are done. • Serve very hot.

Serves: 4 • Prep: 5 min • Cooking: 15 min • Level: 1

Roast leg of lamb with aromatic herbs

Cosciotto d'agnello alle erbe aromatiche

Preheat the oven to 375°F (190°C/gas 5). • Cut the crusts off the bread and chop in a food processor with the garlic and aromatic herbs (leaves only). Season with salt and a generous grinding of pepper. • Melt the butter in a roasting pan in the oven for a few minutes. • Place the lamb in the roasting pan, drizzle with the oil, and scatter with the chopped herbs and bread. • Return to the oven and roast until the meat is tender, about 1 hour 30 minutes. Baste from time to time with the wine. • Transfer to a heated serving dish and serve hot.

Serves: 6–8 • Prep: 10 min • Cooking: 1 hr 45 min • Level: 1

- 3 slices sandwich bread
- 2 cloves garlic
- mixture of aromatic herbs: 4 leaves sage, 1 sprig rosemary, 1 sprig thyme, 1 sprig marjoram, 1 large bunch parsley
- salt and freshly ground black pepper
- 2 tablespoons butter
- 4 lb (2 kg) leg of lamb
- 1/4 cup (60 ml) extra-virgin olive oil
- 2/3 cup (150 ml) dry white wine

PORK

In Italian, pork is known as *maiale,* a name that derives from the ancient Roman custom of sacrificing a pig to the earth goddess Maia. In Christian times, the pig became associated with the Egyptian saint, Anthony the Great, and came to be a symbol of his victory over sins of the flesh, such as sloth, selfishness, lust, greed, and gluttony. Whatever its symbolism, the pig has always been an important source of meat in Italy, especially for people of humble origin. Nowadays many of Italy's best-known food products, most notably prosciutto (Parma ham), but also mortadella, pancetta, coppa, cotechino, zampone, and a host of other deli meats, are all pork products. In this chapter we have gathered some 21 recipes, for everything from roasts and stews to pork chops, but also some for pork products, such as salsicce, zampone, and cotechino (see recipes on pages 324, 325, and 326).

Sausages with grapes (see page 326)

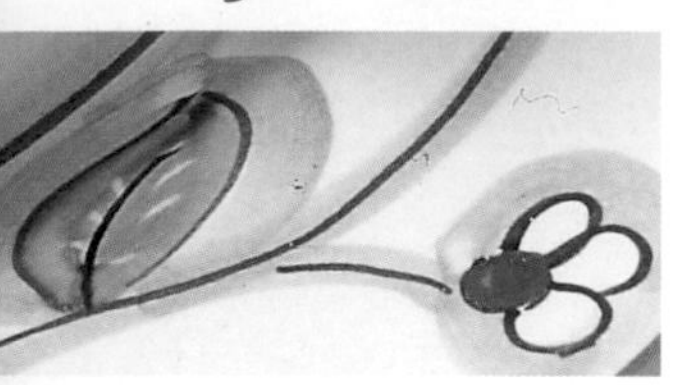

Roast pork loin with potatoes

Roast pork loin rib with potatoes

Carré di maiale arrosto con patate

- 4 lb (2 kg) pork loin rib roast (bones in)
- 3–4 cloves garlic, peeled and cut in half
- salt and freshly ground black pepper
- 2 tablespoons fresh rosemary leaves
- 1/4 cup (60 ml) extra-virgin olive oil
- 2 tablespoons butter
- 1/2 cup (125 ml) dry white wine
- 2 lb (1 kg) small round starchy (baking) potatoes

Preheat the oven to 350°F (180°C/gas 4). • Tie the pork with kitchen string. Use a sharp knife or skewer to make deep holes in the meat. Season the garlic generously with salt and pepper. Fill the holes with pieces of garlic and rosemary. • Heat the oil and butter in a large roasting pan over medium-high heat. Add the pork and brown well on the bottom and sides. • Pour in the wine and sauté until it evaporates. • Roast in the oven for 45 minutes. Add the potatoes and roast until the meat is tender and the potatoes are crisp, about 45 minutes. • Serve hot or at room temperature.

Serves: 4–6 • Prep: 20 min • Cooking: 1 hr 30 min Level: 1

Roast pork with red wine

Cosciotto di maiale al chianti

This Tuscan recipe calls for dry red wine and is usually made using the region's famous Chianti wine. You may substitute with any robust dry red.

- 5 lb (2.5 kg) pork loin roast, with bone
- salt and freshly ground black pepper
- 1 teaspoon ground cinnamon
- 1/3 cup (50 g) all-purpose (plain) flour
- 2 onions, coarsely chopped
- 4 bay leaves
- 1/4 cup (60 ml) extra-virgin olive oil
- 1 cup (250 ml) robust red wine
- 1 cup (180 g) raisins
- 6 oz (180 g) green olives

Preheat the oven to 400°F (200°C/gas 6). • Season the pork with salt, pepper, and cinnamon, then dust with the flour. • Place in a roasting pan with the onions and bay leaves and drizzle with the oil. • Bake for 30 minutes, drizzle with half the wine, and return to the oven. • Soak the raisins in a small bowl of tepid water for 15 minutes. Drain well. • After another 30 minutes, drizzle the pork with the remaining wine, and sprinkle with the raisins and olives. Return to the oven and roast until tender, about 1 more hour. • Serve hot.

Serves: 6 • Prep: 10 min • Cooking: 2 hr • Level: 1

Roast spareribs

Rosticciana

- 5 lb (2.5 kg) spareribs
- salt and freshly ground black pepper
- 2 tablespoons fresh rosemary leaves
- 1/4 cup (60 ml) extra-virgin olive oil
- 4 cloves garlic, peeled and cut in half

Preheat the oven to 350°F (180°C/gas 4). • Place the spareribs in a large roasting pan. Season with salt and pepper, sprinkle with the rosemary, and drizzle with the oil. Use a sharp knife to make 8 incisions in the meaty parts of the spareribs and fill each one with garlic. • Roast the spareribs until tender and cooked through, about 50 minutes. The exact cooking time will depend on how much meat is on the spareribs • Serve hot.

Serves: 6 • Prep: 10 min • Cooking: 50 min • Level: 1

Roast suckling pig with vegetables

Maialino al forno

- 2 onions, 2 carrots, 2 stalks celery, 2 zucchini (courgettes), 3 potatoes, all diced
- 1 leek, sliced
- 1/3 cup (90 ml) extra-virgin olive oil
- dash of salt
- 1/2 suckling pig, about 5 lb (2.5 kg)
- 10 black peppercorns
- 2 bay leaves
- 1 cup (250 ml) dry white wine
- 1 tablespoon finely chopped parsley
- 2 cloves garlic, finely chopped

Preheat the oven to 400°F (200°C/gas 6). • Sauté the vegetables in a large saucepan with 2 tablespoons of oil over high heat for 5–6 minutes. • Sprinkle with salt and stir well. Remove from the heat and set aside. • Add the remaining oil to the same pan and brown the pork. • Transfer the meat and any liquid it has produced to a roasting pan. Sprinkle with a little more salt and the peppercorns. Add the bay leaves and turn the meat in its juices. • Roast until tender, about hours, basting frequently and gradually adding the wine. After the pork has been cooking for 1 hour, add the vegetables and sprinkle with the garlic and parsley. • Arrange on a serving dish with the vegetables and serve hot.

Serves: 6 • Prep: 10 min • Cooking: 2 hr 15 min • Level: 1

Pork chops in onion sauce

PORK CHOPS COOKED IN TOMATO

Braciole di maiale al pomodoro

- 4 large pork chops, on the bone
- 1/4 cup (60 ml) extra virgin olive oil
- 1 small onion, finely chopped
- 1 clove garlic, finely chopped
- 3 tablespoons white wine vinegar
- 1/3 cup (90 ml) dry white wine
- 1 (14-oz/400-g) can tomatoes, with juice
- 1 bay leaf
- salt and freshly ground black pepper
- 2 tablespoons butter

Pound the meat lightly to flatten. • Heat the oil in a Dutch oven or earthenware dish over medium heat. Add the onion and garlic. Sauté until softened, about 5 minutes. • Add the chops, making sure that they do not overlap. Sauté until the meat is lightly browned all over, 3–4 minutes each side. • Drain off the oil and add the vinegar. Cook until the vinegar has evaporated, 1–2 minutes. • Add the white wine and cook until it has almost all evaporated, 2–3 minutes. • Add the tomatoes and bay leaf. Season with salt and pepper. Turn the chops several times, until evenly coated in the sauce. Lower the heat and simmer until the meat is tender and the sauce is thick, about 40 minutes. Add a little water if the sauce begins to stick to the dish. Remove from the heat. • Transfer the chops to a heated serving dish. • Add the butter to the dish and mix until melted. Spoon the sauce over the chops and serve hot.

Serves: 4 • Prep: 10 min • Cooking: 1 hr • Level: 1

PORK CHOPS IN ONION SAUCE

Cipollata

- 1 1/2 lb (750 g) pork chops
- 10 cups (2.5 liters) water
- salt
- 2 1/2 lb (1.2 kg) onions
- 1 stalk celery, chopped
- 1 carrot, chopped
- 1/4 cup (60 ml) extra virgin olive oil
- 4 oz (125 g) Italian pork sausages, skinned and crumbled
- 1/2 cup (60 g) pancetta or bacon, chopped
- 4–6 slices of crusty white bread
- 2 cloves garlic
- freshly made mashed potatoes, to serve

Place the pork chops in a large saucepan, cover with the water, and season with salt. Chop one of the onions into chunks. Add the celery, carrot, and chopped onion to the saucepan. Bring to a boil over medium heat. Cover and simmer over low heat until the meat begins to come away from the bones, about 1 hour. Transfer the chops to a large bowl using a slotted spoon. • Strain the stock through a fine mesh strainer and then return it to the saucepan. Keep the stock warm. • Slice the remaining onions thinly. • Heat the oil in a large saucepan over medium heat. Add the sausage and pancetta and sauté until lightly browned, about 5 minutes. • Add the sliced onions and sauté until softened, about 10 minutes. • Add 2 ladles of the stock and simmer until the mixture is thick and the onions are very tender, 15–20 minutes. • Return the pork chops to the pan. Add the remaining stock and bring to a boil. Season with salt and pepper, and simmer for 15 minutes. Remove from the heat. • Serve hot with mashed potatoes.

Serves: 4–6 • Prep: 25 min • Cooking: 1hr 40 min • Level: 2

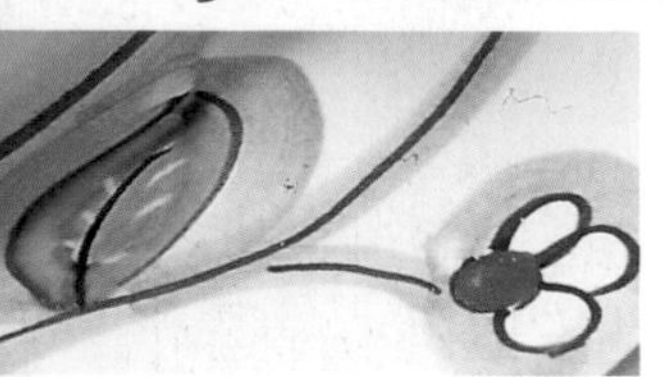

Cotechino with Brussels sprouts

Cotechino con cavolini di bruxelles in umido

- 1 packaged, pre-cooked cotechino sausage
- $1\frac{1}{2}$ lb (750 g) Brussels sprouts, cleaned
- 2 tablespoons butter
- 1 onion, finely chopped
- 2 tablespoons finely chopped parsley
- 1 (14-oz/400-g) can tomatoes, with juice
- 1 bay leaf
- salt and freshly ground black pepper

Cook the cotechino in a large pot of boiling water following the instructions on the package. Cooking time is usually 30–40 minutes. • Blanch the Brussels sprouts in boiling water for 3 minutes. Drain well. • Heat the butter in a heavy saucepan and sauté the onion and parsley until the onion is softened, 3–4 minutes. • Add the Brussels sprouts, tomatoes, and bay leaf. Season with salt and pepper and simmer until the tomatoes have reduced and the Brussels sprouts are tender, about 20 minutes. • Place the Brussels sprouts and sauce in a heated serving dish. Unwrap the cotechino sausage, slice, and place over the Brussels sprouts. • Serve hot.

Serves: 4–6 • Prep: 30 min • Cooking: 30–40 min • Level: 1

Sausages with grapes

Salsicce all'uva

- 8 Italian pork sausages
- 2 tablespoons extra-virgin olive oil
- 2 bunches of seedless white grapes, washed and removed from the stems

Prick the sausages all over with a fork. • Heat the oil in a frying pan over medium heat and add the sausages. Brown the sausages all over, 5–7 minutes. • Drain off the excess fat. • Add the grapes and simmer until the sausages are cooked through, about 5 minutes. Stir often during the cooking time to coat the grapes in the cooking juices but try not to burst them. • Transfer to a serving dish and serve hot.

Serves: 4 • Prep: 5 min • Cooking: 15 min • Level: 1

Zampone with lentils

Zampone con lenticchie

Zampone and cotechino—in the previous recipe—are large, highly flavored pork sausages made in Emilia-Romagna. The filling for zampone is packed inside a pig's foot (trotter). Both sausages are available in Italian delicatessens and supermarkets. Previously they needed to be soaked and simmered for hours but are now available (usually in foil packages) pre-soaked and partially cooked. Read the instructions on the package for the cooking time, as this may vary from one brand to another. Zampone with lentils is traditionally served on New Year's Eve as it is believed that it will bring luck—and wealth—in the coming year.

- 1 packaged, pre-cooked zampone (stuffed pig's foot) sausage weighing about 2 lb (1 kg)
- 2 tablespoons extra-virgin olive oil
- $\frac{1}{2}$ cup (60 g) finely chopped pancetta
- $1\frac{1}{2}$ cups (300 g) lentils (small brown or Puy type)
- 1 medium onion, finely chopped
- 1 bay leaf
- boiling water
- 1 bouillon cube

Cook the zampone in a large pot of boiling water following the instructions on the package. Cooking time is usually 30–40 minutes. • Heat the oil in a heavy saucepan and sauté the pancetta for 2–3 minutes. • Add the onion and bay leaf and sauté until the onion is softened, 3–4 minutes. • Add the lentils and sauté in the oil for 2–3 minutes. • Add sufficient boiling water to cover the lentils completely and crumble the bouillon cube into the water. • Simmer over low heat until tender but not mushy, about 25–30 minutes. Drain and remove the bay leaf. • Unwrap the zampone, slice, and serve very hot, accompanied by the lentils.

Serves: 6–8 • Prep: 15 min • Cooking: about 40 min
Level: 1

VEGETABLES

Almost every Italian lunch or dinner features vegetables, usually as appetizers, salads, or side dishes. In this chapter, we have gathered recipes that are usually served as sides to accompany meat or fish main courses. If you don't want a meat dish to be the main feature of your meal, prepare three or four of these vegetable dishes and serve them together. We have included all the classics, such as Stewed bell peppers (see page 336), Grilled summer vegetables (see page 336), and Baked stuffed tomatoes (see page 332) and Stuffed eggplants (see page 340), as well as a superb variation on the classic Eggplant parmigiana (see page 340) and a wonderful recipe for Stuffed zucchini flowers (see page 348). For best results with these recipes, be sure to use only the freshest in-season vegetables; it is pointless, for example, to grill a zucchini or bell pepper imported from far away in mid-winter—it will be quite tasteless. Use the vegetables of each season, preferably bought at farmers' markets.

Grilled summer vegetables (see page 336)

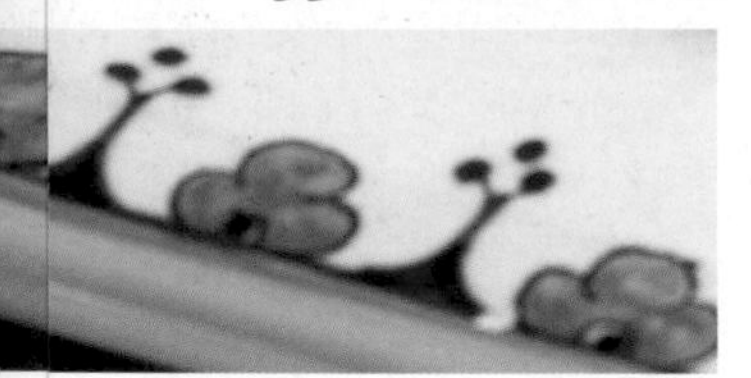

Baked stuffed tomatoes

Mixed vegetable skewers

Spiedini misti di verdure

- 2 zucchini (courgettes)
- 12 cherry tomatoes
- 2 medium onions
- 3 small bell peppers (capsicums), mixed colors
- ½ cup (125 ml) extra virgin olive oil
- salt and freshly ground black pepper
- ½ teaspoon sweet paprika
- juice of ½ lemon
- 1 tablespoon finely chopped fresh or 1 teaspoon dried herbs (oregano, mint, or thyme)

Cut the zucchini in thick wheels. Cut the cherry tomatoes in half. Cut the onions into quarters, then cut each quarter in half. Cut the bell peppers in 1½-inch (5-cm) squares. • Thread the vegetable pieces alternately onto wooden skewers. Set them on a plate. • Place the oil, salt, pepper, paprika, lemon juice, and herbs in a small bowl and beat with a fork until well mixed. • Drizzle over the skewers, cover with aluminum foil, and chill in the refrigerator for 2 hours. • Heat a grill pan or griddle until very hot. Drain the skewers and place half of them in the grill pan. Grill, turning them so that they brown on all sides and basting them with the marinade until tender, about 10 minutes. Repeat with the remaining skewers. • Serve hot.

Serves: 4 • Prep: 25 min + 2 hr to marinate • Cooking: 20 min • Level: 1

Baked stuffed tomatoes

Pomodori ripieni di carne

- 4 large firm tomatoes
- salt and freshly ground black pepper
- ¼ cup (60 ml) extra virgin olive oil
- ¼ cup (60 g) butter
- 1 small onion, finely chopped
- 8 oz (250 g) lean ground (minced) beef
- ⅓ cup (90 ml) beef stock, homemade (see page 104) or bouillon cube
- 4 tablespoons finely chopped parsley
- 3 tablespoons finely chopped basil
- 1 clove garlic
- 4 oz (125 g) mortadella or cooked ham
- ½ cup (60 g) freshly grated Parmesan cheese
- 2 large eggs, lightly beaten
- ½ cup (60 g) fine dry bread crumbs

Preheat the oven to 375°F (190°C/gas 5). • Cut the tops off the tomatoes using a sharp knife. Use a teaspoon to scoop out and discard the seeds. Season the tomatoes with a little salt and pepper. • Heat half the oil and half the butter in a large frying pan over low heat. Add the onion and sauté until softened, 3–4 minutes. • Add the beef and sauté until lightly browned, about 5 minutes. • Add the stock and simmer until the meat is almost cooked, about 10 minutes. Remove from the heat. • Put the parsley, basil, garlic, and mortadella into a food processor and chop finely. • Transfer to a bowl and add the meat, Parmesan, eggs, and half the bread crumbs. Season with salt and pepper and mix well. • Spoon into the hollowed out tomatoes and arrange them in an oiled baking pan. Sprinkle with the remaining bread crumbs. Dot with the remaining butter and drizzle with the remaining oil. • Bake until cooked through and lightly browned, 45 minutes. • Serve hot or at room temperature.

Serves: 4 • Prep: 25 min • Cooking: 1 hr 5 min • Level: 2

Sweet and sour baby onions

Cipolline in agrodolce

- 1 lb (500 g) white baby onions
- ½ cup (60 g) diced prosciutto (Parma ham)
- 1 tablespoon lard (or butter or extra-virgin olive oil)
- salt and freshly ground black pepper
- 1 tablespoon sugar
- 3 tablespoons white wine vinegar
- scant ½ cup (100 ml) cold water

Clean the onions and place in a bowl of cold water. • Sauté the prosciutto in the lard (or butter or oil) in a medium saucepan. • Drain the onions and add to the pan. Season with salt and pepper and add the sugar. Pour in the vinegar and water. • Simmer over medium-low heat until the onions are tender and the cooking juices have almost all been absorbed, about 30 minutes. • Serve hot or at room temperature.

Serves: 4–6 · Prep: 10 min · Cooking: 40 min · Level: 1

Savory onions and tomatoes

Frizon

- ½ cup (125 ml) extra-virgin olive oil
- 2 lb (1 kg) onions, peeled and sliced
- 1 red bell pepper (capsicum) and 1 yellow bell pepper (capsicum), cleaned and cut into small pieces
- 1½ lb (750 g) tomatoes, peeled and chopped
- salt and freshly ground black pepper

Heat the oil in a large heavy saucepan and sauté the onions until soft, 7–10 minutes. • Add the bell peppers and simmer for 10 minutes. • Add the tomatoes and season with salt and pepper. Simmer over low heat until the bell peppers are very tender, about 30 minutes, stirring now and then. • Serve hot or at room temperature.

Serves: 4–6 • Prep: 15 min • Cooking: 50 min • Level: 1

Spinach with pine nuts and anchovies

Spinach soufflé

Soufflé di spinaci

- 1½ lb (750 g) fresh spinach, tough stems removed
- ⅓ cup (90 g) butter
- ¼ cup (30 g) freshly grated Parmesan cheese
- 3 large eggs, separated
- salt
- 3 tablespoons fine dry bread crumbs
- 8 salt-cured anchovy fillets

Preheat the oven to 375°F (190°C/gas 5). • Rinse the spinach under cold running water. Do not drain. Cook over medium heat with just the water left clinging to the leaves. • Chop finely in a food processor. • Place in a small frying pan with ¼ cup (60 g) of butter over medium heat and sauté until the butter has been absorbed. • Place the spinach in a bowl with the Parmesan and egg yolks. Mix until smooth. • Beat the egg whites with a pinch of salt until very stiff. Fold them into the spinach mixture. • Butter an 8-inch (20-cm) soufflé mold and sprinkle with the bread crumbs. • Place half the spinach mixture in the mold and cover with the anchovy fillets. Cover with the remaining spinach. • Chop the remaining butter and scatter over the top of the soufflé. • Bake for 30 minutes. Serve hot.

Serves: 4 • Prep: 15 min • Cooking: 40 min • Level: 2

Spinach with pine nuts and anchovies

Spinaci alla genovese

- 2 lb (1 kg) fresh spinach, tough stems removed
- ⅓ cup (90 ml) extra-virgin olive oil
- 3 salt-cured anchovies, rinsed and chopped
- 2 tablespoons finely chopped parsley
- generous ¼ cup (50 g) golden raisins (sultanas), soaked in warm water for 15 minutes and drained
- generous ¼ cup (50 g) pine nuts
- ¼ teaspoon freshly grated nutmeg
- salt and freshly ground black pepper

• Rinse the spinach under cold running water. Do not drain. Cook over medium heat with just the water left clinging to the leaves. Chop coarsely with a knife. • Heat the oil in a large saucepan over a low heat. Sauté the anchovies and parsley for 2–3 minutes. • Add the spinach, raisins, pine nuts, and nutmeg. Season with salt and pepper. • Mix well and cook for 10 minutes. • Serve hot.

Serves: 4 • Prep: 10 min • Cooking: 25 min • Level: 1

Braised savoy cabbage, Venetian-style

Verze sofegae

- 1 Savoy cabbage, about 4 lb (2 kg)
- $3/4$ cup (90 g) finely chopped fresh lard (replace with butter or extra-virgin olive oil, if preferred)
- 1 sprig, rosemary
- 1 clove garlic, whole but lightly crushed
- salt
- $1/2$ cup (125 ml) dry white wine

Braised Savoy cabbage is a classic side dish for strongly flavored meat dishes, such as pork or sausages.

Discard the tougher leaves of the cabbage; then take the rest apart leaf by leaf, cutting out the hard ribs and rinsing. Cut the leaves into thin strips. • Chop the lard and rosemary leaves together with a mezzaluna (half-moon cutter) or heavy kitchen knife. • Sauté in a heavy saucepan with the garlic, discarding the latter when it starts to color. • Add the shredded cabbage and season with salt. Cover and simmer over low heat, stirring frequently to prevent the cabbage catching and burning, for 1 hour. • Add the wine, cover and simmer for another hour. • Serve hot.

Serves: 6 • Prep: 10 min • Cooking: 2 hr • Level: 1

Cauliflower with tomato and fennel seeds

Cavolfiore in umido

- 2 cloves garlic, finely chopped
- 1 teaspoon fennel seeds
- $1/4$ cup (60 ml) extra-virgin olive oil
- 4–6 peeled and chopped tomatoes
- 1 medium cauliflower
- salt and freshly ground black pepper

Heat the oil in a large frying pan over medium heat. Sauté the garlic and fennel seeds until the garlic is pale gold, 3–4 minutes. • Stir in the tomatoes and simmer for 15 minutes. • Cut the cauliflower into florets, removing the tough pieces of stalk. • Place the cauliflower in the tomato sauce and season with salt and pepper. • Cover and simmer over medium heat until the cauliflower is tender, 15–20 minutes. • Serve hot.

Serves: 4–6 • Prep: 10 min • Cooking: 40 min • Level: 1

Cauliflower with tomato and fennel seeds

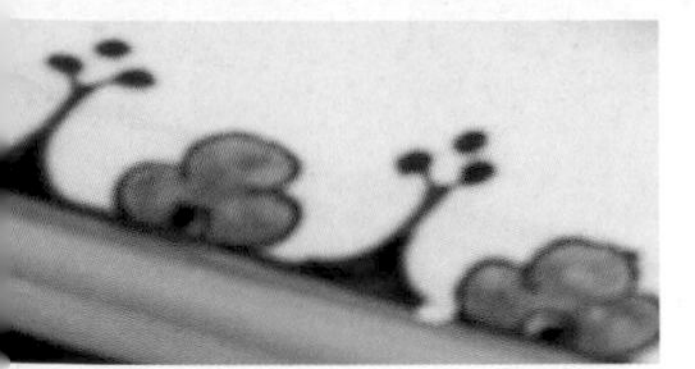

Stewed bell peppers

Stewed bell peppers

Peperonata

- 1/3 cup (90 ml) extra-virgin olive oil
- 6 onions, thinly sliced
- 2 (14-oz/400-g) cans tomatoes, with juice
- 2 red bell peppers (capsicums), seeded and sliced
- 2 yellow peppers (capsicums), seeded and sliced
- 2 green bell peppers (capsicums), seeded and sliced
- 1/3 cup (90 ml) white wine vinegar
- 1 cup (100 g) pitted green olives, coarsely chopped
- salt

Heat the oil in a large frying pan over medium heat. Add the onion and sauté until softened, 3–4 minutes. • Add the tomatoes and bell peppers and mix well. Simmer until the peppers are very tender and the sauce has reduced, about 30 minutes. • Stir in the vinegar. Simmer until the vinegar has evaporated, 5 minutes. • Add the olives and season with salt. Mix well and simmer for 5 minutes. • Serve warm or at room temperature.

Serves: 6–8 • Prep: 5 min • Cooking: 45 min • Level: 1

Baked fennel with Parmesan cheese

Finocchi alla parmigiana

- 6 large bulbs fennel
- 1/2 cup (125 g) butter
- 1/3 cup (50 g) all-purpose (plain) flour
- 1 large onion, thinly sliced
- 1 1/4 cups (150 g) diced ham
- 1/4 cup (60 ml) heavy (double) cream
- salt and freshly ground black pepper
- 1 1/4 cups (150 g) freshly grated Parmesan cheese

Preheat the oven to 375°F (190°C/gas 5). • Clean the fennel by removing the tough outer leaves. Trim the stalks and cut each bulb in half. • Cook in salted boiling water until almost tender, about 8 minutes. • Drain well. Cut each half fennel bulb into 2 or 3 wedges. • Heat half the butter in a frying pan over medium heat. • Dredge the fennel and onion in the flour and sauté in the butter until golden brown, about 5 minutes. • Add the ham and cream and season with salt and pepper. Cover and simmer over low heat for 15 minutes. • Spoon into a buttered baking dish. Sprinkle with the Parmesan and dot with the remaining butter. • Bake until golden brown, about 20 minutes. • Serve hot.

Serves: 4–6 • Prep: 15 min • Cooking: 45 min • Level: 1

Baked bell peppers

Peperoni al forno

- 6 large bell peppers (capsicums), mixed colors, cleaned and cut into small strips
- 20 black olives, pitted and quartered
- 6 salt-cured anchovy fillets, coarsely chopped
- 1/4 cup (50 g) pine nuts
- 2 tablespoons capers
- 12 fresh basil leaves, torn
- 1/3 cup (90 ml) extra-virgin olive oil
- salt
- 1/2 cup (60 g) fine dry bread crumbs

This brightly colored dish is delicious served hot but even better when left to stand at room temperature for 2–3 hours before serving.

Preheat the oven to 375°F (190°C/gas 5). • Rinse the bell peppers and dry with paper towels. Place in a large bowl and add the olives, anchovies, pine nuts, capers, and basil. • Add 1/4 cup (60 ml) of oil and the salt and toss (as if you were tossing a salad). • Grease a large ovenproof dish with the remaining oil and add the bell pepper mixture, pressing down gently. • Sprinkle with the bread crumbs. • Bake until the bell peppers are tender, about 35 minutes.

Serves: 4 • Prep: 15 min • Cooking: 35 min • Level: 1

Grilled summer vegetables

Verdure grigliate

- 4 medium zucchini (courgettes), sliced lengthwise
- 1 red bell pepper (capsicum), seeded and cut in strips
- 1 yellow bell pepper (capsicum), seeded and cut in strips
- 1 large eggplant (aubergine), with peel, sliced
- salt and freshly ground black pepper
- 1/3 cup (90 ml) extra-virgin olive oil

Heat a grill pan over high heat. • Place the zucchini in the pan and grill until tender, about 5 minutes each side. • Place the bell pepper strips in the grill pan and grill until tender, about 10 minutes. • Place the eggplant slices in the grill pan and grill until tender, about 5 minutes each side. • Place all the grilled vegetables on a large serving plate. • Season with salt and pepper. Drizzle with the oil and serve hot or at room temperature.

Serves: 6 • Prep: 15 min • Cooking: 30 min • Level: 1

Potato and vegetable gateau

Potato and vegetable gateau

Gateau di patate e verdure

- 2 lb (1 kg) starchy potatoes, peeled
- 2 large carrots, peeled and sliced
- 10 asparagus tips, cut into 1 inch (3 cm) sections
- 8 oz (250 g) fresh or frozen fava (broad) beans
- 1 cup (150 g) frozen peas
- ½ cup (60 g) freshly grated Parmesan cheese
- 4 oz (125 g) caciotta or other mild firm cheese, cut into small cubes
- generous ⅓ cup (100 ml) milk
- ½ cup (125 ml) heavy (double) cream
- ⅓ cup (90 g) butter, melted
- 4 large eggs, lightly beaten
- ½ teaspoon freshly grated nutmeg
- salt and freshly ground black pepper
- 4 oz (125 g) ham, sliced
- 3 tablespoons fresh bread crumbs

Cook the potatoes in a large pot of salted boiling water until tender, 25–30 minutes. • Drain well and mash until smooth. • Preheat the oven to 375°F (190°C/gas 5). • Oil a 9 inch (23 cm) springform pan. • Cook the carrots in a large pot of salted boiling water until tender, about 10 minutes. Drain well. • Cook the asparagus in a large pot of salted boiling water until tender, 5–7 minutes. Drain well. • Cook the beans in a large pot of salted boiling water until tender, 5–7 minutes. Drain well. • Cook the peas in a large pot of salted boiling water until tender, 5 minutes. Drain well. • Mix the potato, Parmesan, caciotta, milk, cream, ¼ cup (60 g) of the butter, the eggs, and nutmeg in a large bowl. Season with salt and pepper. Add the carrots, peas, beans, and asparagus. Mix well. • Spoon half the mixture into the prepared pan. Level the surface using the back of a spoon. Place the ham on top. Cover with the remaining vegetable mixture. Level the surface with the back of a spoon. Sprinkle with bread crumbs and drizzle with the remaining butter. • Bake until the top is browned, 45 minutes. • Serve hot or at room temperature

Serves: 6 • Prep: 20 min • Cooking: 1 hr 45 min • Level: 1

Asparagus with egg dressing

Asparagi di Bassano

Trim off the tough lower parts of the asparagus stalks. Rinse well under cold running water. • Steam the asparagus until the stalks are tender, about 5 minutes. The cooking time will vary depending on the freshness and thickness of the asparagus. • Take the asparagus carefully out of the saucepan and refresh by rinsing briefly in a colander under cold running water. This will stop them cooking and keep them an attractive fresh green color. • Mash the eggs in a bowl with a fork, blending in the oil, vinegar, salt, and pepper until smooth. • Arrange the asparagus on a serving dish and spoon the dressing over the tips. • Serve hot or at room temperature.

Serves: 6 • Prep: 15 min • Cooking: 15 min • Level: 1

- 3 lb (1.5 kg) very fresh, young asparagus
- 4 hard-boiled eggs
- 3 tablespoons extra-virgin olive oil
- 2 tablespoons white wine vinegar
- salt and freshly ground black pepper

Potato pie

Tortino di patate

- 1½ lb (750 g) firm, waxy potatoes
- ½ cup (125 g) butter
- 8 oz (250 g) Parmesan cheese, sliced
- salt and freshly ground black pepper
- 1 cup (250 ml) milk

Preheat the oven to 400°F (200°C/gas 6). • Boil the potatoes in their skins for about 25 minutes. • Peel while hot and set aside to cool. • Cut into ½-inch (1-cm) slices and arrange in layers in a greased ovenproof dish. Distribute flakes of butter and slices of Parmesan over each layer, then sprinkle with salt and pepper. Pour in the milk. • Bake until golden brown, about 25 minutes.

Serves: 4 • Prep: 20 min • Cooking: 50 min • Level: 1

Carrots in butter sauce

Carote caramellate

Rinse the carrots under cold running water. Cut into sticks about 2 inches (5 cm) long. • Place in a large sauté pan and cover with cold water. Add half the butter. • Cook over high heat until the water evaporates. • Season with salt and pepper, add the remaining butter and sprinkle with the sugar. Sauté the carrots until well-coated with butter. • Add the parsley and serve hot.

Serves: 6 • Prep: 10 min • Cooking: 25 min • Level: 2

- 2 lb (1 kg) carrots,
- ⅓ cup (90 g) butter, chopped
- salt and freshly ground black pepper
- 2 tablespoons sugar
- 2 tablespoons finely chopped parsley

Stuffed eggplants

Melanzane ripiene

- 4 large round eggplants (aubergines), with peel
- 2 tablespoons coarse sea salt
- 4 cloves garlic, finely chopped
- ½ cup (60 g) diced pancetta
- 14 oz sharp Provolone or pecorino romano cheese, cut in small cubes
- ⅓ cup (90 ml) extra-virgin olive oil
- 1 lb (500 g) peeled and chopped fresh tomatoes
- ½ cup (60 g) freshly grated Parmesan cheese
- freshly ground black pepper

Preheat the oven to 375°F (190°C/gas 5). • Cut the eggplants in half lengthwise and use a sharp knife to open crosswise slits in the pulp. Sprinkle with sea salt and let rest for 1 hour. • Combine the garlic, pancetta, and Provolone or pecorino cheese in a bowl. • Pour half the oil into a baking dish and place the eggplants in it. Cover with the filling, pushing it into the slits opened earlier. Cover with the tomato, drizzle with the remaining oil, and sprinkle with the Parmesan. Season with a generous grinding of pepper. • Bake until tender, about 30 minutes. • Serve hot or at room temperature.

Serves: 4 • Prep: 20 min + 1 hr to drain eggplants
Cooking: 30 min • Level: 1

Spicy grilled eggplants

Melanzane in olio piccante

- 3 large round eggplants, with peel
- 2 tablespoons coarse sea salt
- 1–2 finely chopped hot chile peppers
- salt and freshly ground black pepper
- 1 cup (250 ml) extra-virgin olive oil
- 10 fresh basil leaves, torn

Cut the eggplants in ½-inch (1-cm) thick slices. Sprinkle with sea salt and let rest for 1 hour. • Heat a grill pan to very hot and place the slices on it. Press them down with a fork so the eggplant adheres to the grill pan. Turn the slices often. • As soon as the pulp is soft, remove from the grill pan and arrange on a serving dish. • Combine the chile pepper, salt, and pepper in the oil and beat well with a fork. Cover and set aside. • When the eggplants are all cooked, pour the spicy oil over the top and sprinkle with the basil. • Serve at room temperature.

Serves: 4–6 • Prep: 15 min + 1 hr to drain eggplants
Cooking: 20 min • Level: 1

Eggplant parmigiana

Parmigiana di melanzane

Although the name of this dish brings to mind the city of Parma in the north of Italy it is in fact a pillar of southern cuisine. Parmesan is one of the main ingredients and this perhaps helps to explain the name.

- 6 medium eggplants (aubergines), with peel, sliced lengthwise, ⅔ inch (1.5 cm) thick
- coarse sea salt
- 3 large eggs
- ½ cup (50 g) all-purpose (plain) flour
- 1 cup (250 ml) extra virgin olive oil
- salt
- 1 large onion, finely chopped
- 2 tablespoons finely chopped basil
- 1½ lb (750 g) ripe tomatoes, peeled and chopped
- 1½ cups (200 g) freshly grated Parmesan cheese
- 8 oz (250 g) fresh mozzarella cheese, drained and thinly sliced

Sprinkle the eggplants with coarse sea salt and arrange on a slanted cutting board. Cover with a plate and place a weight on top of the plate. Let rest for 2–3 hours so that they degorge their bitter liquid. • Put the eggs in a small saucepan and cover with water. Bring to a boil over medium heat. Cook for 8 minutes from the moment the water reaches the boil. Drain and cool under cold running water. Shell the eggs and slice them. • Rinse the eggplants and place on paper towels. Pat dry using more paper towels. • Dip each slice of eggplant in the flour, making sure it is evenly coated. Shake gently to remove any excess flour. • Heat ⅓ cup (90 ml) of the oil in a large frying pan over medium heat. • Fry the eggplants in small batches until tender, 5–7 minutes per batch. Drain on paper towels. Sprinkle with salt. Add more oil as required to cook the remaining eggplants. • Heat the remaining oil, about ⅓ cup (90 ml), in a large frying pan over medium heat. Add the onion and basil. Sauté until the onion is softened, 3–4 minutes. • Add the tomatoes and simmer until the sauce reduces, about 30 minutes. • Press the sauce through a fine mesh strainer. • Preheat the oven to 375°F (190°C/gas 5). • Oil a large baking dish. • Arrange a layer of the eggplants in the dish and sprinkle with a little of the Parmesan. Add a layer of mozzarella and a layer of eggs. Drizzle with a few spoons of tomato sauce and then add another layer of eggplant. Continue layering the ingredients until they are all in the dish. Finish with a layer of sauce and a layer of Parmesan. • Bake until the top is lightly browned and crisp, about 30 minutes. • Serve hot or at room temperature.

Serves: 6 • Prep: 40 min + 2–3 hr to degorge eggplants
Cooking: 1 hr 10 min • Level: 2

Peas with pancetta, garlic, and wine

Fava bean and pea stew

Frittedda

- 4 artichokes
- 1 lemon
- 1 small onion, finely chopped
- $^{1}/_{4}$ cup (60 ml) extra-virgin olive oil
- 1 lb (500 g) fresh or frozen fava beans
- 3 cups (450 g) hulled (shelled) peas
- $^{1}/_{8}$ teaspoon freshly grated nutmeg
- salt and freshly ground black pepper
- 1 tablespoon finely chopped mint
- 1 teaspoon sugar
- 1 teaspoon vinegar

Remove the outer leaves from the artichokes and trim the tops and stalks. Cut them in half and remove the choke. Cut the tender hearts in thin wedges. Rub all over with the lemon to prevent discoloring. • Sauté the onion in the oil in a large frying pan over medium heat until softened, 3–4 minutes. • Add the artichokes and sauté for 5 minutes. • Add the fava beans, peas, and nutmeg. Season with salt and pepper and cook over medium-low heat until tender, 25 minutes. • Stir in the mint, sugar, and vinegar and simmer for 2–3 minutes. • Serve hot or at room temperature.

Serves: 4–6 • Prep: 15 min • Cooking: 30 min • Level: 1

Peas with pancetta, garlic, and wine

Piselli alla montaperti

- 1 small white onion or shallot, very thinly sliced
- 1 clove garlic, finely chopped
- 2 tablespoon finely chopped parsley
- $^{1}/_{2}$ cup (125 g) diced pancetta
- $^{1}/_{4}$ cup (60 ml) extra-virgin olive oil
- 4 cups (600 g) frozen peas
- salt and freshly ground black pepper
- $^{1}/_{2}$ cup (125 ml) dry white wine
- $^{1}/_{2}$ cup (125 ml) beef stock, homemade (see page 104) or bouillon cube

Sauté the onion, garlic, parsley, and bacon together in the oil over medium heat for 2 minutes. • Add the peas and season with salt and pepper. Pour in the wine, cover, and simmer gently until tender, 15–20 minutes, stirring occasionally. Moisten with a little stock as necessary. • Serve hot.

Serves: 4–6 • Prep: 10 min • Cooking: 25 min • Level: 1

Green beans with tomatoes

Baggianata piemontese

- 1 lb (500 g) ripe tomatoes
- 2 tablespoons lard (or butter)
- 1 clove garlic, finely chopped
- 8 leaves fresh basil, finely chopped
- 2 tablespoons finely chopped parsley
- 2 lb (1 kg) green beans, trimmed
- 1/2 cup (125 ml) dry red wine
- salt and freshly ground black pepper

Plunge the tomatoes into a pot of boiling water for 1 minute. Drain and place in cold water. Peel and cut in half. Squeeze out as many seeds as possible and chop coarsely. • Melt the lard in a large frying pan and add the garlic, basil, and parsley. Sauté over medium-high heat for 5 minutes. • Add the green beans, tomatoes, and wine, and season with salt and pepper. Cover and simmer over low heat until the beans are tender, about 30 minutes. • Serve hot or at room temperature.

Serves: 4–6 • Prep: 15 min • Cooking: 35 min • Level: 1

Cauliflower mold with black olives

Sformato di cavolfiore con olive

- 2 lb (1 kg) cauliflower head
- 1 quantity Béchamel sauce (see page 151)
- salt and freshly ground black pepper
- 1/4 teaspoon freshly grated nutmeg
- 1/2 cup (60 g) freshly grated Parmesan cheese
- 20 black olives, pitted and chopped
- 3 eggs, beaten until foamy

preheat the oven to 350°F (180°C/gas 4). • Divide the cauliflower into large florets and trim the stems. Cook in a pot of salted, boiling water until tender, 5–7 minutes. Drain and set aside. • Prepare the Béchamel sauce. • Chop the in a food processor until smooth. • Combine the cauliflower purée with the Béchamel, Parmesan, olives, eggs, salt, pepper, and nutmeg. • Grease a ring mold about 10 inches (25 cm) in diameter with a little butter and sprinkle with bread crumbs. Pour the mixture into the mold and place the mold in a larger container filled with water. • Bake until set, about 45 minutes. • Invert the mold onto a platter while still hot. Serve hot or at room temperature.

Serves: 6 • Prep: 25 min • Cooking: 55 min • Level: 2

Green beans with tomatoes

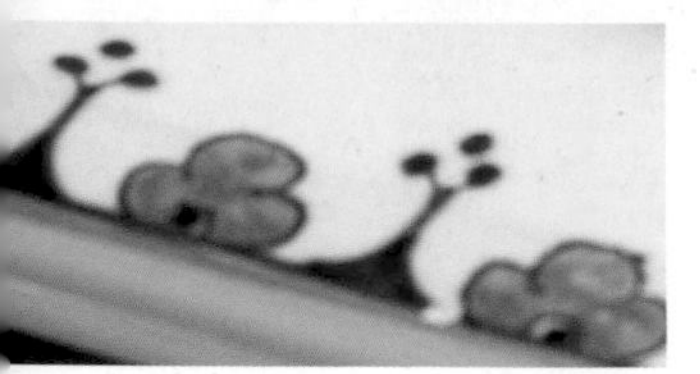

Sweet and sour artichokes

Caponata di carciofi

- 8 very young fresh artichokes
- 1/2 lemon
- 3 tablespoons all-purpose (plain) flour
- 1/3 cup (90 ml) extra-virgin olive oil
- 1 small onion, finely chopped
- 1 tablespoon salt-cured capers
- 12 green olives, pitted and finely chopped
- 1 small carrot, cut into small cubes
- 2 stalks celery, finely chopped
- 1/2 cup (125 ml) hot water
- salt and freshly ground black pepper
- 4 tomatoes, chopped
- 1/4 cup (60 ml) red wine vinegar
- 2 teaspoons sugar

Remove the outer leaves of the artichokes and the top third of the leaves. Remove the choke and peel the remaining stalk. Rub all over with the lemon to prevent discoloring. • Cut each artichoke into six wedges. • Roll the artichokes in the flour. • Sauté the artichokes in the oil in a heavy saucepan over high heat for 3 minutes. • Remove the artichokes, leaving the oil in the pan, and set aside. • Add the onion, capers, olives, carrot, celery, and hot water to the pan. Season with salt and pepper. Simmer over medium heat for 10 minutes. • Add the tomatoes and artichokes. Cover and simmer over low heat for 25 minutes. • Mix the vinegar and sugar and stir into the vegetables. Cook for 5 minutes more. • Serve hot or at room temperature.

Serves: 4 • Prep: 25 min • Cooking: 40 min • Level: 1

Southern vegetable stew

Stufato di verdure

Sauté the bell peppers in the oil in a large frying pan until softened, 5–7 minutes. • Set aside. • In the same pan, sauté the garlic and onion until golden, about 5 minutes. • Add the eggplant, potatoes, zucchini, and tomatoes. Season with salt and pepper. Cover and simmer over low heat for 20 minutes. • Add the bell peppers, parsley, and basil. Simmer for 3 minutes. • Add the capers and olives. • Serve hot or at room temperature.

Serves: 6 • Prep: 15 min • Cooking: 35 min • Level: 1

- 3 yellow and red bell peppers (capsicums), seeded, cut into strips
- 1/3 cup (90 ml) extra-virgin olive oil
- 1 clove garlic, finely chopped
- 1 onion, thinly sliced
- 2 eggplants (aubergines), coarsely chopped
- 2 potatoes, peeled and chopped
- 2 zucchini (courgettes), cut in rounds
- 12 oz (350 g) tomatoes, quartered
- salt and freshly ground black pepper
- 1 tablespoon finely chopped parsley
- 1 tablespoon torn basil
- 2 tablespoons capers
- 3 oz (90 g) black olives

Jewish-style artichokes

Carciofi alla giudia

- 8 large artichokes
- juice of 1 lemon
- 1 cup (250 ml) extra-virgin olive oil
- salt

Clean the artichokes by trimming the tops and stalk (leave a short stalk attached). Remove all the tough outer leaves so that only the pale, inner part remains. As you clean the artichokes, place them in a large bowl of cold water with the lemon juice (this will stop them from discoloring). • Drain and bang each artichoke down on the bench so that the leaves open out a little. • Heat the oil in a large frying pan and add the artichokes. Cook over medium heat for 15–20 minutes. • When the artichokes are tender, turn up the heat and brown them for 2–3 minutes. They should turn a lovely golden brown at this stage. • Drain on paper towels, season with salt, and serve at once.

Serves: 4 • Prep: 10 min • Cooking: 25 min • Level: 2

Carrot and zucchini mold

Sformato di carote e zucchine

Preheat the oven to 400°F (200°C/gas 6). • Sauté the carrots and onions in the oil for 5 minutes. • Add the zucchini, cover the pan, and sauté until the vegetables are tender, 10–15 minutes. • Prepare the Béchamel sauce. Let cool. • Combine the Béchamel with the Parmesan, eggs, vegetables, and mint. Season with salt and pepper. Mix well. • Grease a 10-inch (25-cm) ring mold with the butter and sprinkle with bread crumbs. • Pour the mixture into the mold. • Place the mold in a larger container filled with water. • Bake until set, about for 50 minutes. • Let stand for 10 minutes, then invert onto a serving dish and serve hot.

Serves: 4–6 • Prep: 10 min • Cooking: 1 hr 30 min • Level:

- 4 medium carrots, finely chopped together
- 2 medium onions, sliced
- 1/4 cup (60 ml) extra-virgin olive oil
- 1 1/4 lb (600 g) zucchini (courgettes), thinly sliced
- 1 quantity Béchamel sauce (see page 151)
- 1/2 cup (60 g) freshly grated Parmesan cheese
- 2 eggs, beaten until foamy
- 2 tablespoons finely chopped mint
- salt and freshly ground black pepper

Grilled porcini mushrooms

Grilled porcini mushrooms

Capelle di porcini alla griglia

- 4–8 medium porcini mushrooms, cleaned
- salt and freshly ground black pepper
- ½ cup (125 ml) extra-virgin olive oil
- 2 cloves garlic, finely chopped
- 2 tablespoons finely chopped parsley or thyme

Porcini mushrooms are superb when grilled over a barbecue. This dish is very easy and quick to prepare. The mushrooms can be served as a side dish but they are also rich and hearty enough to serve as a main.

Preheat a barbecue, so that you have plenty of glowing embers. • Place the porcini tops upside-down in a large dish. Season with salt and pepper and drizzle with half the oil. • Grill over the embers until tender and well cooked, 10–15 minutes. • Mix the remaining oil in a small bowl with the garlic and parsley or thyme, salt, and pepper. • Drizzle over the cooked mushrooms and serve hot.

Serves: 4 • Prep: 15 min • Cooking: 10–15 min • Level: 1

Mushrooms cooked in foil packages

Funghi incartati

- 5 tablespoons freshly grated pecorino cheese
- 3 tablespoons bread crumbs
- 2 salt-cured anchovies rinsed and finely chopped
- 2 cloves garlic, finely chopped
- 2 tablespoons finely chopped parsley
- 2 teaspoons lemon juice
- salt and freshly ground black pepper
- ¼ cup (60 ml) extra-virgin olive oil
- 4 large or 8 small porcini mushroom caps (or horse, field, or cultivated mushrooms), cleaned

Preheat the oven to 375°F (190°C/gas 5). • Place the cheese, bread crumbs, anchovies, garlic, parsley, lemon juice, salt, pepper, and oil in a large bowl and mix well. • Place each mushroom cap upside-down on a fairly large piece of oiled foil. • Spread an equal part of the mixture over each mushroom. • Bring two sides of the foil up over each mushroom to make a pleat, leaving plenty of air space inside, and fold the ends over. • When all the mushrooms are packaged, place on a baking sheet and bake for 20–25 minutes, depending on the size of the mushrooms. • If using smaller porcini place two in each package. The small porcini or white mushrooms will take only about 15–20 minutes to cook.

Serves: 4 • Prep: 15 min • Cooking: 20–25 min • Level: 1

Potato and cabbage mix

Brustengo di patate e cavolo

- 2 lb (1 kg) starchy potatoes, peeled
- 12 oz (350 g) cabbage, shredded
- 2 cloves garlic, finely sliced
- scant ½ cup (50 g) chopped pancetta or lard
- salt and freshly ground black pepper
- ¼ cup (60 ml) extra-virgin olive oil

Cook the potatoes in a large pot of salted, boiling water until tender, 25 minutes. • Drain and mash. • Cook the cabbage with the garlic, pancetta, and ½ cup (125 ml) salted water in a large saucepan until tender, 10 minutes. Season with salt and pepper. Add the potato and mix well. • Heat half the oil in a large frying pan over a medium heat. • Put the vegetables into the frying pan and smooth the surface with the back of a spoon. • Cook until lightly browned, about 5 minutes. • Slide onto a plate and add the remaining oil to the pan. • Turn back into the pan and cook on the other side until lightly browned, 5 minutes. • Serve hot.

Serves: 4–6 • Prep: 10 min • Cooking: 45 min • Level: 1

Baked mushrooms and potatoes

Porcini e patate al forno

- 2 lb (1 kg) starchy potatoes, peeled
- ¼ cup (60 ml) extra-virgin olive oil
- 1 teaspoon butter
- 1 small onion, finely chopped
- 6 large mushrooms, coarsely chopped
- 1 tablespoon each finely chopped fresh thyme, marjoram, and parsley
- salt and freshly ground black pepper
- 4 eggs, lightly beaten
- ⅓ cup (90 ml) heavy (double) cream

If you can't get porcini mushrooms, use other wild or cultivated mushrooms in their place.

Cook the potatoes in a large pot of salted, boiling water until tender, 25 minutes. • Drain and slice. • Preheat the oven to 350°F (180°C/gas 4). • Heat the oil and butter in a large frying pan over medium heat. Sauté the onions and mushrooms until softened. Add the thyme, marjoram, and parsley. • Beat the eggs and cream in a medium bowl until well mixed. Season with salt and pepper. Add the potatoes and mushroom mixture. • Butter an ovenproof dish. Pour the mixture into the dish. • Bake for 15 minutes, or until golden brown. • Turn out onto a serving plate. • Serve hot.

Serves: 4 • Prep: 15 min • Cooking: 15 min • Level: 1

Stuffed zucchini flowers

Beans with anchovy and garlic sauce

Fagioli in salsa

- 1/4 cup (60 ml) extra-virgin olive oil
- 2 cups (400 g) dried borlotti or red kidney beans
- salt and freshly ground black pepper
- 1 clove garlic, peeled and whole
- 2 tablespoons finely chopped parsley
- 1/4 cup (60 ml) extra-virgin olive oil
- 6 salted-cured anchovies, rinsed and chopped
- 1 cup (250 ml) red wine vinegar

Soak the beans in plenty of cold water overnight. • Drain the beans and place in a saucepan with sufficient cold water to cover. Bring to a boil and simmer gently over low heat until tender, about 2 hours; add salt only just before they are done or their skins will toughen. • Sauté the garlic and parsley gently in the oil in a saucepan. Discard the garlic when it starts to color. Add the anchovies and cook gently until they have dissolved in the oil. • Add the vinegar and a generous grinding of pepper and simmer, uncovered, for 10 minutes. • Drain the beans when cooked and transfer to a serving dish. Drizzle with the dressing and leave to stand at room temperature for an hour to flavor before serving.

Serves: 6 • Prep: 10 min + 12 hr soaking and 1 hr to flavor
Cooking: 2 hr 15 min • Level: 1

Stuffed zucchini flowers

Fiori di zucca ripieni

Place the ham, mozzarella, parsley, and garlic into a medium bowl. Season with salt and pepper. Mix well. • Beat the eggs with a pinch of salt in a bowl. • Put the flour on one plate and the bread crumbs on another. • Fill each of the zucchini flowers with a little of the ham mixture. • Dip the filled flowers firstly in the flour, then in the egg, and finally in the bread crumbs, ensuring that each one is evenly coated. • Heat the oil in a large frying pan over medium heat. • Fry the zucchini flowers lightly browned all over, 5–7 minutes. • Drain on paper towels. • Serve hot.

Serves: 4 • Prep: 20 min • Cooking: 45 min • Level: 1

- 1/2 cup (60 g) very finely chopped ham
- 4 oz (125 g) fresh mozzarella cheese, drained and finely chopped
- 4 tablespoons finely chopped parsley
- 1 clove garlic, very finely chopped
- salt and freshly ground black pepper
- 2 large eggs, l lightly beaten
- 1/2 cup (75 g) all-purpose (plain) flour
- 1 cup (125 g) fine dry bread crumbs
- 12 large zucchini (courgette) flowers
- 1 cup (250 ml) olive oil, for frying

Bean casserole

Fagiolata

- 1 1/2 lb (750 g) fresh borlotti or red kidney beans, net shelled weight
- about 12 oz (350 g) fresh pork rind, cut into 1 inch (2.5 cm) cubes
- 1 large onion, peeled and sliced
- 1–2 tablespoons tomato paste (concentrate)
- 4–5 tablespoons extra-virgin olive oil
- scant 1 tablespoon chopped fresh rosemary leaves
- 2 cloves
- salt and freshly ground black pepper

If you can't get fresh borlotti beans, use 1 1/2 cups (300 g) of dried borlotti or red kidney beans soaked in cold water overnight.

Place the beans, pork rind, and onion in an earthenware casserole or heavy saucepan with just enough cold water to cover them. • Bring to a boil over a high heat, then simmer gently over low heat until tender, about 1 hour 30 minutes, stirring now and then. • The liquid should reduce considerably, but the beans should remain very moist. Add a little more boiling water if necessary. • Add the tomato paste, oil, rosemary, and cloves, and season with salt and pepper. Continue cooking for 30 more minutes over a low heat. • Serve hot.

Serves: 6 • Prep: 15 min • Cooking: 2 hr • Level: 1

Tuscan-style kidney beans

Fagioli all'uccelletto

Sauté the garlic in the oil and as soon as it begins to color, add the tomatoes, sage, salt, and pepper. • Simmer over medium heat for 10 minutes. • When the sauce has reduced a little, add the beans and cook for about 15 more minutes. • Serve hot.

Serves: 4 • Prep: 10 min • Cooking: 25 min • Level: 1

- 4 cloves garlic, finely chopped
- 1/4 cup (60 ml) extra-virgin olive oil
- 1 (14-oz/400-g) can tomatoes, with juice
- 8 leaves fresh sage
- salt and freshly ground black pepper
- 1 (14 oz/400-g) can white kidney beans (or soaked and pre-cooked dry beans)

SALADS

Small salads are served as appetizers or side dishes with most Italian meals. Increasingly too, large salads, called *insalatone*, are served as meals in themselves. These include traditional dishes, such as *Insalata caprese* (Tomato and mozzarella salad, see page 352) and Rice salad with cherry tomatoes (see page 358), as well as recent, cool re-workings of traditional flavor combinations (Spelt salad, photograph left; see page 358 for the recipe), pasta salads (see pages 358, 360), and chicken salad (see page 362). Whatever the salad, it will inevitably be dressed with olive oil, either alone or with vinegar or lemon juice. For salads, always use a top quality, cold pressed, extra-virgin olive oil; don't be tempted by cheaper alternatives and always check the date on the bottle. After 12 months olive oil becomes rancid and should be thrown out.

Spelt salad (see page 358)

Salads

Tomato and mozzarella salad

Tomato and basil salad

Insalata di pomodori e basilico

- 2 lb (1 kg) firm ripe salad tomatoes
- 10 leaves fresh basil, torn
- 2 tablespoons freshly squeezed lemon juice or balsamic vinegar
- salt and freshly ground black pepper
- 1/3 cup (90 ml) extra-virgin olive oil

Slice the tomatoes into quarters and arrange in a salad bowl. Sprinkle with the basil (be sure to tear them with your fingers, so that they don't lose any of their superb fragrance). • Drizzle with the lemon juice or vinegar. Season with salt and pepper and drizzle with the oil. • Toss well and serve.

Serves: 4–6 • Prep: 10 min • Level: 1

Tomato and mozzarella salad

Insalata caprese

Cut the tomatoes in thick slices and arrange on a flat serving dish. • Cut the Mozzarella in slices of the same width and alternate with the tomato. • Sprinkle with basil, salt, and pepper, and drizzle with the oil. • Serve at once.

Serves: 4–6 • Prep: 10 min • Level: 1

- 8 large ripe salad tomatoes
- 1 lb (500 g) fresh mozzarella cheese
- 20 large basil leaves, torn
- salt and freshly ground black pepper
- 1/3 cup (90 ml) extra-virgin olive oil

Italian salad

Insalata italiana

- 12 oz (350 g) potatoes, peeled and boiled
- 8 oz (250 g) red beet, boiled and peeled
- 8 oz (250 g) green beans, boiled in salted water
- 1 tablespoon white wine vinegar
- 1/4 cup (60 ml) extra-virgin olive oil
- salt and freshly ground black pepper
- 4 leaves basil (optional)

This salad is called "Insalata Italiana" because it has the same colors as the Italian flag.

Cut the potatoes and beets into cubes, and the beans into sections. Place the vegetables in a large salad bowl. • Mix the vinegar, oil, salt, and pepper in a small bowl. • Drizzle over the vegetables just before serving. Garnish with the basil leaves, if using.

Serves: 4 • Prep: 15 min + time to cook vegetables • Level: 1

Caesar's mushroom salad

Insalata di ovoli

Clean the mushrooms and rinse them carefully in cold water. Pat dry with paper towels. • Slice the mushrooms finely and arrange them on a serving dish. • Sprinkle with the walnuts and Parmesan flakes. • Mix the oil, salt, pepper, and lemon juice in a bowl and drizzle over the mushrooms. • Serve immediately, before the flavor begins to change.

Serves: 4–6 • Prep: 10 min • Level: 1

- 14 oz (400 g) Caesar's (royal agaric) mushrooms
- 1 cup (100 g) walnuts, shelled and chopped
- 3 oz (90 g) Parmesan cheese, flaked
- 1/3 cup (90 ml) extra-virgin olive oil
- salt and freshly ground white pepper
- juice of 1 lemon

Orange salad

Insalata di portualla

- 4 ripe, juicy oranges
- 8–10 green or black olives, pitted and cut into quarters
- 1 medium leek, cleaned, trimmed and thinly sliced into rings
- 1 tablespoon finely chopped parsley
- 1/4 cup (60 ml) extra-virgin olive oil
- salt and freshly ground black pepper

This delicious salad works well as an appetizer or as a side dish for meat dishes.

Peel the oranges, removing all the white pith as well as the skin. • Slice them thinly or cut into small pieces. Place in a salad bowl and add the olives, leek, parsley, oil, salt, and pepper. • Toss well and let stand for 10 minutes, then toss again and serve.

Serves: 6 • Prep: 15 min • Level: 1

Cucumber and onion salad

Insalata di cetrioli e cipolla

You may prefer not to peel the cucumbers. However, for many people the peel is not easy to digest. In any case, choose untreated cucumbers.

Peel the onions and slice thinly. • Put the onions in a salad bowl, sprinkle with the salt, pepper, vinegar, and oil. Toss well and set aside for 30 minutes. • Peel the cucumbers and slice very thinly. • Add the cucumbers and capers to the onions and toss again. • Sprinkle with the basil and serve.

Serves: 6–8 • Prep: 15 min + 30 min to rest • Level: 1

- 4 sweet red onions
- salt and freshly ground black pepper
- 1 tablespoon white wine vinegar
- 1/4 cup (60 ml) extra-virgin olive oil
- 2 medium cucumbers
- 1 tablespoon pickled capers, drained
- 6 leaves fresh basil, torn

Artichoke salad with Parmesan

Mixed salad with caprino cheese

Insalata mista con caprini

- 1 lb (500 g) mixed salad greens
- $^{1}/_{4}$ cup (60 ml) extra-virgin olive oil
- salt
- 8 tiny forms French goat cheese
- 4 slices sandwich bread, cut into triangles

This salad is actually a tiny bit French but it's so good we couldn't leave it out. It makes a wonderful starter and a great follow up to a light soup or omelet.

Preheat the oven to 350°F (180°C/gas 4). • Place the salad greens, whole or coarsely torn (depending on their size), in four salad bowls. Season with salt and drizzle with the oil. • Place the cheese on the bread and toast in the oven until lightly browned, 5–10 minutes. • Place the toasted cheese bread on the salads and serve.

Serves: 4 • Prep: 15 min • Cooking: 10 min • Level: 1

Artichoke s

Insalata d

Clean the artichokes by pu
outer leaves down and snap
Cut off the top third of the
the stalk. Cut in half and us
to remove any fuzzy choke
three-quarters of the lemon
finely. Place in a large salad
the carrot and celery. Drizz
remaining lemon juice and
• Drizzle with the oil and s
and pepper. Top with the P
gently, and serve.

Serves: 4–6 • Prep: 15 min • Level:

MIXED SALAD WITH PEAR, PECORINO, AND WALNUTS

Insalata di pere, pecorino e noci

- 1 tablespoon French mustard
- 1 tablespoon white wine vinegar
- ⅓ cup (90 ml) extra-virgin olive oil
- salt
- 8 oz (250 g) mixed salad greens
- 2 celery sticks, sliced
- 2 large ripe pears, peeled, cored, and thinly sliced
- 4 oz (125 g) aged pecorino or Parmesan cheese cut into flakes
- handful of walnuts, coarsely chopped

Beat the mustard, vinegar, oil, and a pinch of salt with a fork in a small bowl to make a smooth dressing. • Put the mixed salad greens and celery into a large salad bowl. • Add the pears to the salad bowl. • Top with the pecorino and walnuts. • Drizzle with the dressing. Toss gently and serve.

Serves: 6 • Prep: 10 min • Level: 1

ARUGULA SA
AN

Insalata di ru

Place the arugula in a large
with the Parmesan. • Cut th
remove the core, and cut in
Drizzle with the lemon juic
salad. Sprinkle with the wa
oil, vinegar, and mustard in
Season with salt and peppe
fork until well mixed. • Dri
over the salad. Toss gently

Serves: 4–6 • Prep: 15 min • Level: 1

Mixed salad with pear, pecorino, and walnuts

Bean salad with onion and bell pepper

RAW VEGETABLES WITH OLIVE OIL DIP

Pinzimonio

- 4 artichokes
- juice of 2 lemons
- 4 carrots (or 8 baby spring carrots)
- 4 celery hearts
- 2 large fennel bulbs
- 12 scallions (green onions)
- 12 radishes
- 1 cup (250 ml) extra-virgin olive oil
- salt and freshly ground black pepper

Place the vegetables on a platter in the middle of the table and give each guest a plate and a small bowl of dip. If liked, add a little red wine vinegar or balsamic vinegar to the oil.

Artichokes: remove the tough outer leaves by pulling them down and snapping them off. Cut off the stem and the top third of the leaves. Cut in half lengthwise and scrape any fuzzy choke away with a knife. Cut each artichoke into wedges and soak in a bowl of cold water with the juice of 1 lemon for 10 minutes. • Carrots: scrub with a brush or peel and soak in a bowl of cold water with the remaining lemon juice for 10 minutes. • Celery: trim off the leafy tops and discard the tough outer stalks. Keep the inner white stalks and the heart. • Fennel: slice off the base, trim away the leafy tops, and discard any blemished outer leaves. Divide into 6–8 wedges, depending on the size. • Scallions: remove the roots and the outer leaves and trim the tops. • Radishes: cut the roots off and trim the tops. • For the dip: beat the oil with salt and pepper with a whisk or blender until well mixed. Pour into 6–8 small bowls.

Serves: 6–8 • Prep: 20 min • Level: 1

BEAN SALAD WITH ONION AND BELL PEPPER

Insalata di fagioli, cipolle e peperoni

- 1 (14-oz/400-g) can cranberry or borlotti beans, drained
- 1 (14-oz/400-g) can cannellini or white-kidney beans, drained
- 1 large red bell pepper (capsicum), seeded and finely sliced
- 1 sweet red onion, thinly sliced
- 1 clove garlic, finely chopped
- 4 tablespoons finely chopped parsley + extra sprigs, to garnish
- 1/4 cup (60 ml) extra-virgin olive oil
- juice of 1 lemon
- salt and freshly ground black pepper
- 5 oz (150 g) lollo rosso (or other) salad greens

Place the beans in a large bowl. • Add the bell pepper, onion, garlic, and parsley and toss well. • Beat the oil and lemon juice in a small bowl with a fork. Season with salt and pepper. • Drizzle the dressing over the salad. Toss well, cover, and let rest for 30 minutes. • Arrange the salad greens in a large salad bowl. • Spoon the bean salad over the top. Garnish with the sprigs of parsley and serve.

Serves: 4–6 • Prep: 15 min + 30 min to rest • Level: 1

PLATTER OF BOILED VEGETABLES

Insalata cotta

- 5 fennel bulbs
- 5 artichokes
- 6 carrots
- 6 zucchini (courgettes)
- 6 potatoes
- 6 beets (red beet)
- 1 lb (500 g) green beans
- 1 cup (250 ml) mayonnaise

Simple and light, this is an Italian classic.

Cook the vegetables whole in a large pot of salted boiling water until tender. Except for the beets, they can all be cooked together, removing the different vegetables as they are ready. • Peel the potatoes and beets after cooking. • When all the vegetables are cooked, drain well and arrange (either sliced or whole) on a large serving dish, divided by types. • Leave to cool. • Serve with the mayonnaise passed separately.

Serves: 6–8 • Prep: 25 min • Cooking: 30 min • Level: 1

ZUCCHINI AND BEAN SALAD WITH PESTO

Insalata di zucchini e fagiolini con pesto

- 14 oz (400 g) green beans, topped and tailed
- 4 zucchini (courgettes), cut in rounds
- 2–4 ripe tomatoes, cut into wedges
- salt and freshly ground black pepper
- 1 quantity pesto (see page 130)

Cook the green beans in salted boiling water until tender, 5–10 minutes. Drain and chop. • Sauté the zucchini in 2 tablespoons of oil in a large frying pan over medium heat until tender, about 5 minutes. Season with salt and pepper and let cool. • Prepare the pesto. • Place the green beans, zucchini, and tomatoes in a salad bowl. Drizzle with the pesto, toss gently, and serve.

Serves: 4 • Prep: 25 min • Cooking: 20 min • Level: 1

Rice salad with cherry tomatoes

Spelt salad

Insalata di farro

- 2 cups (400 g) spelt
- 16 cherry tomatoes, halved
- 8 oz (250 g) fresh mozzarella, drained and cut into small cubes
- 6 scallions (green onions), sliced
- 15 basil leaves, shredded
- 1/3 cup (60 g) capers preserved in brine, rinsed and drained
- 4 small fresh zucchini (courgettes), cut into small cubes
- 1/3 cup (90 ml) extra-virgin olive oil
- salt and freshly ground black pepper

Spelt is an ancient strain of wheat. It contain less gluten than modern strains so is easier to digest. Italian supermarkets now sell parboiled spelt which cooks in 10 minutes. You may substitute spelt for pearl barley, if preferred.

Cook the spelt in a large pot of salted boiling water until tender, about 40 minutes (or 10 minutes, for the parboiled type). Drain well and cool under cold running water. Drain well and place a large salad bowl. • Add the tomatoes, mozzarella, spring onions, basil, capers, and zucchini. Drizzle with the oil and season with salt and pepper. Toss well. • Let rest for 10 minutes before serving.

Serves: 6–8 • Prep: 10 min + 10 min to rest the salad
Cooking: 40 min (or 10 min) • Level: 1

Rice salad with cherry tomatoes

Insalata di riso con pomodorini

- 2 cups (400 g) short-grain rice
- 1 cup (150 g) frozen peas
- 20 cherry tomatoes, cut in half
- 4 oz (125 g) Fontina or Emmental cheese, cut into small cubes
- 1 cucumber, peeled and cut into small cubes
- 1 tablespoon capers preserved in vinegar, rinsed and drained
- 10 black olives, pitted and coarsely chopped
- 1 sweet red onion, chopped
- 8 basil leaves, torn
- 1/4 cup (60 ml) extra virgin olive oil
- salt

Cook the rice in a large pot of salted boiling water until tender, about 15 minutes. Drain well and cool under cold running water. Drain again and place in a large salad bowl. • Cook the peas in a small pot of salted boiling water until tender, about 5 minutes. Drain well and cool under cold running water. Drain again and place in the salad bowl. • Add the tomatoes, cheese, cucumber, capers, olives, onion, and basil. • Drizzle with the oil and season with salt. Toss gently. Let rest for 10 minutes before serving.

Serves: 4–6 • Prep: 10 min + 10 min to rest the salad
Cooking: 15 min • Level: 1

Cool summer pasta salad

Pasta fredda estiva

Place the eggplant slices in a colander and sprinkle with the salt. Let drain for 1 hour. • Chop into 1/2-inch (1-cm) cubes. • Heat the oil in a large deep frying pan until very hot. Fry the eggplant in small batches for until golden brown, 5–7 minutes. • Broil (grill) the bell peppers until the skins are blackened. Wrap them in a paper bag for 5 minutes, then remove the skins and seeds. Cut into 1/2-inch (1-cm) cubes. • Heat 3 tablespoons of the extra-virgin olive oil in a small saucepan and sauté the onion with a pinch of salt over high heat until golden. Cover and sweat over very low heat for 15 minutes. • Add the garlic and sauté until pale gold. • Toast the pine nuts in a nonstick frying pan over medium heat until golden, 2 minutes. • Cook the pasta in a large pot of salted boiling water until al dente. • Drain and run under cold running water until the pasta has cooled completely. • Transfer to a large serving bowl with the fried eggplant, capers, bell peppers, onions, pine nuts, olives, basil, parsley, and oregano.

Serves: 6 • Prep: 1 hr • Cooking: 20 min • Level: 1

- 1 large eggplant (aubergine) weighing about 1 lb (500 g), cut into 1/2-inch (1-cm) thick slices
- 2 tablespoons coarse sea salt
- 2 cups (500 ml) olive oil
- 2 yellow bell peppers (capsicums)
- 1/3 cup (90 ml) extra-virgin olive oil
- 1 medium onion, finely chopped
- 1/2 teaspoon salt
- 2 cloves garlic, finely chopped
- 2 tablespoons pine nuts
- 1 lb (500 g) short pasta (such as ridged ditalini)
- 2 tablespoons salt-cured capers, rinsed
- 1 cup (100 g) green olives in brine, pitted and coarsely chopped
- 1 small bunch basil, torn
- 2 tablespoons finely chopped parsley
- 1 tablespoon finely chopped oregano

MIXED SALAD WITH TUNA, EGGS, AND BASIL

Insalata mista al basilico

- 3 ripe tomatoes, cut into segments
- 2 bell peppers (capsicums), seeded and sliced
- 1 cucumber, peeled and sliced
- 10 radishes, cut into quarters
- 1 small red onion, sliced
- 14 oz (400 g) fresh fava (broad) beans, shelled
- 20 black olives, pitted
- 10 green olives, pitted
- 2 cloves garlic, lightly crushed but whole
- 1 stalk celery, finely chopped
- 6 basil leaves, torn
- 1/3 cup (90 ml) extra-virgin olive oil
- 3 tablespoons white wine vinegar
- salt
- 8 oz (250 g) canned tuna, broken into pieces
- 3 hard-boiled eggs, shelled and cut into segments
- 5 artichoke hearts preserved in oil, drained and cut into segments
- 10 salt-cured anchovy fillets, rinsed

Place the tomatoes, bell peppers, cucumber, radishes, red onion, fava beans, olives, garlic, and celery in a large salad bowl. Toss well. • Beat the basil, oil, vinegar, and salt in a small bowl. • Add the tuna to the salad. • Drizzle with the dressing and toss well. • Discard the garlic. • Arrange the eggs, artichokes, and anchovies on top of the salad in a decorative manner. • Serve at room temperature.

Serves: 4–6 • Prep: 20 min • 10 min • Level: 1

RADICCHIO, SHRIMP, AND RED BEAN SALAD

Insalata di gamberi e fagioli

Wash the radicchio and chicory under cold running water, drain, and dry well. • Strip the red leaves from the radicchio and arrange in the bottom of a large salad bowl. • Chop the chicory coarsely and sprinkle over the radicchio. • Drain the beans and spoon over the salad. • Heat 2 tablespoons of the oil in a frying pan and sauté the shrimp with a little salt over high heat for 2 minutes. • Add the vinegar and lemon zest and cook for 3 minutes more. • Beat the remaining oil, salt, pepper, scallions, celery, and parsley in a bowl with a fork. • Add the shrimp to the salad bowl. Drizzle with the oil mixture. • Serve at once.

Serves: 4 • Prep: 30 min • Cooking: 5 min • Level: 1

- 2 large heads red radicchio
- 2 chicory hearts
- 1 lb (500 g) cooked borlotti or red kidney beans (pre-soaked and boiled for 1 hour, or one 14-oz/400-g can, drained)
- 20 shrimp, shelled
- 1/2 cup (125 ml) extra-virgin olive oil
- 1/4 cup (60 ml) white wine vinegar
- grated zest of 1/2 lemon
- salt and freshly ground black pepper
- 4 scallions (green onions), finely chopped
- 1 celery heart, finely chopped
- 2 tablespoons finely chopped parsley

STEAMED CHICKEN AND VEGETABLE SALAD

Insalata di pollo al vapore con verdure

Steam the chicken over medium heat until cooked through, about 15 minutes. • Remove from the steamer and let cool slightly. • Arrange the celery, scallions, carrot, and bell pepper in a large bowl. Drizzle with the oil and season with salt. • Chop the chicken into small cubes and add to the salad. • Serve at once.

Serves: 4 • Prep: 5 min • Cooking: 15 min • Level: 1

- 2 boneless, skinless chicken breasts. about 1 1/2 lb (750 g)
- 2 stalks celery, finely chopped
- white part of 3 scallions (green onions), finely chopped
- 1 large carrot, finely chopped
- 1/2 yellow bell pepper (capsicum), seeded and finely chopped
- 1/4 cup (60 ml) extra-virgin olive oil
- salt

DESSERTS

An everyday Italian meal will often end with a healthy bowl of fresh fruit filled with peaches, plums, grapes, apples, figs, oranges, or cherries, or whatever else happens to be in season. Throughout the summer months fresh strawberries marinated in wine or lemon juice are another favorite. Try our recipe for Strawberries in white wine (see page 367). There are many light and delicious mousses and creams in the Italian repertoire and we have included a number of classics, such as *Crème caramel* (see page 374), Zabaione (see page 370), and *Panna cotta* (see pages 374 and 376). Ice cream, or gelato, was invented in Italy, and here you will find a good Basic ice cream recipe (see page 378), as well as a classic *Straciatella* (see page 378). For special occasions, try simple and delicious *Tiramisù* (see page 370), Raspberry charlotte (see page 372), Florentine trifle (see page 374), or Sicilian cassata (see page 381).

Italian cheesecake (see page 372)

Berryfruit mousse

STUFFED BAKED PEACHES

Pesche al forno

- 4 large ripe yellow peaches
- 20 amaretti cookies (macaroons), crushed
- 3/4 cup (150 g) granulated sugar
- 2 tablespoons butter
- 1/2 cup (125 ml) dark rum

Preheat the oven to 350°F (180°C/gas 4). • Rinse the peaches under cold running water and dry with paper towels. Cut them in half and remove the pits. Use a teaspoon to make a hollow about the size of a golf ball in each peach half. Place the peach flesh in a bowl and add three-quarters of the amaretti cookies and ½ cup (100 g) of sugar. Mix well and use to fill the peaches. • Use the butter to grease a baking pan large enough to hold all the peach halves snugly in a single layer. Arrange the peaches in the pan. • Drizzle with the rum and sprinkle with the remaining amaretti cookies and sugar. • Bake for 30 minutes. • Serve hot or at room temperature.

Serves: 4 • Prep: 20 min • Cooking: 30 min • Level: 1

STRAWBERRIES IN WHITE WINE

Fragole al vino bianco

Healthy and delicious on their own, these strawberries are excellent when served with freshly whipped cream. Try replacing the white wine with the same amount of red wine or lemon juice (add a little more sugar if using lemon juice).

- 1¼ lb (600 g) fresh strawberries
- ¼ cup (50 g) superfine sugar
- ½ cup (125 ml) dry white wine

Hull the strawberries and rinse under cold running water. Drain well and cut each strawberry in 3–4 pieces. • Place the strawberries in a serving bowl. Sprinkle with the sugar and drizzle with the wine. • Chill in the refrigerator to rest for at least 1 hour before serving.

Serves: 4–6 • Prep: 5 min + 1 hr to chill • Level: 1

BERRYFRUIT MOUSSE

Mousse alla fragola con salsa di lampone

Mousse
- 1 oz (30 g) gelatin
- 1/3 cup (90 ml) water
- 12 oz (350 g) strawberries
- 1 cup (250 ml) heavy (double) cream
- 1/3 cup (70 g) granulated sugar
- 2 tablespoons strawberry syrup

Sauce
- 8 oz (250 g) raspberries
- 2 tablespoons raspberry syrup
- 2 tablespoons sugar
- whipped cream and fresh strawberries and raspberries, to garnish

Dissolve the gelatin in the water. • Purée the strawberries in a food processor. Strain the strawberry purée through a fine mesh strainer to remove the seeds. • Whip the cream and sugar until stiff. • Fold into the strawberry purée. • Add the syrup and dissolved gelatin and mix gently. • Pour the mousse into a loaf pan and chill in the refrigerator until set, 2 hours. • Sauce: Purée the raspberries in a food processor (or mash with a fork.) • Strain the raspberry purée through a fine mesh strainer to remove the seeds. • Add the syrup and the sugar and mix well. • Turn the mouse out onto a serving dish. • Garnish with a little whipped cream and serve.

Serves: 4–6 • Prep: 20 min + 2 hr to chill • Level: 2

LEMON CREAM

Biancomangiare

- ½ cup (100 g) granulated sugar
- 1 cup (150 g) all-purpose (plain) flour
- finely grated zest of 2 lemons
- 4 cups (1 liter) milk

Place the sugar, flour, and zest of 1 lemon in a heavy-bottomed pan. Stir in the milk gradually, making sure that no lumps form. • Place the pan over medium-low heat and, stirring continuously, bring to a boil. • Boil for 1 minute, then remove from the heat. • Pour into a 1½-quart (1.5-liter) mold and let cool. Chill in the refrigerator for at least 2 hours. • Sprinkle with the remaining grated lemon zest and serve.

Serves: 4–6 • Prep: 15 min + 2 hr to chill • Cooking: 10 min Level: 1

Tiramisù

Fresh fruit chocolate fondue

Fonduta al cioccolato

- 2 lb (1 kg) fresh fruit (grapes, figs, strawberries, bananas, apples, apricots, plums, peaches)
- 2 cups (500 ml) water
- juice of 1 lemon
- 1 lb (500 g) semi-sweet (dark) chocolate, chopped
- 1 cup (250 ml) heavy (double) cream
- 1/4 cup (60 g) butter
- 4 tablespoons granulated sugar
- 1/3 cup (50 g) each chopped toasted almonds and hazelnuts
- 1/2 cup (30 g) shredded (desiccated) coconut

This dessert is delicious, eyecatching, and fun – a perfect way to finish a dinner party!

Rinse and dry the fruit. Cut the larger pieces into bite-sized chunks. • If using apple, pear, or banana, immerse the chunks in water and lemon juice for a few seconds to prevent the flesh from browning, then dry carefully. • Arrange the fruit in an attractive bowl or serving dish. • Melt the chocolate in a double boiler over barely simmering water. Dilute with the cream, add the butter and sugar and mix thoroughly. • Pour the chocolate mixture into a fondue bowl and keep warm over the flame. • Place bowls filled with the almonds, hazelnuts, and coconut on the table, so that your guests can dip their pieces of fruit into them, after having dipped them in the chocolate sauce.

Serves: 6–8 • Prep: 15 min • Cooking: 15 min • Level: 1

Tiramisù

Tiramisu

- 3 large eggs, separated
- 2 large egg yolks
- 3/4 cup (150 g) granulated sugar
- 1/8 teaspoon salt
- 1 lb (500 g) mascarpone cheese, at room temperature
- 8 oz (250 g) sponge fingers
- 1/4 cup (60 ml) very strong black coffee
- 5 oz (150 g) semisweet (dark) chocolate, coarsely grated
- 2 tablespoons unsweetened cocoa powder

Beat the egg yolks and sugar in a bowl until the mixture is very pale and creamy. • Beat the egg whites with a pinch of salt in a large bowl until stiff. • Stir the mascarpone into the egg yolk mixture. • Fold in the egg whites. • Oil a large dessert dish. • Spoon one third of the mascarpone mixture into the pan and sprinkle with half the chocolate. Add a layer of the sponge fingers, dipping them in the coffee before arranging them in the pan. Add another layer of mascarpone cream. Sprinkle with the remaining chocolate and top with the remaining sponge fingers, dipping them in the coffee before arranging them in the pan. • Cover with the remaining mascarpone cream. Dust with the cocoa and chill in the refrigerator for at least 4 hours before serving.

Serves: 6 • Prep: 20 min + 4 hr to chill • Level: 1

Chocolate egg cream

Bonet

- 6 large eggs
- 1 cup (200 g) granulated sugar
- 2 tablespoons unsweetened cocoa powder, sifted
- 2 tablespoons Amaretto di Saronno (almond) liqueur
- 2 cups (500 ml) milk, very hot
- 6 amaretti cookies, crushed

Preheat the oven to 350°F (180°C/gas 4). • Whisk the eggs and sugar until pale and creamy. • Stir in the cocoa and almond liqueur. • Add the milk gradually, stirring constantly, then add the amaretti cookies. • Pour the mixture into a 10-inch (25-cm) ring mold and place in a roasting pan half-filled with water. • Bake in the oven until set, 1 hour. • Cool for 15 minutes before unmolding onto a serving dish. Serve at room temperature (or chill for several hours in the refrigerator and serve cold).

Serves: 6 • Prep: 30 min • Cooking: 1 hr • Level: 2

Zabaglione

Zabaione

- 4 large egg yolks
- 4 tablespoons granulated sugar
- 1/4 cup (125 ml) dry Marsala wine or dry sherry or Vin Santo (a Tuscan sweet dessert wine)

Beat the egg yolks and sugar in a double boiler with an electric mixer at high speed until pale and very thick • Gradually pour in the Marsala. • Place over barely simmering water and simmer, stirring constantly with a wooden spoon, until very thick, about 10–15 minutes. • Serve right away or place plastic wrap directly on the surface and refrigerate until ready to serve.

Serves: 4 • Prep: 5 min • Cooking: 10–15 min • Level: 1

Raspberry charlotte

ITALIAN CHEESECAKE

Torta al formaggio

- one 10-inch (25-cm) Italian sponge cake (see page 401)

Filling
- 2 cups (500 ml) milk
- 2 tablespoons finely grated lemon zest
- 1/8 teaspoon salt
- 1 cup (200 g) short-grain rice
- 1/4 cup (50 g) granulated sugar
- 1 tablespoon unflavored gelatin
- 1/4 cup (60 ml) water
- 1 cup (250 ml) heavy (double) cream
- 1 cup (250 g) mascarpone cheese
- 1 teaspoon vanilla extract (essence)

Topping
- 14 oz (400 g) mixed red berryfruit
- 1/2 cup (125 g) apricot preserves (jam)

Prepare the cake and let cool. • Filling: Bring the milk, lemon zest, and salt to a boil in a saucepan over medium heat. Stir in the rice and sugar and simmer until the rice is very tender, about 25 minutes. Remove from the heat and let cool. • Sprinkle the gelatin over the water in a saucepan. Let stand 1 minute. Stir over low heat until completely dissolved. Stir the gelatin into the rice mixture and refrigerate for 15 minutes • Beat the cream in a large bowl until stiff. • Stir the mascarpone, vanilla, and cream into the rice mixture. • Cut the cake in half horizontally. Place a layer on the bottom of a buttered 10-inch (25-cm) springform pan. Place the sides of the springform pan around the cake and tighten. Spoon the filling over the cake. Refrigerate until set, 3 hours. • Decorate with the berries. • Warm the preserves in a saucepan over low heat. Brush over the fruit. Refrigerate for 15 minutes. • Loosen and remove the pan sides.

Serves: 6–8 • Prep: 15 min + tim to make cake • Cooking: 4–5 min • Level: 1

STRAWBERRY BAVARIAN CREAM

Bavarese di fragole

- 2 tablespoons unflavored gelatin (or 8 sheets leaf gelatin)
- 1/3 cup (90 ml) cold water
- 1/3 cup (90 ml) boiling water
- 1 lb (500 g) strawberries (or raspberries), crushed
- 3/4 cup (150 g) granulated sugar
- 2 tablespoons cold water
- 4 large egg whites

Soak the gelatin in the first measure of cold water and dissolve in the boiling water. • Stir the strawberries into the gelatin and water. Refrigerate until the mixture begins to set. • Cook the sugar and the second measure of cold water in a small saucepan until a few drops form a soft ball in cold water. • Remove from the heat and gradually add to the egg whites, beating constantly. Continue beating gently until cool. • Combine the egg whites and sugar with the strawberry gelatin and place in a 1½-quart (1.5-liter) pudding mold. Refrigerate until set. • To serve, unmold on a plate and garnish with fresh strawberries.

Serves: 6–8 • Prep: 15 min + 2 hr to chill • Cooking: 10 min Level: 2

MONT BLANC

Monte Bianco

- 8 oz (250 g) chestnuts
- 1/2 cup (75 g) unsweetened cocoa powder
- 2/3 cup (100 g) confectioners' (icing) sugar
- 2 tablespoons white rum
- 1 cup (250 ml) heavy (double) cream, whipped
- candied chestnuts, to decorate

Place the chestnuts in a saucepan and cover with cold water. Bring to the boil, then simmer for about 40 minutes. • Drain and peel the chestnuts, removing the inner skin. Mash them with a potato-masher while still hot. Place in a large bowl and stir in the cocoa powder, sugar, and rum. • Put the purée through a potato-ricer, letting it drop onto the serving dish in a little mound. • Chill in the refrigerator for at least 1 hour. • Cover with whipped cream and decorate with the candied chestnuts just before serving.

Serves: 4–6 • Prep: 20 min • Cooking: 40 min • Level: 2

RASPBERRY CHARLOTTE

Charlotte ai lamponi

- 2 cups (500 ml) heavy (double) cream
- 2 tablespoons confectioners' (icing) sugar
- 8 oz (250 g) fresh raspberries
- 3 meringues, crushed
- 2 tablespoons raspberry liqueur
- 1/4 cup (60 ml) raspberry syrup
- one 10-inch (25-cm) Italian sponge cake (see page 401), sliced into 1/2-inch (1-cm) layers
- whipped cream and fresh raspberries, to garnish

Whip the cream in a large bowl until stiff. • Fold in the sugar, raspberries, and one-third of the meringue. • Mix the liqueur and raspberry syrup in a bowl. • Crumble a slice of sponge into a bowl. Add the remaining meringue and mix well. • Oil a 1½-quart (1.5-liter) charlotte or pudding mold. Brush with liqueur mixture. Line with slices of sponge dipped in the liqueur mixture. • Spoon half the filling into the case. Add the meringue mixture and cover with the remaining filling. Top with the remaining sponge dipped in the liqueur mixture. • Chill in the refrigerator for 4 hours. • Turn out onto a serving dish. Garnish with cream and raspberries.

Serves: 6–8 • Prep: 30 min + 4 hr to chill • Level: 2

BAKED CARAMEL CUSTARD

Creme caramel

- 2 large eggs + 3 large egg yolks
- 1 cup (200 g) granulated sugar
- 2½ cups (375 ml) milk
- ¼ teaspoon vanilla extract (essence)
- 2 tablespoons cold water

Preheat the oven to 350°F (180°C/gas 4). • Beat the eggs and egg yolks with ¾ cup (150 g) of sugar until very pale and creamy. • Heat the milk and vanilla extract to boiling point over medium heat. Remove from the heat and pour into the eggs and sugar. Stir well until the sugar dissolves. • Put the remaining sugar in a small saucepan with the water over very low heat until it turns to caramel. • Pour the caramel into an ovenproof pudding mold. Strain the milk and egg mixture into the same mold. • Place the mold in a roasting pan half-filled with water. • Bake until set, about for 50 minutes. • Leave to cool, then chill for at least 3 hours in the refrigerator before unmolding to serve.

Serves: 6 • Prep: 30 min + 3 hr to chill • Cooking: 1 hr
Level: 2

PANNA COTTA

Panna cotta

- 2 cups (500 ml) heavy (double) cream
- ⅔ cup (150 ml) milk
- ⅓ cup (75 g) granulated sugar
- 2 teaspoons vanilla extract (essence)
- 2–3 tablespoons peach brandy
- 1 heaped tablespoon unflavored gelatin
- ¼ cup (60 ml) cold water

Panna cotta, *which means "cooked cream" in Italian, is easy to make and delicious. Serve it plain or with melted chocolate or chopped fresh fruit.*

Heat the cream, milk, sugar, vanilla, and peach brandy in a saucepan over medium heat until almost boiling. • Meanwhile, put the cold water in a bowl and sprinkle with the gelatin. Leave to stand for 3 minutes to soften. • Remove the saucepan from the heat and use a whisk to beat in the gelatin until dissolved. • Pour the creamy mixture into little molds or individual glass dishes and set aside to cool. • Chill in the refrigerator for at least 2 hours before serving.

Serves: 6 • Prep: 10 min + 2 hr to chill • Cooking: 8–10 min
Level: 1

FLORENTINE TRIFLE

Zuppa inglese

Florence has long been the home of a large English-speaking community. This recipe is reputed to have come from British Florentines of the 18th century. Alchermes is a sweet red liqueur available in some Italian delicatessens. Substitute with white rum with a few drops of red food coloring.

- 5 large egg yolks
- ¾ cup (150 g) granulated sugar
- ⅓ cup (50 g) all-purpose (plain) flour
- 2 cups/500 ml milk
- few drops of vanilla extract (essence)
- 4 oz (125 g) grated semisweet (dark) chocolate
- ½ cup (125 ml) Alchermes liqueur
- 1/2 cup/125 ml rum
- ¼ cup (60 ml) water
- about 20 sponge fingers
- whipped cream, for decoration

Whisk the egg yolks and sugar until pale and creamy. Stir in the flour. • Heat the milk with the vanilla extract until fairly hot, but not boiling. • Pour the milk into the egg mixture and then simmer for 7–8 minutes in a heavy-bottomed saucepan over a low heat, stirring continuously to prevent lumps forming. • Pour half the custard into a bowl and cover with plastic wrap (cling) touching the surface to prevent a skin forming. • Melt the chocolate in a double boiler over barely simmering water. • Return the remaining custard to the heat and stir in the melted chocolate. Cook for 2 minutes, stirring continuously. • Pour the chocolate custard into a bowl and cover with plastic wrap touching the surface to prevent a skin forming. • Set the custards aside to cool before using. • Mix the Alchermes, rum, and water together in a bowl. • Dip the ladyfingers into the water and liqueur mixture, then use one-third of them to line a 2-quart (2-liter) glass bowl or soufflé dish. • Pour the chocolate custard over the top, cover with another layer of dipped ladyfingers, and spread the plain custard on top. • Finish with the remaining ladyfingers, cover with foil and chill in the refrigerator for at least 12 hours. • Just before serving, decorate with plenty of whipped cream and, if liked, a little more grated chocolate.

Serves: 6–8 • Prep: 20 min + 12 hr to chill • Cooking: 15 min
Level: 1

Stracciatella ice cream

BASIC ICE CREAM

Gelato alla crema

- 4 large egg yolks
- 1 cup (200 g) granulated sugar
- 2 cups (500 ml) milk
- 1 cup (250 ml) heavy (double) cream

This basic recipe can be flavored with vanilla extract, coffee, chocolate, or many different types of spices, flavorings, and liqueurs to make a wide variety of ice creams. Basic instructions for making ice cream without an ice-cream maker have also been included.

Whisk the egg yolks and sugar until pale and creamy. • Place the milk and cream in a heavy-bottomed saucepan and bring to a boil. Remove from heat and cool slightly. Gradually stir into the egg and sugar. • Simmer in a double boiler over barely simmering water until it coats the back of a spoon. Make sure it does not come to a boil at any point. • Remove from the heat and let cool completely. • If you have an ice cream maker, pour the mixture into it and follow the instructions on your machine. • If you don't have an ice cream maker, pour it into a large bowl and place in the freezer. After 3 hours, stir the mixture to make sure it freezes evenly. After another 3 hours, whisk it for a few minutes and return to the freezer for another 3 hours before serving.

Serves: 4 • Prep: 30 min + 9 hr to freeze (without ice-cream maker) • Cooking: 15 min • Level: 2

STRACCIATELLA ICE CREAM

Gelato stracciatella

- 2 cups (500 ml) milk
- zest of 1/2 a lemon, removed using a sharp knife
- 1/2 vanilla pod
- 3/4 cup (150 g) granulated sugar
- 5 large eggs
- 1/3 cup (100 ml) heavy (double) cream
- 4 oz (125 g) semisweet (dark) chocolate, finely chopped

Place a large bowl into the freezer to chill. • Place the milk, lemon zest, vanilla pod, and half the sugar in a large saucepan over medium heat. Mix well and bring to a boil. • Remove from the heat as soon as it reaches a boil. Let cool. Discard the lemon zest and vanilla pod. • Beat the eggs and remaining sugar in a large bowl until pale and creamy. • Gradually add the milk mixture, stirring well. • Return to the saucepan and simmer over very low heat, stirring constantly with a wooden spoon, until the mixture coats the back of a spoon, 7–10 minutes. Be careful not to let the custard boil. • Remove from the heat and transfer to the chilled bowl. Let the custard cool completely, stirring from time to time. • Transfer the mixture to an ice cream machine and freeze following the manufacturer's instructions. • Whip the cream in a large bowl until stiff. When the ice cream is half frozen, add the cream and chocolate.

Serves: 4–6 • Prep: 30 min + freezing time • Cooking: 15 min • Level: 2

MELON SORBET WITH PORT

Sorbetto di melone al Porto

- 2 small canteloupe (rock) melons
- 1 1/3 cups (200 g) confectioners' (icing) sugar
- 1 large egg white
- 1/4 cup (60 ml) port
- 4 sprigs fresh mint, to garnish

Cut the melons in half horizontally. Remove and discard the seeds. Use a spoon to remove the flesh. Place in a bowl and set aside. • When the melon halves are cleaned, place them in the freezer. • Process the melon flesh in a food processor or blender with the confectioners' sugar, egg white, and Port. • Spoon the purée in ice cube trays and freeze for about 3 hours. • Before serving, return the melon ice cubes to the blender and process until finely chopped. • Pour the sorbet into the melon halves. Garnish with the mint and serve on dessert plates.

Serves: 4–6 • Prep: 20 min + 3 hr to freeze • Level: 2

Sicilian cassata

SICILIAN CASSATA

Cassata siciliana

- 1 Italian sponge cake (see page 401), cut into 1/2-inch (1-cm) slices
- 1/4 cup (60 g) apricot preserves (jam)
- 2 teaspoons water

Filling
- 1 1/2 cups (150 g) granulated sugar
- 1 tablespoon water
- 1/2 teaspoon vanilla extract (essence)
- 2 cups (500 g) fresh ricotta cheese, drained
- 2 cups (400 g) mixed candied fruit peel, finely chopped, + extra, to decorate
- 2 tablespoons pistachios, coarsely chopped
- 2 teaspoons kirsch

Glaze
- 1 1/3 cups (200 g) confectioners' (icing) sugar
- 1/2 cup (125 g) apricot preserves (jam)
- 2 teaspoons orange-flower water

Oil a 10-inch (25-cm) springform pan. Line with the cake slices. • Warm the preserves and water in a small saucepan over low heat until liquid. Fill the spaces in the pan with the preserves. • Filling: Warm the sugar, water, and vanilla in a saucepan over medium heat, stirring constantly, until the sugar has dissolved. • Place the ricotta in a large bowl and gradually beat in the sugar mixture. • Stir in the candied fruit peel and pistachios. Add the liqueur. • Spoon into the pan over the cake slices. • Top with the remaining cake slices. • Refrigerate for 2 hours. • Dip the pan briefly into cold water. Invert onto a serving plate and release the sides. • Glaze: Stir the confectioners' sugar, preserves, and orange-flower water in a saucepan over medium heat until smooth. Drizzle over the cake. • Arrange the candied peel on top in a decorative manner.

Serves: 6–8 • Prep: 1 hr + 2 hr to chill • Level: 2

FLORENTINE ICE CREAM CAKE

Zuccotto

This cake is called Zuccotto in its hometown of Florence. It takes its name (the Italian word 'zuccotto' means skullcap) from the traditional head coverings worn by church dignitaries.

- 1 cup (200 g) granulated sugar
- 1 cup (250 ml) water
- 3 tablespoons brandy
- 3 tablespoons rum
- 1 Italian sponge cake (see page 401), cut into 1/2-inch (1-cm) slices
- 1/3 cup (50 g) confectioners' (icing) sugar
- 1/3 cup (30 g) almonds, finely ground
- 1/3 cup (30 g) hazelnuts, finely ground
- 2 tablespoons mixed candied fruit, chopped
- 6 oz (180 g) semisweet (dark) chocolate, grated
- 2 cups (500 ml) heavy (double) cream, whipped

Mix the sugar and water in a saucepan over medium heat until the sugar has dissolved and it comes to a boil. Boil for 5 minutes. Remove from the heat. Add the brandy and rum and let cool. • Moisten the edges of a domed 2-quart (2-liter) mold or a stainless steel bowl with a little syrup and line with half the cake slices. Brush with the remaining syrup. • Gently fold the confectioners' sugar, nuts, candied fruit, and 5 oz (150 g) grated chocolate into the cream. Spoon the cream into the mold and top with the remaining cake slices. • Chill in the refrigerator for 5 hours. • Dip the mold briefly into cold water. Invert onto a serving plate. Sprinkle with the remaining grated chocolate.

Serves: 8–10 • Prep: 45 min + 5 hr to chill • Level: 2

HAZELNUT ICE CREAM

Gelato al Gianduia

- 1 quantity basic ice cream (see page 378)
- 2 tablespoons unsweetened cocoa powder
- 1/4 cup (50 g) finely ground hazelnuts
- 1/2 cup (125 ml) heavy (double) cream
- 1/4 cup 840 g) chocolate chips

Prepare the ice cream, dissolving the cocoa powder and hazelnuts in the hot milk-and-cream mixture. • When the ice cream is ready, serve in individual ice-cream dishes. Whip the cream until stiff and use it to decorate each serving. Sprinkle with the chocolate chips and serve.

Serves: 6 • Prep: 30 min + 9 hr to freeze (without ice-cream maker) • Cooking: 15 min • Level: 2

NEAPOLITAN ICE CREAM CAKE

Torta gelata alla napoletana

- 1 1/2 cups (270 g) candied cherries, finely chopped
- 2 cups (500 ml) kirsch
- 1 Italian sponge cake (see page 401)
- 2 cups (500 g) pistachio ice cream, softened
- 2 cups (500 g) chocolate ice cream, softened
- 1/3 cup (50 g) confectioners' (icing) sugar, to dust
- handful candied cherries, to decorate

Oil a 10-inch (25-cm) springform pan. • Soak the cherries in the kirsch, 1 hour. • Place the cake in the prepared pan. Freeze for 30 minutes. • Drain the cherries, reserving the liqueur. Drizzle over the cake. Spread with the pistachio ice cream. Arrange the cherries on top of the ice cream and spread with the chocolate ice cream. • Freeze for 4 hours. • Dip the pan briefly into cold water. Invert onto a serving plate. • Dust with the confectioners' sugar and decorate with the candied cherries.

Serves: 6–8 • Prep: 15 min + time to make cake and 4 hr 30 min to freeze • Level: 2

Brutti ma buoni

Brutti ma buoni

- $2^2/_3$ cups (400 g) blanched almonds or hazelnuts
- $1^1/_2$ cups (300 g) granulated sugar
- $^1/_4$ teaspoon ground cinnamon
- $^1/_2$ teaspoon vanilla essence (extract)
- 6 large egg whites

Ugly but good—the name says it all! In some regions the almonds are substituted with hazelnuts so try that too.

Preheat the oven to 350°F (180°C/gas 4). • Put the almonds on a baking sheet and toast in the oven until pale golden brown, 5 minutes. • Let cool slightly. Chop very finely in a food processor with the sugar, cinnamon, and vanilla. • Beat the egg whites in a large bowl until very stiff. • Place the beaten egg whites in a double boiler and fold in the almond mixture. • Stir constantly over very low heat until the mixture is very thick, 30 minutes. • Line a large baking sheet with waxed paper. • Drop spoonfuls of the mixture onto the baking sheet. • Bake until firm and lightly browned, 20–25 minutes. • Cool on a rack.

Makes: about 24 cookies • Prep: 15 min • Cooking: 1 hr Level: 2

Pine nut and raisin cookies

Zaletti

- $^1/_2$ cup (100 g) golden raisins (sultanas)
- 2 cups (300 g) yellow cornmeal
- $1^1/_2$ cups (200 g) all-purpose (plain) flour
- $^1/_2$ cup (100 g) granulated sugar
- $^1/_8$ teaspoon salt
- finely grated zest of 1 lemon
- $^2/_3$ cup (150 g) butter, melted
- $^1/_4$ cup (60 ml) milk
- 4 tablespoons pine nuts
- confectioners' (icing) sugar, to dust

These tasty delicacies made with cornmeal are an old specialty of central Italy.

Preheat the oven to 400°F (200°C/gas 6). • Soak the raisins in warm water, drain well, and squeeze out excess moisture. • Place the cornmeal , flour, sugar, salt, and lemon zest in a large bowl. • Gradually stir in the butter and milk. The dough should be firm but not crumbly. Add a little more milk if necessary. • Stir in the raisins and pine nuts. • Break off pieces of dough about the size of a walnut. Shape into balls, then flatten slightly. • Place, well spaced out, onto oil cookie sheets. • Bake until pale golden brown, 15 minutes. • Cool on a rack. Dust with confectioners' sugar before serving.

Makes: about 30 cookies • Prep: 40 min • Cooking: 15 min Level: 1

Almond macaroons

Amaretti

- $1^1/_4$ cups (150 g) almonds, toasted
- 3 teaspoons bitter almonds, toasted
- 1 cups (200 g) granulated sugar
- 3 large egg whites

Preheat the oven to 400°F (200°C/gas 6). • Butter 2 baking sheets. • Chop the sweet and bitter almonds together with a little of the sugar. • Add half the sugar, then one of the egg whites, followed by the remaining sugar and the second white. • Mix by hand to form a smooth batter and roll into long cylinders about 1 inch (2.5 cm) in diameter. Cut into slices about $^1/_2$-inch (1-cm) thick. Shape into balls and flatten slightly. • Arrange on the baking sheets. • Bake until golden brown, 30 minutes. • Cool on a rack.

Makes: about 25 cookies • Prep: 20 min • Cooking: 30 min Level: 2

Ladies kisses

Baci di dama

- 7 tablespoons butter, softened
- $^3/_4$ cup (150 g) superfine (caster) sugar
- $1^1/_4$ cups (150 g) hazelnuts, toasted and finely ground
- 1 cup (150 g) all-purpose (plain) flour
- $^1/_8$ teaspoon salt

Filling

- 3 oz (90 g) semisweet (dark) chocolate
- $^1/_3$ cup (90 ml) heavy (double) cream

Preheat the oven to 300°F (150°C/gas 2). • Butter 2 baking sheets. • Beat the butter and sugar in a large bowl with an electric mixer at high speed until creamy. • Use a large rubber spatula to fold in the hazelnuts, flour, and salt. Shape into balls the size of walnuts. • Place on the prepared sheet. • Bake until lightly browned, 25–30 minutes. Cool completely on a rack. • Filling: Melt the chocolate in a double boiler over barely simmering water. • Heat the cream in a small saucepan until warm. Stir the warm cream into the melted chocolate and mix until cooled. • Spread the filling onto half the cookies. Join the halves together.

Makes: about 20 cookies • Prep: 20 min • Cooking: 25–30 min • Level: 1

Dusted butter cookies

DUSTED BUTTER COOKIES

Canestrelli

- $3^1/_3$ cups (500 g) all-purpose (plain) flour
- $1^2/_3$ cups(400 g) butter, softened
- scant 1 cup (180 g) sugar
- 2 large eggs, separated
- $^1/_2$ cup (75 g) confectioners' (icing) sugar, to dust

Preheat the oven to 350°F (180°C/gas 4). • Sift the flour onto a clean work surface. Use your fingertips to rub in the butter until the mixture resembles coarse crumbs. • Stir in the sugar. • Make a well in the center and add the egg yolks. Mix to make a soft dough. • Roll out the dough on a lightly floured work surface to $^1/_2$-inch (1-cm) thick. Cut out the cookies with various shaped cookie cutters. • Use a spatula to transfer to an oiled baking sheet and brush with the lightly beaten egg whites. • Bake until golden brown, about 20 minutes. • Dust with the confectioners' sugar.

Makes about: 60 cookies • Prep: 10 min • Cooking: 20 min Level: 2

JAM-FILLED TURNOVERS

Tortelli di marmellata

- 3 cups (450 g) all-purpose (plain) flour
- 1 cup (200 g) granulated sugar
- $^1/_8$ teaspoon salt
- $^2/_3$ cup (150 g) butter, cut up
- 3 large eggs
- 3 tablespoons rum
- $1^1/_2$ cups (450 g) Morello cherry or plum preserves (jam)
- $^1/_2$ cup (75 g) confectioners' (icing) sugar

Preheat the oven to 350°F (180°C/gas 4). • Place the flour, sugar, and salt in a bowl. Make a well in the center and add the butter, eggs, and rum. Combine well, without working the dough too much; it should be just smooth. • Shape into a ball, cover with plastic wrap (cling film), and let rest for 1 hour. • Roll the dough out to just under $^1/_4$ inch (5 mm) thick. Use a glass or cookie cutter to cut out 3-inch (8-cm) disks. • Place a teaspoon of jam in the center of each and fold in half to form a half-moon shape. Press the edges together to seal. • Place the filled turnovers on a greased baking sheet. • Bake until pale golden brown, about 30 minutes. • Cool on a rack., Dust with confectioners' sugar before serving.

Makes: about 20 cookies • Prep: 1 hr + 1 hr to rest Cooking: 30 min • Level: 1

CREAM CRESCENTS

Crestine alla crema

- 3 cups (450 g) all-purpose (plain) flour
- 1 cup (200 g) granulated sugar
- 1 cup (250 g) butter, softened
- finely grated zest of 1 lemon
- 2 egg yolks
- $^1/_8$ teaspoon salt
- 3 teaspoons baking powder

Filling

- 3 large egg yolks
- 3 tablespoons sugar
- 3 tablespoons all-purpose (plain) flour
- 2 cups (500 ml) milk
- $^1/_8$ teaspoon salt
- $^1/_2$ teaspoon vanilla extract (essence)
- 6 tablespoons confectioners' (icing) sugar

Preheat the oven to 350°F (180°C/gas 4). • Place the flour in a bowl and make a well in the center. Add the sugar, butter, lemon zest, egg yolks, and salt. • Work the ingredients together quickly, then add the baking powder. • Roll the dough out to a thickness of $^1/_4$ inch (5 mm) and cut into large disks using a glass or cookie cutter. • Filling: Whisk the egg yolks and sugar until pale and creamy, then stir in the flour. • Bring the milk to a boil with the salt and vanilla and stir into the egg mixture. Simmer over low heat, stirring constantly, until thickened. • Set aside to cool, then cover with a layer of plastic wrap that touches the surface of the custard (to prevent a skin from forming). • Place spoonfuls of the filling on each disk of pastry and fold in half to form a crescent-shaped parcel, pressing down on the edges to seal. • Place on a greased and floured baking sheet. • Bake until pale golden brown, 20 minutes. • Dust with confectioners' sugar and serve.

Makes: about 20 cookies • Prep: 20 min • Cooking: 20 min Level: 2

NEAPOLITAN CHRISTMAS FRITTERS

Struffoli

- 3½ cups (500 g) all-purpose (plain) flour, sifted
- 4 large eggs
- 2 tablespoons superfine sugar
- ½ cup (125 ml) liqueur (Strega or anise)
- ⅛ teaspoon salt
- 2 cups (500 ml) oil, for frying
- ¾ cup (200 g) honey
- 1 cup (80 g) each candied orange and lemon peel, diced
- ¼ cup (30 g) sprinkles

Combine the flour with the eggs, sugar, liqueur, and salt in a mixing bowl and beat until smooth and well-mixed. Set aside to rest for 2 hours. • Scoop out tablespoonfuls of the dough and roll them into sticks about the thickness of a pencil. Cut into pieces about ½-inch (5-mm) long. • Heat the oil to very hot in a large frying pan and fry the fritters in small batches until light golden brown. Scoop the fritters out of the oil with a slotted spoon and drain on paper towels. • Heat the honey in a large, heavy-bottomed saucepan until thoroughly melted. Add the Struffoli and the candied orange and lemon peels. Stir carefully until they are all coated with honey. • Place the Struffoli on a serving dish. Decorate with the sprinkles and serve.

Makes: about 40 fritters • Prep: 1 hr • Cooking: 30 min
Level: 2

LEMON RICE FRITTERS

Frittelle di riso

- 1 cup (200 g) short-grain, pudding rice
- 2¼ cups (500 ml) milk
- 1 tablespoon butter
- 3 tablespoons sugar
- grated zest of ½ lemon or orange
- 2 large eggs
- ⅛ teaspoon salt
- ¼ cup (50 g) all-purpose (plain) flour
- ⅓ cup (50 g) golden raisins, soaked in warm water for 15 minutes, drained and squeezed
- ¼ cup (60 ml) rum
- 1 cup (250 ml) olive oil for frying
- ⅔ cup (100 g) confectioners' (icing) sugar

Cook the rice in the milk until the grains have almost disintegrated, about 1 hour. • Stir the butter into this mixture and remove from the heat. • Add the sugar and zest. Add the eggs, one at a time, until just blended after each addition. • Stir in the salt, flour, raisins, and rum. Chill in the refrigerator for 1 hour. • Heat the oil in a frying pan until very hot. To test, drop a tiny piece of fritter into the oil. If bubbles form around it immediately, it is hot enough. • Use a tablespoon to drop spoonfuls of the fritter mixture into the oil. Fry until golden brown, 3–4 minutes. • Drain on paper towels. Dust with the confectioners' sugar. Serve hot.

Makes about 15 fritters • Prep: 20 min + 1 hr to rest
Cooking: 1 hr 25 min • Level: 2

SICILIAN CANNOLI

Cannoli alla siciliana

This is a traditional Sicilian pastry, a kind of fried wafer, filled with a rich ricotta cream. They are best eaten freshly made, as the pastry does not remain crisp for long when they are filled. To make them you will need some stainless steel cannoli mold. They are available from all good kitchenware stores.

Filling
- 14 oz (400 g) fresh ricotta cheese
- 1 cup (200 g) granulated sugar
- ¾ cup (75 g) chopped candied peel
- 2 tablespoons orange blossom water or orange liqueur
- 2 oz (60 g) semisweet (dark) chocolate, finely chopped
- 1 tablespoon unsweetened cocoa powder

Pastry
- 1⅔ cups (250 g) all-purpose (plain) flour
- 1 tablespoon sugar
- 1 tablespoon unsweetened cocoa powder
- ⅓ cup (90 ml) Marsala wine
- 1 teaspoon instant coffee (optional)
- ⅛ teaspoon salt

- 2 cups (500 ml) oil, for frying

To garnish
- strands of candied peel
- glacé cherries
- 2 tablespoons confectioners' (icing) sugar

Filling: Press the ricotta through a fine mesh strainer. • Mix the ricotta, sugar, candied peel, orange blossom water, and chocolate in a large bowl. • Divide the mixture into 2 bowls. Add the cocoa to one of the bowls and mix well. Pastry: Mix the flour, sugar, cocoa, Marsala, coffee, and salt in a large bowl to make a soft dough. Cover the dough and chill in the refrigerator for 1 hour. • Roll out the dough on a lightly floured surface until it is ⅛-inch (3-mm) thick. • Cut into ovals large enough to wrap around the cannoli molds. Wrap an oval of pastry around each mold. Overlap the pastry where it meets and seal each one using a little of the egg white. • Heat the oil in a deep fryer over medium heat. Fry the pastry coated tubes until the pastry is golden brown, 3–4 minutes. • Drain on paper towels and let cool. • Slip the pastry cases off the molds. • Fill each cannolo with the plain ricotta mixture from one end and the chocolate ricotta mixture from the other end. • Garnish by pressing pieces of candied peel and cherries into the filling at the ends of each cannolo. • Dust with confectioners' sugar and serve.

Makes: 12 cannoli • Prep: 30 min + 1 hr to chill the dough
Cooking: 15 min • Level: 3

CAKES & PIES

Traditional Italian cakes and pies are often based on in-season fruit and nuts, and on grains such as polenta and wheat. In this chapter we have gathered 26 regional recipes for cakes and pies, many of which are not widely known outside Italy. Try, for example, the Umbrian King's salami cake (see page 401), the Ligurian Chiavari cake (see page 401), or the Tuscan chestnut cake (see page 409). We have also included some old favorites, including Panforte (see page 409), *Pastiera napoletana* (Neapolitan pie; see page 406), and *Sabbiosa* (Venetian crumble cake; see page 404).

Rustic apple and polenta cake (see page 405)

Chiavari cake

KING'S SALAMI CAKE

Salame del re

- 2 tablespoons butter
- generous 1/3 cup (60 g) cornstarch (cornflour)
- 2 cups (500 ml) milk
- 1¼ cups (250 g) granulated sugar
- grated zest and juice of 1 lemon
- 8 oz (250 g) semisweet (dark) chocolate, chopped
- 5 large eggs, separated
- 3/4 cup (125 g) all-purpose (plain) flour
- 1 teaspoon baking powder
- 1/2 teaspoon vanilla extract (essence)
- 1/8 teaspoon salt
- 1/4 cup (60 ml) Alchermes or other sweet red liqueur
- 4 tablespoons confectioners' (icing) sugar, to dust

This cake is a specialty of Città di Castello and is traditionally baked to celebrate a baptism.

Melt the butter in a saucepan over low heat. • Remove from the heat, add the cornstarch, and mix well. Add the milk a little at a time and mix well after each addition to prevent lumps from forming. • Add half the sugar and half the lemon zest. Return the saucepan to the heat and simmer, stirring constantly, until the custard thickens, 5–10 minutes. • Remove from the heat and add the chocolate. Mix well to melt the chocolate. • Preheat the oven to 350°F (180°C/gas 4). • Line a large jelly roll (swiss roll) pan with parchment paper. • Beat the egg yolks and remaining sugar in a large bowl until pale and creamy. • Gently fold in the flour, baking powder, and vanilla. Add the lemon juice and remaining lemon zest. • Beat the egg whites with the salt in a large bowl until stiff. Gently fold them into the batter. • Spoon the batter into the prepared pan. • Bake until well risen and springy to the touch, 10–12 minutes. • Remove from the oven and turn out onto a clean cloth sprinkled with confectioners' sugar. • Peel off the parchment paper. Let cool. • Brush the cake with the liqueur and spread with the chocolate mixture. Roll up the cake, using the cloth as a guide. Chill in the refrigerator for 2 hours before serving.

Serves: 8 • Prep: 35 min + 2 hr to chill • Cooking: 20 min Level: 2

ITALIAN SPONGE CAKE

Pan di Spagna

- 6 large eggs
- 1 cup (200 g) granulated sugar
- 2 teaspoons grated lemon zest
- 1 cup (150 g) all-purpose (plain) flour
- 1/2 cup (75 g) cornstarch (cornflour)
- 1/8 teaspoon salt

This recipe for sponge cake is used as the basis of many other cakes and desserts. It is relatively simple to make and will keep for up to a week in an airtight container. It also freezes well. .

Preheat the oven to 375°F (190°C/gas 5). • Place the eggs and sugar in a double boiler (or in a small saucepan placed in a larger pan of simmering water over low heat) and whisk until frothy. • Remove from the heat, add the lemon zest and continue to whisk until cooled. • Fold in both flours and the salt carefully so that the egg mixture does not collapse. • Butter and grease a 10-inch (25-cm) springform pan and fill with the sponge mixture. • Bake until well risen, golden brown, and springy to the touch, about 40 minutes.

Serves: 6 • Prep: 30 min • Cooking: 40 min • Level: 2

CHIAVARI CAKE

Torta di Chiavari

Zabaione
- 3 large egg yolks
- 4 tablespoons sugar
- 1/4 cup (60 ml) dry Marsala wine

- 25–30 lang de chat or other very thin sweet cookies
- one (10-inc/25-cm) Italian sponge cake, (see recipe above)
- 1/4 cup (60 ml) curaçao
- 1/2 cup (125 ml) heavy (double) cream, whipped
- 6 amaretti cookies, crushed
- 2 tablespoons rum
- 2 tablespoons cake crumbs, toasted

Beat the egg yolks, sugar, and Marsala in a double boiler over barely simmering water until very thick, 10–15 minutes. • Remove from the heat and let cool. • Grease a large serving dish with a little butter and arrange the cookies around the edge of the dish. • Cut the sponge cake in half horizontally. • Brush the bottom half with curaçao and put it in the center of the circle of cookies. • Spread the cake with a thin layer of cream. Moisten the amaretti with the rum and sprinkle over the cream. Spread with the zabaione. Spread with add another thin layer of cream. • Brush the other half of the sponge cake with the remaining curaçao and place on top. • Spread the remaining cream over the top of the cake. • Sprinkle with the toasted cake crumbs. Keep the cake refrigerated until you serve it. • Serve in slices.

Serves: 6–8 • Prep: 15 min + time to prepare the cake Cooking: 10–15 min • Level: 2

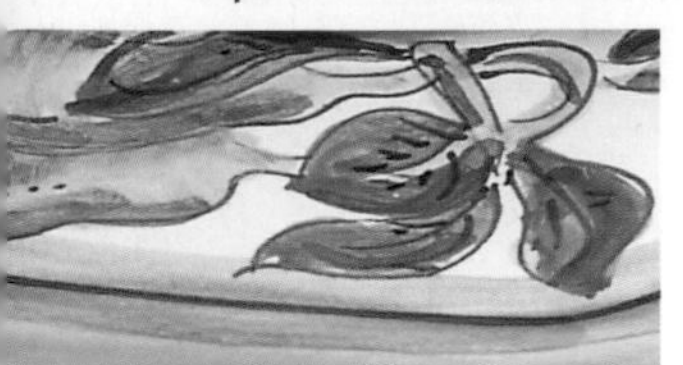

Modena cake

Bensone

- $3\frac{1}{3}$ cups (500 g) all-purpose (plain) flour
- $\frac{3}{4}$ cup (150 g) sugar
- $\frac{1}{8}$ teaspoon salt
- finely grated zest of 1 lemon
- 3 teaspoons baking powder
- $\frac{1}{2}$ cup (125 g) butter, chopped in small pieces
- 3 large eggs, lightly beaten
- 2–3 tablespoons milk
- 3 oz (90 g) sugar grains (crystals/nibs)

Preheat the oven to 350°F (180°C/gas 4). • Sift the flour into a large bowl. Mix in the sugar, salt, lemon zest, and baking powder. • Make a well in the center and fill with the butter and eggs (reserving 1 tablespoon of beaten egg to glaze the cake). • Beat these ingredients together, gradually combining them with the flour, and adding 2–3 tablespoons of milk. Beat or stir the dough until only just smooth. • Butter a baking sheet and dust with flour. • Shape the dough into a long, thick sausage and arrange it in an S-shape on the baking sheet. • Brush the surface with the reserved egg and sprinkle with the roughly crushed sugar. Using a sharp, pointed knife, make an incision along the center of the entire length of the cake. • Bake until a skewer inserted into the center comes out clean, about 40 minutes. • Let cool on a rack before serving.

Serves: 6–8 • Prep: 25 min • Cooking: 40 min • Level: 1

Florentine carnival cake

Schiacciata alla fiorentina

This cake is baked in Florence during the lead up to Carnivale in the spring. Serve fresh the day it is baked and cut in half and fill with cream the next day.

Dissolve the yeast in the warm water. Set aside until foamy, 10–15 minutes. • Sift the flour into a bowl. Add the yeast and enough of the flour to make a soft dough. Shape into a ball, cover and let rise for 1 hour. • Place the remaining flour on a work surface. Make a well in the center and add the risen dough, eggs, sugar, butter, orange zest, and salt. Mix with to make a soft dough. • Knead until smooth and elastic, 10–15 minutes. • Butter an 8 x 12-inch (20 x 30-cm) baking pan. • Fill with the dough. Let rise for 2 hours. • Preheat the oven to 375°F (190°C/gas 5). Bake until well risen and golden brown, about 30 minutes. • Let cool slightly then turn out onto a rack to cool completely. Dust with confectioners' sugar and serve.

Serves: 8 • Prep: 30 min + 3 hr to rise • Cooking: 30 min Level: 2

- 1 oz (30 g) fresh yeast or 2 ($\frac{1}{4}$-oz/7-g) packets active dry yeast
- $\frac{1}{4}$ cup (60 ml) lukewarm water
- $3\frac{1}{3}$ cups (500 g) all-purpose (plain) flour
- 4 large eggs, lightly beaten
- $\frac{3}{4}$ cup (150 g) granulated sugar
- generous $\frac{1}{3}$ cup (100 g) butter, melted
- grated zest of 1 orange
- $\frac{1}{8}$ teaspoon salt
- $\frac{1}{4}$ cup (60 g) confectioners' (icing) sugar
- 1 cup (250 ml) heavy (double) cream (optional)

Almond polenta cake

Sbrisolona

- 8 oz (250 g) almonds, blanched
- $\frac{3}{4}$ cup (150 g) granulated sugar
- $1\frac{1}{3}$ cups (200 g) all-purpose (plain) flour
- 8 oz (250 g) polenta (coarse-ground cornmeal)
- finely grated zest of 1 lemon
- 1 teaspoon vanilla sugar
- $\frac{1}{8}$ teaspoon salt
- $\frac{1}{2}$ cup (125 g) butter, cut in small pieces
- 3 oz (90 g) lard, cut in small pieces
- 2 large egg yolks, beaten

Preheat the oven to 375°F (190°C/gas 5). • Chop the almonds in a food processor with two-thirds of the sugar. • Transfer to a work surface and add the flour, cornmeal, lemon zest, remaining sugar, vanilla sugar, and salt. Shape into a mound and make a well in the center. • Combine the butter and lard with the egg yolks, and add to the flour mixture. Working quickly, use your fingertips to combine the mixture until it is smooth and crumbly. • Place the dough in a buttered and floured 10-inch (25-cm) springform pan, pressing down lightly with your fingertips to make an uneven surface. • Bake for 40 minutes. • If liked, dust with confectioners' (icing) sugar before serving.

Serves: 6 • Prep: 20 min • Cooking: 40 min • Level: 1

Bread and milk cake

Torta Nicolotta

Preheat the oven to 350°F (180°C/gas 4). • Place the rum and raisins in a bowl and soak for 30 minutes. • Cut the bread into small pieces and place in a large bowl. • Bring the milk to a boil, add the butter and sugar, and stir briefly. Pour over the bread. • When the bread has absorbed all the milk (this will take about 30 minutes), add the lightly beaten eggs, the drained raisins, and lemon zest. • Mix well and transfer to a 10 inch (25 cm) springform pan. • Bake until pale golden brown, about 30 minutes. • Serve hot or at room temperature.

Serves: 6 • Prep: 15 min + 1 hr to soak • Cooking: 30 min Level: 1

- $\frac{1}{2}$ cup (125 ml) dark Jamaica rum
- 8 oz (250 g) golden raisins (sultanas)
- 12 oz (350 g) day-old white bread
- 4 cups (1 liter) milk
- $\frac{1}{3}$ cup (90 g) butter
- $1\frac{1}{4}$ cups (250 g) granulated sugar
- 5 large eggs
- finely grated zest of 1 lemon

CHRISTMAS PIE

Spongata

Filling
- 1 cup (125 g) walnuts
- 1 cup (250 g) chunky apricot preserves (jam)
- 1 cup (809 g) fine dry bread crumbs
- 1¾ cups (200 g) honey
- ½ up (125 ml) water
- ½ cup (60 g) seedless golden raisins, soaked in water, well drained
- ½ cup (100 g) pine nuts
- ¼ teaspoon ground cinnamon

Pastry
- 2½ cups (375 g) all-purpose (plain) flour
- ½ cup (200 g) granulated sugar
- ¼ teaspoon salt
- finely grated zest of 1 lemon
- ⅔ cup (150 g) butter, cut into small pieces
- 1 large egg + 2 large egg yolks
- confectioners' sugar, to dust

Spongata is one of the oldest cakes in Italy. Records show that it was already being served in Emilia-Romagna as a Christmas cake during the 15th century.

Filling: Preheat the oven to 350°F (180°C/ gas 4). • Chop the walnuts finely. • Spread the bread crumbs out on a shallow baking sheet. bake until lightly browned, 3–4 minutes. • Chop the the chunky preserves into very small pieces. • Place the preserves, walnuts, and bread crumbs in a bowl. • Pour the honey into a small saucepan with the water and bring slowly to a boil. • Stir into the bowl with the nut and bread crumb mixture. Add the raisins, pine nuts, and cinnamon. Mix well. • Cover the bowl and refrigerate for 2–3 days. • Pastry: Preheat the oven to 375°F (190°C/ gas 5). • Sift the flour into a large bowl. Add the sugar, salt, and lemon zest and mix well. • Turn out onto a pastry board and heap up into a mound. Make a well in the center, add the butter, and use your fingertips to rub it into the flour. The mixture should resemble fine bread crumbs. • Add the egg and yolks and combine, working the pastry dough briefly. Shape into a ball and wrap in plastic wrap (cling film). Chill in the refrigerator for 1 hour. • Divide the dough in two portions, one slightly larger than the other. Roll them out into two disks, trimming one to 9½ inches (24 cm), the other to 11 inches (28 cm) in diameter. • Place a sheet of baking paper on a baking sheet and transfer the smaller disk carefully onto it. • Give the filling a final stir and spoon it onto the pastry dough, spreading it out, but leaving a ½-inch (1-cm) border around the edge. • Cover with the larger disk, pressing the edges to seal well (trim off any overlapping dough from the larger disk). Bake for 25 minutes. • Leave to cool before sprinkling with sifted confectioners' sugar.

Serves: 8–10 • Prep: 2 hr + 2–3 days to rest the filling • Cooking: 25 min • Level: 3

NEAPOLITAN PIE

Pastiera napoletana

Pastry
- 3⅓ cups (500 g) all-purpose (plain) flour
- 1 cup (200 g) granulated sugar
- generous ¾ cup (200 g) butter, cut into pieces
- 2 large eggs + 2 egg yolks

Filling
- 1 cup (250 g) cooked wheat, drained
- generous ¾ cup (200 ml) milk
- scant ¼ cup (50 g) butter
- 1 cup (100 g) chopped candied cedar or candied peel
- 1 tablespoon all-purpose (plain) flour
- 1½ lb (750 g) fresh ricotta cheese, drained
- 7 large eggs + 3 large egg yolks
- ¼ teaspoon ground cinnamon
- 2½ cups (500 g) granulated sugar
- 2 tablespoons orange blossom water
- 2 tablespoons icing sugar

Pastry: Place the flour, sugar, and butter in a food processor and blend until the mixture is the consistency of bread crumbs. Add the eggs and mix to make a soft dough. • Turn the dough out onto a piece of plastic wrap (cling film). Wrap the dough and chill in the refrigerator for 1 hour. • Filling: Simmer the wheat, milk, and butter in a saucepan over low heat for 10 minutes. Remove from the heat and let cool. • Preheat the oven to 350°F (180°C/gas 4). • Toss the candied peel in the flour and then add it to the wheat mixture. • Blend the ricotta in a food processor until smooth. Add the eggs one at a time, mixing well after each addition. Add the cinnamon, sugar, and orange blossom water. Mix well. • Transfer the wheat mixture to a large bowl. Add the ricotta mixture and mix well. • Roll out three-quarters of the pastry on a lightly floured work surface until ¼ inch (5 mm) thick. • Oil a deep 10 inch (25 cm) pie pan. • Line the pan with the pastry. Spoon the filling into the pastry case. • Roll out the remaining pastry and cut it into ½-inch (1.5 cm) ribbons. • Decorate the pie by making a lattice pattern with the pastry ribbons. • Bake until cooked through and lightly browned, about 1 hour 30 minutes. • Let cool in the pan.

Serves: 8 • Prep: 30 min + 1 hr to chill the pastry • Cooking: 1 hr 40 min • Level: 2

Panforte

PANFORTE

Panforte

- 1 cup (100 g) candied orange peel, coarsely chopped
- 2 tablespoons candied lemon peel, chopped
- 1⅔ cups (250 g) unblanched, toasted almonds, coarsely chopped
- 1 cup (100 g) walnuts, coarsely chopped
- 1 cup (150 g) all-purpose (plain) flour
- 1 teaspoon each ground coriander, mace, cloves, and nutmeg
- 1 cup (200 g) firmly packed brown sugar
- ½ cup (125 ml) honey
- ½ cup (125 ml) water
- 4 tablespoons confectioners' (icing) sugar, to dust (optional)

Panforte—*literally, in Italian, "strong bread"—is a wonderfully chewy cake made every fall in the beautiful medieval town of Siena, in Tuscany.*

Preheat the oven to 350°F (180°C/gas 4). • Line a baking sheet with rice paper. • Mix the candied peels, nuts, flour, and spices in a large bowl. • Heat the brown sugar, honey, and water in a medium saucepan over medium heat, stirring constantly, until the sugar has dissolved. • Wash down the sides of the pan with a pastry brush dipped in cold water to prevent sugar crystals from forming. Cook, without stirring, until small bubbles form on the surface and the syrup registers 234°F (114°C) on a candy thermometer. • Remove from the heat and beat into the nut mixture. • Spoon onto the prepared sheet. Shape the dough into a round about H-inch (1-cm) thick. • Bake for about 35 minutes, or until golden brown. • Cool the cake completely on the baking sheet. • Remove the excess rice paper from the edges before serving. If using, dust with the confectioners' sugar.

Serves: 10–12 • Prep: 25 min • Cooking: 35 min • Level: 2

TUSCAN CHESTNUT CAKE

Castagnaccio

- 3 cups (450 g) sweet chestnut flour
- 1½ cups (375 ml) water
- ⅔ cup (150 ml) extra-virgin olive oil
- pinch of salt
- ½ cup (75 g) small seedless white raisins, soaked in warm water for 15 minutes, drained and squeezed
- ⅓ cup (30 g) pine nuts
- a few young, tender rosemary leaves

This flat cake comes from Tuscany where it is popular in late fall when the new season's chestnuts are in.

Preheat the oven to 400°F (200°C/gas 6). • Sift the flour into a mixing bowl, make a well in the center and pour in the water, 1 tablespoon of the oil, and the salt. Stir well to obtain a thick, lump-free, pouring batter. • Stir in the drained raisins and the nuts. Pour into an oiled 9 x 13 inch (23 x 33 cm) baking pan. • Sprinkle with the rosemary leaves and drizzle with the remaining oil. • Bake until a thin crust has formed, about 30 minutes. • Serve hot or warm.

Serves: 4 • Prep: 15 min • Cooking: 50 min • Level: 3

SICILIAN EASTER CAKE

Torta pasquale siciliana

- 3 large eggs, at room temperature + 1 large egg, lightly beaten
- 1 cup + 1 tablespoon superfine sugar
- 1 teaspoon vanilla extract (essence)
- 5 cups (750 g) all-purpose (plain) flour
- ½ cup (125 ml) milk
- 2 teaspoons baking soda
- ⅓ cup + 1 tablespoon olive oil
- 4 large eggs, to decorate

Preheat the oven to 400°F (200°C/gas 6). • Butter and flour a rectangular baking sheet. • Beat the eggs, superfine sugar, and vanilla in a large bowl with an electric mixer at high speed until pale and thick. Sift the flour in a large bowl and make a well in the center. Stir in the egg mixture. • Warm the milk and baking soda in a saucepan until the soda has dissolved. Add enough of the milk mixture and oil to the flour mixture to make a smooth dough. • Knead until smooth and elastic, 5 minutes. • Break off a piece slightly larger than an egg and set aside. • Divide the remaining dough into 3 pieces. Use your hands to roll the dough into three ropes about 10 inches (25 cm) long. • Press the ends of the ropes together and braid (plait) the dough. • Transfer to the prepared baking sheet. Press the ends of the braid together to form a ring. • Roll the remaining dough into strips. • Carefully press the 4 eggs reserved for decoration securely into the braid and cross the dough strips over each egg. • Brush with the beaten egg. • Bake for 30–35 minutes, or until golden. Cool the cake completely on the sheet. Transfer to a serving plate.

Serves: 12–15 • Prep: 1 hr • Cooking: 30–35 min • Level: 2

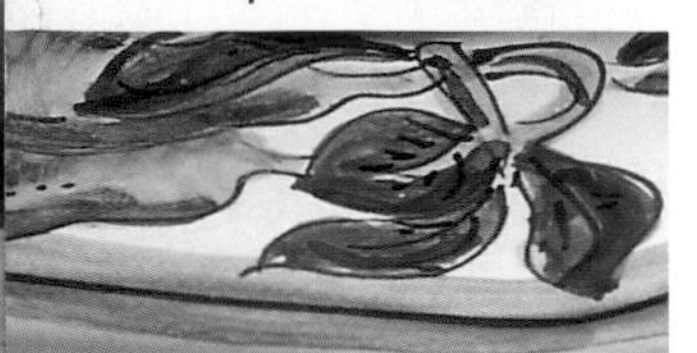

Fresh fruit crostata

Crostata di frutta fresca

Vanilla custard
- 2 cups (500 ml) milk
- 3/4 cup (150 g) granulated sugar
- 6 large egg yolks
- 1 teaspoon vanilla extract

Pastry
- 1 cup (150 g) all-purpose (plain) flour
- 2 tablespoons granulated sugar
- 1/8 teaspoon salt
- 1/3 cup (90 g) cold butter, cut up
- 1 egg yolk, at room temperature
- 1 tablespoon ice water

Topping
- 1–2 cups sliced fresh fruit or whole berries
- 1/4 cup (60 g) apricot preserves (jam)

This eye-catching crostata must be made with the best quality fruit. If you are using bananas, brush with lemon juice to prevent discoloring.

Vanilla custard: bring the milk and 1/4 cup (50 g) of sugar to a boil in a saucepan. • Beat the egg yolks and remaining 1/2 cup (100 g) sugar in a large bowl with an electric mixer at high speed until pale and thick. • Stir the milk into the yolks. Return to the saucepan. Cook over low heat, stirring constantly with a wooden spoon, until the mixture lightly coats a spoon or registers 160°F (80°C) on an instant-read thermometer. Remove from the heat and add the vanilla. Set aside to cool. • Pastry: stir together the flour, sugar, and salt in a large bowl. Use a pastry blender to cut in the butter until the mixture resembles coarse crumbs. Add the egg yolk and water and, working quickly, using your hands, work the pastry until smooth. Shape into a disk, wrap in plastic wrap, and refrigerate for 30 minutes. • Roll the dough out on a lightly floured surface to a 14-inch rectangle. Fit into a 13 x 4-inch rectangular tart pan, trimming the edges if needed. • Preheat the oven to 375°F (190°C/gas 5). • Line the pastry shell with foil and fill the foil with dried beans or pie weights. Bake for 15 minutes. Remove the foil with the beans and bake for 15–20 minutes more, or until crisp. Cool completely in the pan on a rack. • Topping: Spread with custard and arrange the fruit on top. Warm the preserves in a saucepan over low heat. Brush with preserves.

Serves: 6–8 • Prep: 1 hr • Cooking: 45 min • Level: 2

Pear pie

Crostata di pere

- 2 lb (1 kg) firm cooking pears
- 3/4 cup (150 g) superfine (caster) sugar
- 1 1/4 cups (300 ml) full-bodied dry red wine
- pinch of ground cinnamon
- 2 tablespoons unsweetened cocoa powder
- 12 amaretti cookies, coarsely crushed
- 2 cups all-purpose flour
- 1 cup (150 g) fine yellow cornmeal
- 1/8 teaspoon salt
- 2/3 cup (180 g) butter, at room temperature
- 3 large egg yolks

Rinse the pears and dry well. Peel them, then cut lengthwise into quarters, and core. Cut each quarter lengthwise into 3 slices. • Place the slices of pear in a saucepan just large enough to hold them. Add 1/4 cup (50 g) of the sugar, the wine, and cinnamon, and simmer over low heat for 10 minutes. • Pour off the cooking liquid, then sprinkle the pears with the cocoa powder. Set aside to cool. • To make the pastry, begin by mixing the two types of flour thoroughly in a bowl. Stir in the sugar and salt. • Using a fork, stir in the butter, followed by the egg yolks. Work the ingredients quickly together to form a mixture that resembles fine bread crumbs. Gather these together by hand and combine (do not knead) to form a soft ball of pastry dough which is not in the least elastic. • Use two-thirds of the pastry to line the bottom and sides of an ungreased, fairly shallow 9-inch (23-cm) pie pan. Do this by placing the pastry in the pie pan and gradually working it into a lining of even thickness using your fingertips. • Chill the uncooked pie shell in the refrigerator for 1 hour. • Wrap the remaining pastry dough in plastic wrap and put it a cool place (not in the refrigerator as it still has to be rolled out.) • Preheat the oven to 400°F (200°C/ gas 6). • Take the pie shell out of the refrigerator. Sprinkle evenly with the crumbled amaretti cookies and arrange the pears on top. • Roll out the remaining pastry dough into a round slightly larger than the diameter of the pie pan. Place this on top of the pears, pinching the pastry edges together to seal. Pierce a few little holes in the pie lid with a fine skewer. • Bake until golden brown, about 40 minutes. • Let cool slightly in the pan. Serve at room temperature.

Serves: 6 • Prep: 30 min + 1 hr to chill • Cooking: 40 min Level: 2